Postgraduate Research in Music

Postgraduate Research in Music

A Step-by-Step Guide to Writing a Thesis

Victoria Rogers

OXFORD
UNIVERSITY PRESS

Oxford University Press is a department of the University of Oxford. It furthers
the University's objective of excellence in research, scholarship, and education
by publishing worldwide. Oxford is a registered trade mark of Oxford University
Press in the UK and certain other countries.

Published in the United States of America by Oxford University Press
198 Madison Avenue, New York, NY 10016, United States of America.

© Oxford University Press 2024

All rights reserved. No part of this publication may be reproduced, stored in
a retrieval system, or transmitted, in any form or by any means, without the
prior permission in writing of Oxford University Press, or as expressly permitted
by law, by license, or under terms agreed with the appropriate reproduction
rights organization. Inquiries concerning reproduction outside the scope of the
above should be sent to the Rights Department, Oxford University Press, at the
address above.

You must not circulate this work in any other form
and you must impose this same condition on any acquirer.

Library of Congress Cataloging-in-Publication Data
Names: Rogers, Victoria, 1948– author.
Title: Postgraduate research in music : a step-by-step guide to writing a thesis / Victoria Rogers.
Description: [1.] | New York : Oxford University Press, 2024. |
Includes bibliographical references and index.
Identifiers: LCCN 2023003842 (print) | LCCN 2023003843 (ebook) |
ISBN 9780197616048 (paperback) | ISBN 9780197616031 (hardback) |
ISBN 9780197616062 (epub) | ISBN 9780197616079
Subjects: LCSH: Musicology—Methodology. | Dissertations, Academic.
Classification: LCC ML3797 .R64 2023 (print) | LCC ML3797 (ebook) |
DDC 780.72/1—dc23/eng/20230127
LC record available at https://lccn.loc.gov/2023003842
LC ebook record available at https://lccn.loc.gov/2023003843

DOI: 10.1093/oso/9780197616031.001.0001

Paperback printed by Marquis Book Printing, Canada
Hardback printed by Bridgeport National Bindery, Inc., United States of America

For the two Davids

Contents

Examples	*xv*
Tables	*xvii*
Figures	*xix*
Preface	*xxi*
About the Companion Website	*xxv*

Introduction	**1**
What Is a Thesis?	2
Aims and Approach	3
Features	4
How to Use This Book	5
Companion Website	5
Chapter Outline	5
Reading List	8
1. Finding a Topic	**9**
Reading List	11
2. Searching for Sources Part 1: Key Resources and Resource Portals	**12**
Primary, Secondary, and Tertiary Sources	12
Overlaps and Ambiguities	14
Key Resources and Resource Portals	16
Writings about Music	16
Books and E-books (Electronic Books)	16
Journal Articles	17
Historical Treatises and Documents	19
Encyclopedias and Dictionaries of Music	19
Theses and Dissertations	21
Conference Proceedings	22
Album Notes, Liner Notes, Accompanying Notes, and Program Notes	22
Newspapers, Periodicals, and Magazines	23
Official Records and Reports	24
Archival Sources	24
An Archive and a Library Compared	25
Finding Archival Sources	25
Accessing Archival Content	25
Planning a Visit to an Archive	26
Scores, Editions, and Collections	26
Finding Scores, Editions, and Collections	29
Finding Musical Sources	31

viii　Contents

Thematic Catalogues	31
Music Iconography	33
Sound Recordings, Films, and Videos	34
Search Engines and Websites	36
Social Media, Blogs, and Podcasts	37
Coda	37
Exercises	37
Reading List	37

3. Searching for Sources Part 2: Strategies for Locating Information **41**

Searching Databases	41
Strategy 1: Basic and Advanced Searches, and the Use of Filters	41
Strategy 2: Selecting a Search Field	43
Searching by Keyword	44
Searching by Subject	44
Comparing Keyword and Subject Searches	46
Searching by Phrase	46
Searching by Author	47
Searching by Title	47
Uniform Titles	47
Strategy 3: Boolean Operators and Nesting Terms	49
Strategy 4: Truncation	55
Strategy 5: Wildcard Symbols	56
Strategy 6: Proximity Operators	56
Strategy 7: Explore All Possibilities	57
Concluding Thoughts on Strategies	57
Planning a Search	58
Step A: Which Sources Will Be Accessed?	58
Step B: Which Search Terms Will Be Used?	61
Step C: Which Search Strategies Will Be Used?	62
Step D: How Will the Search Results Be Saved?	64
Step E: Searching for Sources as an Ongoing Process	65
Step F: Managing Anxiety and Other Emotions	66
Coda	66
Exercises	67
Reading List	70

4. Writing a Literature Review **72**

Why Write a Literature Review?	72
Which Sources Belong in a Literature Review?	73
How Recent Should the Sources Be?	74
The Skills Needed for Reviewing Sources	75
Critical Thinking: The Foundation of Good Scholarship	75
Guidelines for Critical Thinking	76
Expanded Critical Skills for the Music Scholar	76
Note Taking	76
Begin by Noting the Full Publication Details for Each Source	78

Contents ix

Note the Page Numbers of Each Documented Segment 78
Direct Quotes and Paraphrasing 78
What to Record, and How Much? 78
The Habit of Critical Reading and Critical Note Taking 78
Filing Information 79
Legitimate Shortcuts 80
Writing Skills 81
Guidelines for Writing a Literature Review 81
Location of the Literature Review 81
How Many References? 82
Clustering the References 82
Organizing the References within Each Cluster 83
How to Begin 83
Reviewing the Sources 83
Providing a Citation for Each Reference 84
The Style of a Review 84
Precision and Concision 84
Building a Case through Critical Engagement 84
Creating a Cohesive Narrative 85
Which Person to Use 85
Which Tense to Use 86
Which Voice to Use 88
Distinguishing between the Voice of the Source and the Voice of
the Reviewer 89
How to End a Literature Review 89
Six Common Pitfalls in Writing a Literature Review 90
Guidelines for Writing an Annotated Bibliography 90
Cluster the References 91
How to Begin 91
Reviewing the Sources 91
Style 92
How to End an Annotated Bibliography 92
A Literature Review and an Annotated Bibliography in Summary 93
Coda 93
Exercises 93
Reading List 97

5. **Writing a Research Proposal** 99
Title Page 100
Project Title 102
Table of Contents 104
List of Tables, List of Figures, List of Musical Examples 106
Abstract 106
Introduction 108
Hypothesis or Research Question 109
Literature Review 110
Aims and Rationale 111

x Contents

Aims Compared With Hypothesis or Research Question	112
Anticipated Outcomes	112
Significance	113
Methodology	113
Music as Artifact and Music as Activity	114
Music as Artifact	114
Digital Musicology	114
Historical Musicology	115
Music Analysis	115
Music as Activity	116
Key Methods in Qualitative Research	117
Key Methods in Quantitative Research	118
Practice-Based Research	118
Concluding Thoughts on Methodology	120
Structure of the Thesis	121
Timeline	121
Ethics Clearance	125
Budget	125
Bibliography/Reference List	126
Referencing Styles	126
Notes and Bibliography Referencing	126
Author-Date Referencing	127
The Importance of Accurate Referencing	127
Information That Must Be Referenced	128
Information That Does Not Need to Be Referenced	128
How to Approach Referencing	129
Clustering Sources	130
Formatting of References	130
Dealing with Irregular Sources	130
Footnotes and Endnotes	130
Appendices	132
Coda	132
Exercises	133
Reading List	144
6. Writing a Thesis Part 1: Content, Organization, and Presentation	**148**
Content, Organization, and Presentation	148
Front Matter	149
Title Page	149
Declaration of Originality	151
Copyright Statement	151
Dedication	152
Abstract	152
Table of Contents	153
List of Musical Examples	156
List of Tables	156
List of Figures	156

List of Definitions	156
List of Abbreviations	156
List of Symbols	156
Preface	157
Acknowledgements	157
Chapters (Main Text)	157
Introduction	158
When Should an Introduction Be Written?	159
What is the Difference Between an Abstract and an Introduction?	159
Organization and Presentation of the Research Findings	160
Organization of the Findings	160
Presentation of the Findings	161
Illustrations	162
Conclusion	165
Back Matter	165
Endnotes	165
Bibliography/Reference List	166
Appendices	166
Formatting	166
Margins	166
Justification of Margins	166
Font and Font Size	167
Line Spacing	167
Begin Each Major Element on a New Page	167
Headings	167
Indentation of Paragraphs	169
Exercises	169
Reading List	171

7. Writing a Thesis Part 2: Style in Academic Writing — 174

Key Elements of the Academic Style	174
Defining Terms	174
The Notion of Argument	175
Evidence and the Analytical Process	175
Objectivity	176
Unity and Cohesion	177
Quoting Sources	178
Direct Quotations	179
Single or Double Quotation Marks	179
Introducing and Quitting Quotations	180
Punctuation Preceding a Quotation	181
Punctuation Following a Quotation	181
Changing a Punctuation Mark at the End of a Quotation	182
Capitalization and Lowercase	182
Omissions, Insertions, and Emphases	183
Citations for Quotations	183

xii   Contents

Referencing a Quotation within a Quotation	184
Quotations from Interview or Survey Data	185
Paraphrasing	185
Avoidance of Plagiarism	187
Language Usage in the Academic Style	188
Precision and Concision	188
Which Person to Use?	190
Which Tense to Use?	192
Documenting the Aims: Present Tense	192
Documenting the Methodology: Present, and Present Perfect Tenses	192
Reporting the Research Findings: Past Tense	193
Discussing the Research Findings: Present Tense	193
Evaluating the Research Findings: Present, Future, and Conditional Tenses	193
Which Voice to Use?	194
Avoidance of Contractions, Colloquialisms, and Clichés	194
Use of Acronyms	195
Gender-Neutral Language	195
Italics for Emphasis	197
Matters of Punctuation	197
Exercise	197
Reading List	199

8. Writing a Thesis Part 3: The Musical Lexicon   202

Capitalization	202
Historical Periods, Musical Styles, and Artistic Movements	202
Centuries	203
Genres and Forms	203
Movements and Sections within a Composition	204
Church (Ecclesiastical) Modes	204
Major and Minor	205
Scale Types	205
Scale Degrees	205
Dynamics, Tempo, and Other Performance Instructions	206
Musical Instruments	206
Artists' Names	207
First and Subsequent Mentions	207
Multiple Spellings, and Identification of Family Members	207
Diacritics	208
Particles in Last Names	208
Possessives	208
Titles of Musical Works	209
Generic Titles	209
Content and Formatting	210
Key	210
Thematic Catalogue Number	210

Contents   xiii

Examples of Generic Titles	211
Individual Titles	212
Content and Formatting	212
Examples of Individual Titles	212
Common Usage Titles	213
Examples of Common Usage Titles	213
Titles within a Work	213
Examples of Titles within a Work	214
Liturgical Titles	214
Titles Referred to in Two Languages	214
Notes and Note Names	214
Note Names as Compound Adjectives	215
Accidentals	215
Plurals	216
Succession of Notes or Keys	216
Time Signatures	216
Chords	216
Non-English Terms	217
Numbers	217
Abbreviations	218
Coda	219
Exercise	220
Reading List	222

9. Writing a Thesis Part 4: Efficiency and Effectiveness   224

Finding a Way into Each Chapter	224
Getting the Ideas Down on Paper	225
Building in Breaks	225
Good Scholarship Is Slow Scholarship	226
Making the Most of Supervision	226
Editing	226
Saving and Backing Up	227
Coda	229

10. Beyond the Thesis   230

Conference Papers	230
Where to Present	230
What to Present	230
How to Prepare and Present a Conference Paper	231
Publications	232
Where to Publish	233
What to Publish	233
How to Prepare and Present a Publication Submission	234
Coda	235

xiv Contents

Appendix A: Referencing in the Chicago Notes and Bibliography Style*
Appendix B: Referencing in the Style of the American Psychological
Association (APA Style)*
Appendix C: Guidelines for Musical Examples*
Appendix D: Guidelines for Tables*
Appendix E: Guidelines for Graphical Formats*
Appendix F: Guidelines for Punctuation*
Notes   237
Index   247

*Please note that the Appendices can only be accessed on the companion website, located at: www.oup.com/us/PostgraduateResearchinMusic.

Examples

Please note that both Examples appear only in the Appendices, which can be accessed on the companion website.

C.1. Glanville-Hicks, *Nausicaa*, prologue, mm. 1–5

C.2. Glanville-Hicks, *Sinfonia da Pacifica*, movt. 3, mm. 86–96

Tables

2.1. Primary, secondary, and tertiary sources	13
2.2. Subscription journal databases and their characteristics	20
2.3. Planning a visit to an archive	27
3.1. Keyword and subject searches: Advantages and disadvantages	46
3.2. Record of search terms and filters	65
4.1. Guidelines for critical thinking	77
4.2. The number of references included in a literature review	82
4.3. Connecting words and phrases	86
4.4. Guidelines for the review essay	96
5.1. Two approaches to abstract writing	107
5.2. Timeline template	124
5.3. Hypothetical budget for archival research	125
6.1. Two approaches to abstract writing	153
6.2. Abstract and introduction compared	160
6.3. Formatting of captions in Chicago and APA styles	163
6.4. Line spacing in a thesis	167
6.5. Hierarchy of headings	168
8.1. Capitalization of historical periods	203
8.2. Particles in last names	209
9.1. Supervisor and student roles and responsibilities	227
9.2. Editorial checklist	228
D.1. Frog song in Antarctica: Distribution by pitch collection and region	
D.2. *Frog Song*, scene 1, mm. 1–125	
F.1. Uses of the hyphen	
F.2. Uses of the en dash	
F.3. Uses of the em dash	

Figures

2.1.	*Ulrichsweb* search for the journal *Early Music*	18
2.2.	*Ulrichsweb* search for the journal *Early Music*: Further details about the journal	18
2.3.	*Grove Music Online*'s listing of collected editions for the music of Anton Bruckner	30
2.4.	Extract from *Grove Music Online*'s listing of Anton Bruckner's works	31
2.5.	RISM's advanced search screen with source types menu	32
2.6.	RISM's advanced search screen with search fields menu	32
2.7.	RIdIM database search page	34
3.1.	Advanced search in the RILM database, with filters	42
3.2.	Search filters in a typical library catalogue	43
3.3.	Search fields in RILM, a typical database of academic research	43
3.4.	Search fields in a typical library catalogue	44
3.5.	Subjects listed within "performance practice" in the RILM thesaurus	45
3.6.	Subjects information embedded in a typical library catalogue entry	46
3.7.	Boolean operators in the RILM database	50
3.8.	A search for two terms connected by the Boolean operator **AND**	51
3.9.	Narrowing the search results by adding search terms and applying filters	51
3.10.	A search using the Boolean operator **OR**	52
3.11.	Search using nesting and Boolean operators	52
3.12.	Search using nesting and Boolean operators in RILM	53
3.13.	An expanded search using additional search terms, nesting, and Boolean operators	53
3.14.	An expanded search using nesting, additional search terms, and Boolean operators in RILM	54
3.15.	A search on "early music," **NOT** "ornamentation," with further filters applied	54
3.16.	A search using Boolean operators, nesting, and truncation	55
3.17.	A search using Boolean operators, nesting, and truncation in RILM	55
4.1.	Filing system for the fictitious research project on the music of Diego Ferrera	80
5.1.	Content and ordering of a title page	101

xx Figures

5.2. Content and ordering of a title page: Alternative version with additional information 102

5.3. Table of contents for the fictitious study of the musical language of Diego Ferrera 105

5.4. Abstract for the fictitious study of the musical language of Diego Ferrera 108

5.5. Aims and rationale for a masters-level study entitled *John Blacking: Composer and Ethnomusicologist* 112

5.6. Thesis structure for the fictitious study of the musical language of Diego Ferrera 122

6.1. Title page for the fictitious doctoral thesis on the musical language of Diego Ferrera 150

6.2. Abstract for the doctoral thesis on the music of Diego Ferrera 154

6.3. Table of contents for the doctoral thesis on the music of Diego Ferrera 155

E.1. Frog song in Antarctica: Distribution by region

E.2. Frog song in Antarctica: Distribution by region and pitch collection (as a grouped bar chart)

E.3. Frog song in Antarctica: Distribution by region and pitch collection (as a stacked bar chart)

E.4. Concert attendance by year and genre, lost city of Atlantis, 2000–2012

E.5. Concert attendance by genre, lost city of Atlantis, 2000–2012

Preface

This book had its genesis in a course I taught for many years in my capacity as Associate Professor of Musicology at The University of Western Australia. The course was entitled "Introduction to Music Research" and was directed to honors and postgraduate music students. When I began teaching the course in 2007, I found an extensive general literature about how to do research, but very little about how to do *music* research—for music research is unique in its subject matter, the sources it draws upon, and how it is conducted. Ruth Watanabe's *Introduction to Music Research* was by then somewhat dated.[1] Texts by Jonathan Bellman, Trevor Herbert, and Richard Wingell were directed to undergraduate music students.[2] Style guides by D. Kern Holoman, Demar Irvine, and James Cowdery focused on the musical lexicon.[3] And there was the second edition of Phillip Crabtree and Donald Foster's *Sourcebook for Research in Music*, which documented the sources that were available for music research.[4] Notably absent, however, were books about how to undertake postgraduate research in music.

Over the next decade, the music-specific literature grew with the publication of bibliographic texts by Pauline Bayne, Jane Gottlieb, and Laurie Sampsel.[5] These three books, which dealt predominantly with the resources that are available for music research, were significant additions to the literature. New editions of Herbert's *Music in Words*, Holoman's *Writing about Music*, and Crabtree and Foster's *Sourcebook for Research in Music* were also published, and Thomas Donahue's *A Style and Usage Guide to Writing about Music* was published for the first time.[6] Considered both individually and collectively, these resources marked a significant step forward, but they only partially met the needs of the students who had been entrusted to my pedagogical care.

What was needed, I realized, was a comprehensive resource that considered all aspects of the research process, guiding students from the initial stages of a research project through to completion of the thesis. What was also needed was a music-specific focus, with contexts and examples to which music students could relate. The idea that I might be the person to write this book emerged gradually—perhaps somewhat reluctantly, for working out how to write the book preoccupied me for the year before writing began in early 2018. There was no precedent to draw upon; no-one had done quite what I had in mind.

xxii Preface

I was fortunate to have a starting point, a conceptual framework from which I could work. When I had begun teaching "Introduction to Music Research," I had inherited a small, fourteen-page course booklet written by my predecessor, Emeritus Professor David Tunley—a wonderful pedagogue and scholar who had seen the lacuna in the existing literature and set about addressing it. Each time I taught "Introduction to Music Research," the booklet grew in size and scope as I became increasingly aware of the knowledge and skills students needed to develop. That humble, though effective, course booklet became the starting point for *Postgraduate Research in Music*.

No book of this kind could find its way into the world without the help and support of many people, and I am deeply grateful to them all. I am indebted to David Tunley, who generously gave me his course booklet, and, in so doing, inadvertently sowed the seed for this book. I am grateful beyond measure to David Symons, who has been an endless source of support and encouragement, an invaluable sounding board for many of the ideas in the book, an indefatigable reader of drafts, and a believer in the project when my own conviction faltered. Many thanks are due to Geoffrey Lancaster, whose enthusiasm and belief in the project fueled my own, who fed me issues and ideas that are scattered throughout the book, and who gave valuable feedback on draft chapters. Amanda Myers, with her specialist knowledge of music librarianship, provided invaluable ideas and advice on chapters 2 and 3 of the book. Margaret Warburton's extremely helpful reading of the penultimate draft led to many improvements, and to greater concision in the writing.

Thanks are also due to Jenny Wildy and Linda Papa, music librarians at the University of Western Australia, whose input into the early versions of the course booklet has, more than a decade later, filtered through to the exercises in chapter 3; to Brian Dawson for his contribution to chapter 2, and for his enthusiastic support; to Sally Knowles, whose encouragement helped the project to get off the ground; to Susan Cochrane, for assistance in finding difficult-to-locate references; to Stuart James, for advice on the music notation references; to Jonathan Marshall, for ideas on reflective practice and practice-based research; to Craig McLaren, for his impeccable setting of the musical examples in appendix C; to Jordan Proctor, for his exemplary work in preparing the illustrations in appendix E, and for checking the database exercises in chapter 3; to Cyrus Meher-Homji, for helpful ideas on the musical lexicon; and to Jangoo Chapkhana and Lynn Blenkinsop for support, encouragement, and feedback.

I am also grateful to Tracie Dawson, who provided me with access to EBSCO-host academic databases, and to Naomi Perley, who gave me permission to log into *MGG Online* and the *RILM Music Encyclopedias*; chapters 2 and 3 would have been considerably poorer without their help. I also thank

Taylor & Francis for copyright permission to reproduce content from my 2009 book, *The Music of Peggy Glanville-Hicks*.

My students past and present have played a crucial role in this book, showing me what they needed to know and furnishing me with examples that elevate the book from a litany of do's and don'ts to something that is (hopefully) a little less arduous for readers.

I also thank Edith Cowan University and Jonathan Paget for providing a supportive and congenial research environment.

Finally, thanks are due to Oxford University Press for recognizing the need for a book of this kind, and for having the conviction to run with it; and to the OUP reviewers from whose critiques the book has benefitted greatly.

Reading List

Bayne, Pauline Shaw, and Edward M. Komara. *A Guide to Library Research in Music*. 2nd ed. Lanham, Maryland: Rowman & Littlefield, 2020.

Bellman, Jonathan. *A Short Guide to Writing About Music*. 2nd ed. New York: Pearson Longman, 2007.

Cowdery, James R., Carl Skoggard, and Barbara Dobbs Mackenzie. *How to Write about Music: The RILM Manual of Style*. 2nd ed. New York: *Répertoire International de Littérature Musicale*, 2006.

Crabtree, Phillip D., and Donald H. Foster. *Sourcebook for Research in Music*. Revised by Allen Scott. 2nd ed. Bloomington: Indiana University Press, 2005. [A 3rd edition was published in 2015.]

Donahue, Thomas. *A Style and Usage Guide to Writing about Music*. Lanham, Maryland: Scarecrow Press, 2010.

Gottlieb, Jane. *Music Library and Research Skills*. 2nd ed. New York: Oxford University Press, 2017.

Herbert, Trevor. *Music in Words: A Guide to Researching and Writing About Music*. London: Associated Board of the Royal Schools of Music, 2001. [A 2nd edition was published in 2012.]

Holoman, D. Kern. *Writing About Music: A Style Sheet from the Editors of 19th-Century Music*. Berkeley: University of California Press, 1988. [A 3rd edition was published in 2014.]

Irvine, Demar. *Irvine's Writing About Music*. Revised by Mark A. Radice. 3rd ed. Portland, Oregon: Amadeus Press, 1999.

Sampsel, Laurie J. *Music Research: A Handbook*. 3rd ed. New York: Oxford University Press, 2019.

Watanabe, Ruth. *Introduction to Music Research*. Englewood Cliffs, New Jersey: Prentice Hall, 1967.

Wingell, Richard. *Writing About Music: An Introductory Guide*. 4th ed. Upper Saddle River, New Jersey: Pearson Prentice Hall, 2007.

About the Companion Website

Oxford University Press has created a companion website featuring six appendices to accompany *Postgraduate Research in Music: A Step-by-Step Guide to Writing a Thesis*. The appendices include guidelines for referencing in the Chicago and APA styles; how to format musical examples, tables, and graphs; and information about punctuation marks that are often poorly understood and wrongly deployed in academic writing. These materials are available at www.oup.com/us/PostgraduateResearchinMusic.

Introduction

This book is in a sense a travel guide, a step-by-step itinerary that guides postgraduate music students on a journey from the starting point (a blank page) to the destination of a thesis. At the heart of the journey are the six questions of which Rudyard Kipling wrote in *Just So Stories*:

I keep six honest serving men;
(They taught me all I knew)
Their names are What and Why and When
And How and Where and Who.[1]

Although Kipling did not have postgraduate research in mind when he penned these lines, his "six honest serving men" nonetheless epitomize what research is, why it is done, what it involves, and what it contributes. Defined in a more conventional way, research is "any creative systematic activity undertaken in order to increase the stock of knowledge, including knowledge of man, culture and society, and the use of this knowledge to devise new applications."[2] Research may also be defined as "a process of investigation leading to new insights, effectively shared."[3] Considered together, these two definitions encapsulate what research is and what it does. Research involves investigation that is creative and systematic. It leads to new insights and knowledge that are communicated in an effective manner. And it puts the research outcomes to use in some way. Kipling's "six honest serving men," or questions, provide a framework for the research process.

Research is also an extension of what musicians do as creative artists. Research *enhances* the creative capacity of musicians. Through research, artistic practice becomes more considered, more informed, more broadly based . . . simply *better*. There is, then, good reason to undertake research, and to use it not only as an opportunity to enrich artistic practice, but also to learn skills that will be needed in the professional world of music. Research may be needed, for example, to compare different writings on instrumental technique, or to delve into early music treatises for a concert of early music, or to write program notes, or to evaluate different teaching philosophies and

Postgraduate Research in Music. Victoria Rogers, Oxford University Press. © Oxford University Press 2024.
DOI: 10.1093/oso/9780197616031.003.0001

2 Introduction

methods. Research is more than an obligatory addendum to a postgraduate degree in music. It is an important life skill and presents a rich opportunity for those who undertake it.

What Is a Thesis?

The vehicle for postgraduate research is a document referred to as a thesis—or a dissertation; this book will refer to it as a thesis. The term "thesis" stems from the word "hypothesis," which is a statement that is tested through the presentation of evidence, and through argumentation. A thesis sets out original research findings and draws upon a number of key principles:

- The articulation of a meaningful hypothesis or research question.
- The presentation of data, or evidence, to address the hypothesis or research question.
- The use of argument and logic to discuss and evaluate the data, or evidence.
- The formulation and articulation of new insights and knowledge arising from this process.

Put simply, a thesis states a hypothesis or asks a question, investigates it, presents and discusses the evidence, returns to the hypothesis or question posed at the beginning, and draws conclusions.

A thesis has a clear resonance with many of the concepts musicians work with on a daily basis. Musicians are well acquainted with the inherent quality of music as dialogue and argument. Eighteenth-century repertoire, for example, has, as its key philosophical underpinning, "principles of oration and argument established by Greek rhetoricians [that] were thought of as analogous to musical ideas and forms."[4] Musicians are also used to working with large-scale musical structures that correlate broadly with the architecture of a thesis. Not least of these are the tripartite musical forms which, in a general sense, mirror the three main parts of a thesis: an introduction in which the initial ideas (musical or, in the case of a thesis, conceptual) are set out; a middle section in which the ideas are developed, or argued; and a final section that draws the threads together with a return to the original ideas (either musical or conceptual) and a summation of the key content.

The process of writing a thesis is also, in many respects, analogous to the process of creating music. The shaping of musical phrases and the finessing of intonation and other musical details can be seen to correspond to the chiseling of sentences, phrases, and words to evoke subtle inflections of meaning. Every note is important; every word is important. The only difference is that in writing a thesis, musicians are working with a different language. Writing, like playing an instrument or composing a piece of music, is about structure, logic, feeling, creativity, imagination, and insight.

Aims and Approach

Postgraduate Research in Music is a "how to" book, a practical guide that sets out, step by step, how to write a thesis. Its aims are fivefold:

- To equip students with the skills and knowledge that are needed for postgraduate research in music.
- To consider all key aspects of the research process in the order in which they are encountered, from the initial stages of a research project through to completion of a thesis.
- To provide information that is useful and relevant for *all* music research, regardless of the sub-discipline in which it is conducted.
- To present a music-specific focus, with explanations and examples that are immediately relevant, and which take into account the special characteristics of music as a discipline.
- To provide a teaching framework for lecturers, bypassing the need to extrapolate information from books designed for other disciplines.

Like all books, *Postgraduate Research in Music* speaks from a particular position. It comes from the pen of a musicologist, and the thinking and examples in the book reflect this. A key aim of the book, however, is to be relevant for *all* postgraduate music students, regardless of whether they are performers, composers, or musicologists, and regardless of their area of research. There are certain principles that underpin all good scholarship, and it is these principles that this book seeks to distil. This applies no less to practice-led research, a more recent research area which has, as its goal, the production of an artistic outcome of some kind, or the investigation of an artistically creative process. In writing of this, Henk Borgdorff observes:

> Even if one accepts that the knowledge embodied in art is of a different order than the more "conventional" forms of academic or scientific knowledge, that does not mean

4 Introduction

the methods for accessing, retrieving, and disseminating such knowledge are also different.[5]

There is an obligation, writes Borgdorff, "to situate each study in a broader research context and to elucidate both the process and the outcome in accordance with customary standards."[6] The elucidation of those "customary standards" is the concern of this book—standards that apply to all research, regardless of the discipline or sub-discipline within which it is conducted.

Some topics in this book are discussed in greater detail than others because the information they contain is generically applicable to all of the sub-disciplines of music research. Other topics, for example methodological matters, are so vast as to preclude a detailed discussion. In such cases, a broad overview is provided and readers are referred to texts that focus on specific research areas.

When there is more than one way of approaching a particular issue, the alternatives are set out. When sources are drawn upon directly to inform the content of this book, those sources are acknowledged. When sources inform the text in a general way, they are included in the reading lists.

Much of the content in *Postgraduate Research in Music* is structured around Kipling's "six honest serving men," who provide a simple formula for each topic: what, why, and how. Kipling's three other "men" (when, where, and who) make cameo appearance when and where needed.

Features

Postgraduate Research in Music contains a number of features:

- All key concepts are illustrated with music-relevant examples, making it easier for readers to grasp the concepts being discussed. The operation of databases, for example, is illustrated by screenshots taken from typical music databases; the types of sources that are appropriate for a literature review are explored through examples taken from both real and imagined research projects; and the discussions of abstract writing are supplemented with examples.
- Exercises, and in some chapters class seminar topics as well, are included to reinforce the concepts that have been discussed in the chapters. Detailed pedagogical guidelines are also provided.
- Reading lists are included at the end of most chapters, enabling students to explore topics in greater depth.

- The book explores issues for which there is little or no guidance in other texts. How to use quotations, for example, is often a vexed issue for student scholars.
- The book is highly integrated, with frequent cross referencing between chapters. There are also threads that run through more than one chapter. The abstract for a research proposal, for example (chapter 5), is transformed into one written for a thesis (chapter 6), enabling students to see which information can be replicated and which cannot.

How to Use This Book

This book is designed to be used in two ways: first, as a text for courses in how to undertake music research; and second, as a reference to be consulted on an ongoing basis throughout the research process, and beyond.

Companion Website

There are six appendices, all of which are hosted on the Oxford University Press companion website (www.oup.com/us/PostgraduateResearchinMusic). These appendices contain information that is supplementary to the main text, but at the same time intrinsic to the design of this book. They are important and should not be consigned to the back burner of optional extras.

Chapter Outline

The chapters in this book fall into four segments. Chapters 1–3 are concerned with getting started. Chapters 4 and 5 lay the foundation for the thesis. Chapters 6–9 discuss different aspects of writing a thesis. Chapter 10 explores what lies beyond the thesis.

Chapter 1, Finding a Topic

The first step in getting the research process under way is finding a good topic. Exactly what defines a good topic, however, is not always self-evident. A good idea is not necessarily a good topic, nor is something that is simply of interest

6   Introduction

to the researcher. The matter of what constitutes a good topic, and how one might be found, are the subject of this brief opening chapter.

Chapter 2, Searching for Sources Part 1: Key Resources and Resource Portals

Chapter 2 is the first of two chapters that discuss a pivotal aspect of the research process: searching for sources of information. The chapter begins by identifying the three categories into which sources of information can be divided: primary, secondary, and tertiary. The remainder of the chapter sets out the key resources and resource portals that are used in music research, their value, and where they can be found.

Chapter 3, Searching for Sources Part 2: Strategies for Locating Information

Chapter 3 addresses the "how" of searching for sources, focusing in particular upon electronic databases. The first part of the chapter explores different ways of searching databases, documenting why and how the various search functions are used. The second part provides guidelines for planning a search, drawing together the information and strategies set out in chapters 2 and 3.

Chapter 4, Writing a Literature Review

Chapter 4 explores the next step in the research process: writing a literature review. The chapter begins by addressing the reasons for writing a review of the literature, the sources it includes, and the skills that are needed. Guidelines are then provided for writing a review, and for writing an annotated bibliography—an exercise that is often undertaken as preparation for the literature review itself.

Chapter 5, Writing a Research Proposal

Chapter 5 discusses a further milestone in the research process: writing a research proposal. The chapter introduces students to what a research proposal is and why it is important, and sets out the what, the why and the how of each of the elements within a proposal.

Chapter 6, Writing a Thesis Part 1: Content and Organization

Chapter 6 is the first of four chapters that discuss what is involved in writing a thesis. It considers what a thesis includes, how its content is organized and presented, and how it is formatted.

Chapter 7, Writing a Thesis Part 2: Style in Academic Writing

Chapter 7 explores style in academic writing. It identifies the key elements of the academic style and examines the stylistically appropriate use of language within an academic context.

Chapter 8, Writing a Thesis Part 3: The Musical Lexicon

Whether to capitalize major and minor, the church modes, and scale degrees; how to document artists' names and the titles of musical works; how to refer to notes and note names . . . these are some of the many confusions that arise when writing about music. Chapter 8 brings clarity to the issue by discussing the documentation of key elements within the musical lexicon.

Chapter 9, Writing a Thesis Part 4: Efficiency and Effectiveness

Chapter 9 is the last of the four chapters that explore different aspects of writing a thesis. Where the preceding three chapters have focused on content, style, and the musical lexicon, chapter 9 considers matters of efficiency and effectiveness in the writing process.

Chapter 10, Beyond the Thesis

With the skills acquired through writing a thesis, students are now equipped to take on new challenges: those of presenting their research findings at conferences and in publications. This chapter offers an overview of the where, the what, and the how of presenting a conference paper, and of publishing the research in academic journals and books.

8 Introduction

Reading List

"Annex C: Definitions of Research and Impact for the REF." REF 2021 Research Exercise Framework Guidance on Submissions. Accessed December 20, 2021. https://www.ref.ac.uk/media/1447/ref-2019_01-guidance-on-submissions.pdf.

Borgdorff, Henk. *The Conflict of the Faculties: Perspectives on Artistic Research and Academia.* Leiden: Leiden University Press, 2012.

"Glossary of Statistical Terms: Research and Development—UNESCO." OECD. Accessed December 20, 2021. https://stats.oecd.org/glossary/detail.asp?ID=2312.

Kipling, Rudyard. *Just So Stories.* London: Macmillan, 1902.

Marney, Dylan. "The Application of Musico-Rhetorical Theory to Stretto, Double, and Triple Fugue: Analyses of Contrapuncti V–XI from J. S. Bach's *The Art of the Fugue* BWV 1080." DMA diss., University of Arizona, 2013. Quoted in Geoffrey Lancaster, *Through the Lens of Esoteric Thought: Joseph Haydn's The Seven Last Words of Christ on the Cross* (Crawley, Western Australia: UWA Press, 2019).

Vickers, B. "Figures of Rhetoric/Figures of Music?" *Rhetorica: A Journal of the History of Rhetoric* 2, no. 1 (1984): 21. Quoted in Geoffrey Lancaster, *Through the Lens of Esoteric Thought: Joseph Haydn's The Seven Last Words of Christ on the Cross* (Crawley, Western Australia: UWA Press, 2019).

1
Finding a Topic

A thesis begins with an idea. Nothing more. Just an idea. That idea—if it is the *right* idea—becomes a topic. And that topic—if it is a *good* topic—grows into a thesis. Finding the *right* idea, and a *good* topic, are the starting point in writing a thesis.

Exactly what defines a good topic, however, is not self-evident. A good idea is not necessarily a good topic, nor is something that is simply of interest to the researcher. The matter of what constitutes a good topic, and how one might be found, therefore need some discussion.

First and foremost, a good topic must be original; it must not duplicate existing research, for research involves new and original discovery. It must investigate something that is meaningful—that is worth investigating. It must be feasible in scope—not too broad and not too narrow—and take into account the time frame and word count of the thesis. A study of *all* of Beethoven's compositions, for example, would be far too broad and would take too long to complete. A good topic has the potential for probing research that burrows beneath the surface of a subject; a topic that only produces a shopping list of facts is not a good topic. Perhaps above all, a good topic must fascinate the researcher. This fascination will be needed to sustain the research through its inevitable ups and downs, and through the commitment of time that will be needed to bring the project to a successful conclusion.

Sometimes a topic emerges quickly and easily, but often a considerable amount of reading and reflection are needed before a suitable topic takes shape. The following guidelines will facilitate this process.

1. Identify one or more broad areas of interest that can be explored as possible research topics and write them down—such things as Baroque music; women composers; performance wellness; historical performance practice; a particular composer or time period; serialism; or music pedagogy.
2. Read extensively around each area of interest, drawing upon a wide range of sources. *Grove Music Online* is often a good starting point as it offers authoritative overviews of a large number of research areas,

Postgraduate Research in Music. Victoria Rogers, Oxford University Press. © Oxford University Press 2024.
DOI: 10.1093/oso/9780197616031.003.0002

together with bibliographies that can be drawn upon to generate further reading.[1] The sub-disciplinary reach of *Grove Music Online* is extensive. It incorporates updated versions of six previous *Grove* publications: *The New Grove Dictionary of Music and Musicians*; *The New Grove Dictionary of Jazz*; *The New Grove Dictionary of Opera*; *The Norton Grove Dictionary of Women Composers*; *The Grove Dictionary of American Music*; and *The Grove Dictionary of Musical Instruments*. The print version of *Grove*, the *New Grove Dictionary of Music and Musicians*, can also be used as a starting point, although it is more limited in scope than *Grove Music Online*.[2] Before embarking upon this program of reading, chapters 2 and 3 of this book should be studied ("Searching for Sources" Parts 1 and 2), as well as two sections from chapter 4 ("Writing a Literature Review"): critical thinking skills and note-taking skills.

3. Keep a note of the sources that have been accessed. Be sure to record the key bibliographic information for each source, including the author, title, publisher, date, journal volume and issue, web address, and so on as appropriate. Document what each source is about, as well as any ideas generated by the reading. This information will form the basis of the review of literature that is included in both the research proposal and the thesis. There is no need for polished writing at this stage; the main thing is to keep track of the sources and the ideas.

4. From this survey of the existing research, identify any gaps that might form the nucleus of a thesis topic—in other words, aspects of a subject that have not yet been researched. If, for example, the existing research on a particular composer were to have focused solely on the orchestral and chamber works but not upon the operas, the gap in the existing research—the operas—might form the topic of a thesis.

5. Working from the gaps that have been identified, make a list of possible research topics. Direct the following questions to each topic:
   - Is the topic original? Is it new, distinctive, and different from the research that has gone before?
   - Is the topic meaningful? Is it worth investigating? Will it add something of value to the existing body of research?
   - Is the topic of appropriate scope for an honors, masters, or doctoral thesis (whichever is the case)? How might it be shaped to accommodate the required word count? Does it need to be trimmed to focus on one, or a few, aspects? Does it need to be broadened?
   - Does the topic have the potential for analytic depth?
   - Are there appropriate resources to support the topic? If, for example, essential research material is housed in archival collections, can it be

accessed? If the topic requires the study of unpublished scores, can copies be obtained? If the study is of rare historic recordings, can digital/study copies be made? If survey and interview data will form the core of the research findings, can enough participants be found?

- Does the topic *fascinate* and *excite* you?

6. Discuss the possible topics with supervisors and anyone who will listen! This will help to clarify the ideas and test the feasibility of the topics.

7. Come to a decision based on the evidence and ideas that have been gathered from the above process. Write down the topic you have selected and the reasons for choosing it.

It is important to document each of these steps as it is undertaken, progressively rather than retrospectively. If this is not done, it is likely that key sources, good ideas, and justifications for a topic will be forgotten. It is also important to form the habit of writing as early as possible in the research process, because writing becomes easier the more it is done.

Regardless of whether a good topic emerges quickly or whether it takes longer to take shape, an extensive program of reading will be needed. This raises two important issues: first, *where* to look for information; and second, *how* to look. These topics will be discussed in chapters 2 and 3.

Reading List

Bayne, Pauline Shaw, and Edward M. Komara. *A Guide to Library Research in Music*. 2nd ed., 4–8. Lanham, Maryland: Rowman & Littlefield, 2020.

Booth, Wayne C., Gregory C. Colomb, Joseph M. Williams, Joseph Bizup, and William T. Fitzgerald. *The Craft of Research*. 4th ed., 33–63. Chicago: University of Chicago Press, 2016.

Root, Deane, ed. *Grove Music Online*. Oxford University Press, 2001. http://www.oxfordmusiconline.com.

Sadie, Stanley, and John Tyrrell, eds. *New Grove Dictionary of Music and Musicians*. London: Macmillan, 2001.

Turabian, Kate. *A Manual for Writers of Research Papers, Theses and Dissertations: Chicago Style for Students and Researchers*. 9th ed., 10–24. Chicago: University of Chicago Press, 2018.

2

Searching for Sources Part 1

Key Resources and Resource Portals

Chapter 2 is the first of two chapters that discuss the next step in the research process: searching for sources of information. With the ever-increasing amount of published research, the development and digitization of archival collections, and the proliferation of audio and video content, the music scholar has access to a vast body of information. Searching for sources must therefore be extensive, comprehensive, and discriminating.

This chapter identifies the sources that are used in music research, their value, and how they can be found. The chapter is divided into two parts: a discussion of primary, secondary, and tertiary sources; and an examination of key resources and resource portals. As a general introduction to a highly specialized field of knowledge, the information in this chapter may need to be supplemented with three texts that focus on bibliographic matters: *A Guide to Library Research in Music*, by Pauline Shaw Bayne and Edward M. Komara; *Music Library and Research Skills*, by Jane Gottlieb; and *Music Research: A Handbook*, by Laurie J. Sampsel.[1]

Primary, Secondary, and Tertiary Sources

Sources of information can be divided into three categories: primary, secondary, and tertiary. These categories signal the sort of information that is available for music research, where it can be found, and the role it plays in a thesis. Some discussion is therefore in order.

Primary sources are original sources of information. They provide direct, or firsthand, evidence that has been preserved in either written, aural, visual, or electronic form, and has not been subjected to interpretation or evaluation. Primary sources provide a foundation upon which new, original research is built. They include holograph, autograph, and facsimile scores; diaries and letters; and historical treatises. A listing of primary sources is provided in table 2.1.

Postgraduate Research in Music. Victoria Rogers, Oxford University Press. © Oxford University Press 2024.
DOI: 10.1093/oso/9780197616031.003.0003

Table 2.1. Primary, secondary, and tertiary sources

Primary	Secondary	Tertiary
• Album notes, liner notes, and accompanying notes • Artefacts (e.g., an historical instrument) • Artwork, including paintings and photographs • Autobiographies • Autograph, holograph, and facsimile music scores • Books • Concert reviews • Conference papers • Email communication • Eyewitness accounts • Films and videos • Government documents • Historical documents • Interviews • Journal articles • Letters and diaries • Liner notes • Memorabilia • Newspaper and magazine articles • Novels, poems, and other literary works • Performances • Phone communication • Program notes • Recordings • Speeches • Theses • Treatises • Websites, blogs, and social media	• Album notes, liner notes, and accompanying notes • Books • Book reviews • Collected editions of early music • Commentaries • Concert reviews • Conference papers • Documentaries • Edited collections of letters • Edited scores • Films and videos • Historical accounts • Journal articles • Liner notes • Newspaper and magazine articles • Performances • Programme notes • Recordings • Textbooks • Theses • Websites, blogs, and social media	• Almanacs • Bibliographies • Chronologies • Dictionaries • Directories • Encyclopaedias • Fact books • Guidebooks • Handbooks • Indices • Manuals • Textbooks • Websites, blogs, and social media

Secondary sources are derivative sources of information. They describe, discuss, analyze, synthesize, and evaluate primary sources; they also draw upon other secondary sources. Secondary sources inform research in many ways. A critical commentary in a collected edition of early music, for example, can provide valuable insights into the performance practices of a particular historical period or repertoire. Secondary sources include collected editions of music, historical accounts, and textbooks. A listing of secondary sources is provided in table 2.1. It should be noted that some of these sources may also be categorized as primary sources, and some as tertiary sources. Such overlaps and ambiguities will be discussed in the next section.

14   Postgraduate Research in Music

Tertiary sources are also derivative sources of information. They compile, synthesize, and organize information that has been harvested from both primary and secondary sources. Tertiary sources function as general references for such things as definitions, dates, and facts, and are often used in the early stages of a research project. Tertiary sources include dictionaries, encyclopedias, and bibliographies. A listing of tertiary sources is provided in table 2.1.

Overlaps and Ambiguities

Whilst there are generally clear-cut distinctions between primary, secondary, and tertiary sources, there are times when a particular source might be classified in either of two ways, depending upon its content and context. A composer's holograph, for example, would be classified as a primary source and seen as a definitive, or near definitive, indication of compositional intention. A subsequent printed edition of that score, with editorial emendations, would be defined as a secondary source. These two versions of the same musical work would play different roles in a research project and would generally be housed in different places—the holograph in an archive and the printed score in a library.

Content also determines whether academic journal articles should be classified as primary or secondary sources. An article that sets out an original research design and/or findings is classified as a primary source. On the other hand, one that offers the analysis, interpretation, or evaluation of a research design and/or other research findings is seen as a secondary source.

Newspaper articles can also be classified as either primary or secondary sources. An article that records a journalist's firsthand account of an event is classified as a primary source; one that documents the impressions of bystanders to this same event is described as a secondary source. Similarly, a critic's review of a concert is classified as a primary source, but an article that describes the impressions of concertgoers is a secondary source.

Also spanning two categories are encyclopedias, bibliographies, and textbooks, in this case the categories of secondary and tertiary. An encyclopedia, for example, may present an analysis and interpretation of other sources, in which case it would be described as a secondary source and function as a catalyst for discussion. It may also compile facts derived from primary and/or secondary sources; as such it would be defined as a tertiary source and be used for such things as definitions.

Online sources, too, can be classified in different ways. Social media and blogs can be either primary or secondary sources, depending upon whether their content is original or derivative. Websites span all three categories. A primary source website, for example, might function as a key source of information about a contemporary composer. One such example is the website of the composer Cat Hope (http://www.cathope.com/), which sets out her compositional philosophy and recorded performances, together with explanatory notes.[2] *The Alan Hovhaness Website* (http://www.hovhaness.com/Hovhaness.html), on the other hand, is almost entirely a compilation of information about Hovhaness. As such it is best classified as a tertiary source.[3]

Recordings can also be complex in their classification. They may be seen as primary sources—that is, as original sources of information. They may also be seen as secondary sources—in other words, as an exercise of interpretation in which the score is the primary source and the recording a second layer that is added. In fact, recordings are generally classified as secondary sources. There are times, however, when they can be considered to be primary sources.[4] If, for example, a research project were to investigate style and interpretation in the pianism of Alfred Cortot, the historic recordings upon which the research would draw would be classified as primary sources.

A more ambiguous example is a recording of Indeterminate music. Because every rendition of the work is different, a primary source classification may seem logical. Every note and/or fragment, however, has been set out in the score; the variable element is its manner of performance. It is therefore the score that is the primary source. Each recording is an interpretation of the score, regardless of how many different recordings are generated, or the uniqueness of each. Such recordings would therefore be classified as secondary sources. If, on the other hand, a research project were to focus upon a particular performer's realization of Indeterminate scores, the recordings would be considered to be primary sources.

An edited collection of a composer's letters may also be confusing in its classification. It may appear to be a primary source. It is, however, a secondary source because editorial decisions have determined which letters are included, and the ordering of the letters. There might also be translations from the original language, and editorial amendments as well. Such a collection needs to be distinguished from the original letters held in an archive; they would be classified as primary sources.

It is important to be aware of the nature of sources as primary, secondary, or tertiary because, as noted earlier in the chapter, it indicates not only the kind of information that is available and where it can be found, but also the role it plays in a thesis. Secondary sources, for example, form the basis of a literature review because this is where the existing writings on or around a topic are discussed. Primary sources, on the other hand, generally belong in the methodology because they inform how the research will be conducted. A more nuanced and expansive discussion of this matter is set out in chapter 4 ("Writing a Literature Review") in the section entitled "Which Sources Belong in a Literature Review?"

Key Resources and Resource Portals

Notwithstanding the proliferation of research resources in recent decades, the university library remains the central and most significant access point for the music scholar. The contemporary library is far more than a building that stores books. It is also a gateway to electronic sources that are not freely available on the World Wide Web. Through WorldCat, for example, the library has access to catalogues from libraries around the world. The library is a vital starting point in the search for sources, providing a portal to both hard copy and electronic resources.

The search for sources also needs to extend beyond the boundaries of the library. Archival collections (both hard copy and electronic) and websites, for example, often contain significant research material. The diverse range of resources that can be accessed either within, through, or beyond the library all need to be taken into consideration in the search for sources. These sources can usefully be grouped into eight categories: (1) writings about music; (2) archival sources; (3) scores, editions, and collections; (4) thematic catalogues; (5) music iconography; (6) sound recordings, films, and videos; (7) search engines and websites; and (8) social media, blogs, and podcasts.

Writings about Music

Writings about music vary widely in content and purpose. This section sets out the various categories and the sort of material they contain, whether they are peer-reviewed (also referred to as refereed), their use and value, and where they can be found.

Books and E-books (Electronic Books)

The academic book, a stalwart of scholarship in past centuries, remains a key resource for music research. The reason for this is that academic books, whether published in hard copy or digital (electronic) format, are peer-reviewed—in other words, they are scrutinized by experts from the same field of study before being accepted for publication. This ensures that the research is rigorous and that the scholarship is of a high standard. Academic books are reliable and authoritative sources of information. They yield original research outcomes and speak with a voice of authority that carries weight in the world of scholarship.

Books are generally located through online library catalogues and academic databases (see chapter 3 for a discussion of how to use catalogues and databases). They can also be found through Google Books (https://books.google.com.au/), Google Scholar (https://scholar.google.com.au), the Internet Archive (http://archive.org/details/texts), and the Hathi Trust Digital Library (https://www.hathitrust.org). Google Books generally duplicates the search results presented through other sources, but it sometimes finds items that other sources miss. For this reason it should be included in a search for sources, together with Google Scholar, which locates both books and other scholarly writings. The Internet Archive is a free online database that contains millions of scanned books and other sources that are in the public domain (out of copyright) and not easily available elsewhere. It covers a wide range of subject areas, including music, and can be useful for locating historic publications. The Hathi Trust Digital Library is a vast collection of digitized books that are managed by academic and research libraries. Like the Internet Archive, the Hathi Trust includes music in its subject areas.

Journal Articles

Journal articles, like academic books, are an important source of reliable, authoritative information. The journals in which they appear are usually specific to a particular sub-discipline of music research (for example, *Ethnomusicology*, *Journal of Music Theory*, and *Early Music*); the journals are published at regular intervals, either in hard copy or e-format or both. Current journal articles contain more up-to-date research than books because the lead time for publication is shorter—a matter of months compared with years. In scope, too, a journal article differs from a book, presenting a narrow slice of research that equates more or less with the length of a single book chapter.

Most scholarly journals are peer-reviewed, and whilst research published in non-reviewed journals can also be valuable, it is important to be aware of the academic standing of a journal. For this there is a database, called *Ulrichsweb*, that provides detailed information about more than 300,000 periodicals.[5] *Ulrichsweb* indicates whether a journal is peer-reviewed; it also provides details such as the starting date of the journal, how often it

18 Postgraduate Research in Music

is published, and its areas of focus. *Ulrichsweb* can generally be accessed through the online portals of university libraries. If a library does not subscribe to *Ulrichsweb*, information about an individual journal can be found on the journal's own website in a section that is typically labeled "About," or "Author guidelines."[6]

After a journal title has been typed into the *Ulrichsweb* home page, a page appears with basic information about the journal (see figure 2.1). If the journal is peer-reviewed, a black icon (the image of a referee's jacket) appears to the left of the title. Further information about the journal can be found by clicking on the journal title (see figure 2.2).

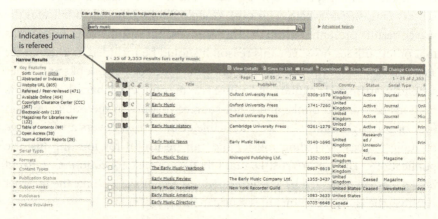

Figure 2.1. *Ulrichsweb* search for the journal *Early Music*

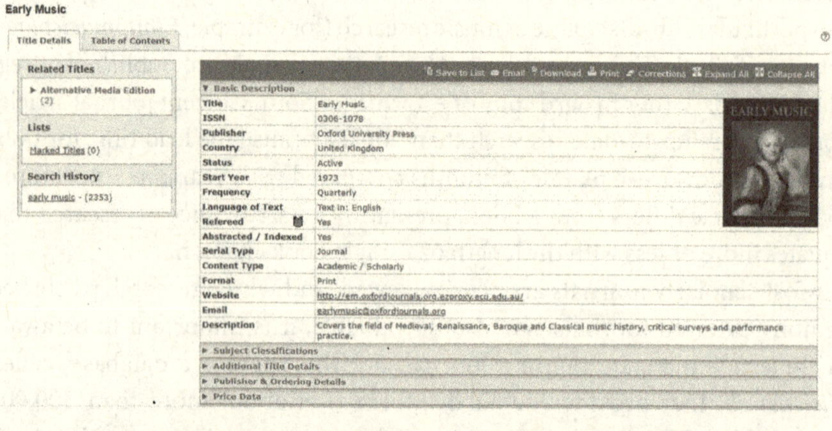

Figure 2.2. *Ulrichsweb* search for the journal *Early Music*: Further details about the journal

There are three key databases that provide access to the journals in which music research is published: Music Index; Music Periodicals Database; and RILM Abstracts of Music Literature (*Répertoire international de la littérature musicale*). Two further databases may also be useful: the Performing Arts Periodicals Database, which extends across the broader gamut of the performing arts; and JStor, which, although not music- or arts-specific, sometimes presents search results missed by other resources. These five databases and their characteristics are set out in table 2.2.[7] They can be accessed through the online portals of university libraries, which generally subscribe to some or all of them.

A further useful resource is JURN (an acronym with no particular meaning; www.jurn.org).[8] JURN is a search tool for locating full-text academic articles and book chapters that are freely available online (referred to as open access). JURN's particular strength is the arts and humanities; it focuses mainly on content published after 1994. A list of the journals included in JURN, together with links to the journals, can be found at http://www.jurn.org/directory/. Another open-access resource is DOAJ (Directory of Open Access Journals; https://doaj.org/). Like JURN, DOAJ is multi-disciplinary in scope, and includes research in the arts and humanities.

The search for journals may also extend to music organizations and associations that publish their own journals. *The Ralph Vaughan Williams Society Journal* (https://rvwsociety.com/society-journal/), for example, contains articles about Vaughan Williams' life and work, and although the journal is not peer-reviewed, the articles it contains are written by authorities in the field. It is therefore a credible source for academic research.

Historical Treatises and Documents

Treatises and other historical documents such as diaries and correspondence are an important resource for music scholars. These are primary sources and provide information that other sources cannot offer. They are generally housed in archival collections; some treatises can also be accessed through the Internet Archive.

Encyclopedias and Dictionaries of Music

Encyclopedias and dictionaries of music contain information on a broad range of music-related topics. They are authoritative, reliable sources and include such things as definitions, overviews of artists and subjects, lists of composers' works, and bibliographies. They are of particular value in the early stages of a research project when a general introduction to a topic is needed.

Encyclopedias and dictionaries of music are extensive in both number and scope. Sampsel provides a comprehensive listing in chapter 3 of *Music*

20   Postgraduate Research in Music

Table 2.2. Subscription journal databases and their characteristics

Database	Characteristics
Music Index and Music Index with Full Text	• Coverage is from 1964 to the present. • Music Index provides indexing and abstracts for well over 800 journals, as well as reviews of performances, sound recordings and videos. • Music Index with Full Text includes the content of the Music Index, as well as full text for more than 200 journals. • Music Index and Music Index with Full Text cover every aspect of classical and popular music, including film music, vocal performance, music and society, music theory, music therapy, music education, musicology, and performance.
Music Periodicals Database	• Includes journal articles that date as far back as 1874, although most are more recent. • Provides indexing and abstracts for more than 600 international music periodicals, plus full text for over 200 journals. • Covers a wide range of subject areas, including music education, performance, ethnomusicology, musical theater, theory, popular music, and composition.
RILM Abstracts of Music Literature (*Répertoire international de la littérature musicale*) and RILM Abstracts of Music Literature with Full Text[a]	• Some content extends back to the late 18th century; most dates from the early 1800s to the present. • RILM Abstracts of Music Literature includes citations, abstracts, and indexing for around 2,000 music journals. • RILM Abstracts of Music Literature with Full Text includes, in addition, full-text content from around 250 periodicals published from the early 20th century to the present. • Subject areas include composition, ethnomusicology, jazz studies, musicology, music analysis, music iconography, music librarianship, music pedagogy, music perception, music therapy, organology, performance practice, and popular music.
Performing Arts Periodicals Database	• Includes titles from as early as 1864; coverage is mostly from 1998. • Indexes over 600 scholarly and trade journals, magazines, books, and newspapers. • Subjects include theater, dance, film, television, stagecraft, broadcast arts, and opera.
JStor	• Covers seventy-five academic disciplines, of which music is one. • Is not as comprehensive as the databases specific to music, but occasionally presents sources missed by other databases.

[a]*Note*: RILM (*Répertoire international de littérature musicale*) is one of four international, co-operative bibliographic projects, the others being RISM (*Répertoire international des sources musicales*), RIPM (*Répertoire international de la presse musicale*), and RIdIM (*Répertoire international d'iconographie musicale*).

Research: A Handbook.[9] There are also useful listings in Gottlieb's *Music Library and Research Skills,* in Bayne and Komara's *A Guide to Library Research in Music,* and in Scholes and Wagstaff's article in *The Oxford Companion to Music.*[10] These texts should be used to supplement the brief overview that is provided in this chapter.

The New Grove Dictionary of Music and Musicians and its online version, *Grove Music Online,* are key sources.[11] The subject reach of *Grove Music Online* is particularly extensive; as noted in chapter 1, it incorporates updated versions of six previous *Grove* publications, including *The New Grove Dictionary of Music and Musicians. Grove Music Online* is available by subscription to individuals and institutions.

Another general encyclopedia is *Die Musik in Geschichte und Gegenwart* (*Music in History and the Present;* MGG), which, like *Grove,* is available in both print and online formats.[12] MGG covers both Western and non-Western musics. The online version includes a bilingual English/German interface, as well as instant translation from German into more than one hundred languages. It is available by subscription to individuals and institutions.

The Garland Encyclopedia of World Music is a comprehensive encyclopedia of music from around the world.[13] It comprises ten volumes, nine of which are devoted to the music of particular geographical regions (Africa, Southeast Asia, etc.). It is of particular value for ethnomusicological research. *The Garland Encyclopedia* is published in both print and online formats; the online version includes audio recordings and is available through individual or institutional subscription.

There are, in addition, three single-volume sources that provide succinct entries on a wide range of subjects, as well as useful definitions of terms: *The Oxford Companion to Music* (a new, online-only edition is included with a subscription to *Grove Music Online*); *The Oxford Dictionary of Music* (also included with a subscription to *Grove Music Online*; it is available in print and online); and *The Harvard Dictionary of Music.*[14]

Theses and Dissertations

A considerable amount of postgraduate music research is now available online through databases that are either subscribed to by university libraries or open access.

There are two subscription databases that can be accessed through the online portals of university libraries: ProQuest Dissertations & Theses Global, and RILM Abstracts of Music Literature. Of these, ProQuest is devoted solely to masters and doctoral theses. RILM includes theses along with other resources such as journal articles and books.

22   Postgraduate Research in Music

Of the databases that are freely available online, four should be included in the search for sources: Doctoral Dissertations in Musicology (DDM; https://www.ams-net.org/ddm/); e-theses online service (EThOS; https://ethos.bl.uk/Home.do); Networked Digital Library of Theses and Dissertations (NDLTD; http://www.ndltd.org/resources/find-etds); and EBSCO Open Dissertations (https://biblioboard.com/opendissertations).

DDM is an initiative of the American Musicological Society. It is an international database that contains bibliographic records for both completed dissertations and new dissertation topics in music research. It does not include the dissertations themselves.

EThOS is hosted by the British Library. It includes bibliographic records of doctoral theses awarded by universities in the United Kingdom. In some cases, there are links to the theses themselves.

NDLTD is an international organization that promotes access to electronic theses and dissertations worldwide. The NDLTD website provides access to e-copies of dissertations which are hosted on the repositories of individual institutions.

EBSCO Open Dissertations provides bibliographic records of theses and dissertations from around the world. It includes URLs that take users to e-copies of the dissertations, which are hosted on institutional repositories.

Theses and dissertations are inconsistent in quality and need to be considered in this light. At best they contain significant research findings, as well as leads to bibliographies and other sources. At worst, they should be disregarded entirely.

Conference Proceedings
Research findings are often reported at conferences and published soon after in conference proceedings that aggregate all, or a selection, of the conference papers into hard-copy or e-publications. With a short lead time between presentation and publication, conference proceedings can be a useful source of recent research findings. Many conference proceedings are peer-reviewed and can therefore be considered to be authoritative sources. The authority of proceedings that are not peer-reviewed is less assured, but these sources should not be discounted. Conference proceedings are included in some academic databases.

Album Notes, Liner Notes, Accompanying Notes, and Program Notes
Album notes for LP (vinyl) recordings, liner notes for CD recordings, accompanying notes for streaming services such as *Naxos*, and program

notes for concerts, can be significant and authoritative sources of information. Although they are not peer-reviewed, they sometimes provide information that is not available elsewhere. A commentary by a composer whose work features in a program of new music, for example, or descriptive notes by an artist featured in a recording of early music, can yield significant insights.

Newspapers, Periodicals, and Magazines

Although newspapers, periodicals, and magazines are usually directed to a generalist audience, they can yield rich data for music research.[15] They include such things as concert and recording reviews, interviews with artists, and essays on musical issues. As historical sources, they also shed light on the social and cultural contexts with which music is intertwined.

Many historical newspapers, periodicals, and magazines are now available online through digitization programs that are being undertaken throughout the world. Foremost amongst them are *Le Répertoire international de la presse musicale* (RIPM), ProQuest Historical Newspapers, Gale Historical Newspapers, Google News Archive, and digitization programs run by government instrumentalities.

RIPM provides online access to primary source literature about musical activities from ca. 1760 to ca. 1966. It focuses on Europe and the Americas and includes music journals, daily newspapers, literary periodicals, theatrical journals, and magazines de mode.[16] RIPM is available through institutional subscription.

Where RIPM focuses on the musical press, ProQuest Historical Newspapers, Gale Historical Newspapers, and Google News Archive provide general news coverage. ProQuest Historical Newspapers offers online access to newspapers from the late 1700s to the early 2000s. It concentrates mostly on the United States; there is also some Canadian and international coverage, as well as an Australian collection.[17] It is available through institutional subscription. Gale Historical Newspapers spans the period from the eighteenth century to the present; it has a global reach and is available through subscription.[18] The Google News Archive is freely available online. It, too, is global in scope and spans the period from the 1700s to the early 2000s.[19]

There are also digitization programs that are sponsored by governments around the world, each with its own national focus. Chronicling America, for example, is a digital repository of historic newspapers in the United States from 1690 to the present (https://chroniclingamerica.loc.gov/).[20] In the United Kingdom, the British Newspaper Archive contains digitized copies of hundreds of newspapers from the United Kingdom and Ireland from the eighteenth century to the present day (https://www.britishnewspaperarchive.co.uk/).

A pivotal resource for locating digitized newspapers by country (with a further breakdown of the United States by state) is the website of the International Coalition on Newspapers (ICON; http://icon.crl.edu/digitization.php). Wikipedia also has a valuable country-by-country listing (https://en.wikipedia.org/wiki/Wikipedia:List_of_online_newspaper_archives).

A large number of historical newspapers, periodicals, and magazines are yet to be digitized and can only be accessed through hard-copy archival collections, or through microfilm and microfiche (largely obsolete technology that is available through university and other libraries). Archival sources are discussed in the ensuing section.

Official Records and Reports

Official records and reports are important sources of statistical data. A study of the gendered distribution of orchestral players, for example, would be likely to draw upon statistics that have been documented in reports commissioned by government instrumentalities or arts organizations. Official records and reports are meticulously compiled and are credible and reliable sources of information.

There is no universal formula for accessing official records and reports, for each jurisdiction operates under a different legislation. Official records can generally be accessed through state or federal records offices or their online portals. Reports can often be accessed through legal (mandatory) deposit copies lodged in state and national libraries, or through the commissioning bodies themselves.

Archival Sources

For the scholar-detective, archival research is an enticing prospect, offering the possibility of unimagined information that may fill gaps in the research puzzle. The term "archive" has two related meanings. It refers to a building where historical records are kept; it also refers to a collection of historical items. Broadly defined, an archive contains historical records of some kind. These records comprise such things as letters, diaries, scores, treatises, recordings, newspapers, and photographs. They may be stored in hard copy (in a building) or electronically (in digital format), and are administered by an institution or organization.

An Archive and a Library Compared

The nature of an archive sets it apart from a library. Archival holdings are usually unique; those held in libraries are usually not. Archives contain primary sources; libraries generally hold secondary and tertiary sources. Archival holdings are not available for loan because of their uniqueness or fragility; library holdings can be borrowed. Archives and libraries also organize and describe their contents differently.[21] Where archival content is grouped into discrete collections, library content is organized by subject matter.

Notwithstanding these differences, the two repositories overlap in one respect. Archives sometimes include the word "library" in their title, and libraries sometimes include archival collections in their holdings (typically referred to as "special collections"). The Library of Congress and the British Library are two such examples.

Finding Archival Sources

Archival sources can be found in a number of ways, including:

- Online searches.
- Secondary sources and their bibliographies.
- Research networks.
- WorldCat (a global network of online library content and services).
- The Archive Finder database, a directory of thousands of primary source collections in the United States and the United Kingdom. Archive Finder is available through institutional subscription.

Accessing Archival Content

Some archival collections have been digitized and their content can be accessed online; one example is the Beethoven-Haus Digital Archives (https://www.beethoven.de/en/archive/list). Digitized collections, however, comprise only a small portion of the material that is held in archives around the world. Most archival content can only be accessed in hard copy.

Archives often compile finding aids that enable researchers to see whether a collection is relevant for their research.[22] A finding aid is, in effect, a table of contents. It includes a listing of the material contained within a collection, as well as a descriptive overview of the collection. Finding aids are generally available online; see, for example, the finding aid for the John Butler Papers in the New York Public Library, https://archives.nypl.org/dan/19816.

If only a small amount of archival material is needed, archives are sometimes willing to provide scanned copies on a fee-for-service basis. Copies of the preliminary sketches of a composition, for example, might be procured

26 Postgraduate Research in Music

in this way. Short, straightforward queries can sometimes be answered gratis by archive staff as part of the service they provide. If a substantial amount of material is needed, however, a visit to the archive will be necessary. For this, a considerable amount of planning is required.

Planning a Visit to an Archive

The following points need to be taken into account when planning a visit to an archive:

- Determine the exact archival content to be accessed. This can be done by consulting the finding aid/s, or by communication with archive staff.
- Estimate how much time will be needed to access the content and formulate a "best-guess" timetable. There will be unknown factors here, but a timetable is a necessary starting point.
- Contact archive staff to arrange a visit. Archive staff also need to plan ahead.
- Find out whether a reader's pass is required, whether it can be obtained online in advance, or whether it needs to be organized upon arrival.
- Find out whether a digital camera can be used to copy documents, and/ or whether any reprographic services are available. This has a bearing on the amount of time that will be needed.
- Check the exact location of the archive. The BBC Written Archives Centre, for example, is located not in Broadcasting House in Central London, but in Reading, a thirty-minute train trip from London.
- Keep a meticulous record of all communications with archive staff.

Planning a visit to an archive needs to be documented step by step. How this might be done is illustrated in table 2.3, which sets out the planning for a hypothetical visit to the BBC Written Archives Centre. This model can be adjusted as appropriate for individual projects.

Scores, Editions, and Collections

It is important for researchers to be aware of the type of score they are working from, particularly in early music research. The following guide describes the various types of scores, editions and collections, and explains the differences between them.[23]

Holograph: A score written in the hand of a composer.[24] Holographs are original sources that are untouched by editorial emendations.

Table 2.3. Planning a visit to an archive

Archive	Archival content to be accessed	Contact person and location	Reader's pass and entry	Notes	Planned access dates
BBC Written Archives Centre	1. Contracts 2. Correspondence relating to broadcasts undertaken for the BBC 3. Scripts from talks and interviews 4. Press cuttings 5. Files relating to ENSA concerts[a] 6. CEMA file relating to a concert tour[b] 7. Concert broadcasts in 1951, 1952, 1953 and 1954: File refs 145, 146, 147 and 148 (12 files in all) 8. Copies of *Radio Times*, *The Listener* and *London Calling*	CONTACT PERSON: Jane Smith, archives researcher LOCATION: BBC Written Archives Centre, Peppard Road, Caversham Park, Reading RG4 8TZ. T: +44(0)20 8008 5661 Reading is half an hour from London by fast train. Train leaves from London Paddington Station. Catch No. 24 bus outside Reading station to the archives	No reader's ticket needed Ring bell on arrival	Open by appointment Wed–Fri, 10am–5pm. Places in the reading room fill up quickly (especially May–June). Book a place asap. Reprographic service available. Can use a digital camera to copy documents	Estimate 5 days, Wed–Fri, 24–26 March; Wed. 31 March; Thurs 1 April Email sent on 11 Feb with these suggested times. Confirmed on 11 Feb

[a] ENSA (Entertainments National Service Association) was an organization established in Britain in 1939 to provide entertainment for the British armed forces.

[b] CEMA (Committee for the Encouragement of Music and the Arts) was a wartime committee set up by the British Government to raise public morale through the Arts.

28   Postgraduate Research in Music

Autograph: A manuscript "written in the hand of a particular person," usually "the hand of its composer."[25] Some sources conflate the terms "holograph" and "autograph," using both terms to refer to a score that is handwritten by a composer.[26] Other sources make a distinction between the terms, suggesting that "the identity of a scribe or copyist is often of prime importance."[27]

Manuscript: "A book, document or piece of music written by hand rather than typed or printed."[28] The term "manuscript" has a broader meaning than "holograph," which refers only to a score. Some scholars use the term "autograph manuscript" to refer to a composer's handwritten score.

Copy: A manuscript written in the hand of another person; it can be distinguished from "autograph."[29]

Facsimile edition: An exact photographic reproduction of a composer's holograph or early printed edition. Facsimiles give scholars access to original or early sources.

Ürtext (original text) edition: Sets a composer's holograph as a printed score, seeking to represent the composer's notation without editorial intervention. The degree to which a composer's notational intentions can be determined, however, and the Ürtext philosophy itself, have been questioned by some scholars (see, for example, the article on Ürtext in *Grove Music Online*[30]).

Critical/scholarly edition: An edited, printed version of a holograph, prepared by a scholar who is an expert in the field and based on one or more primary sources identified by the scholar (for example, a holograph, an early or later sketch, or a first edition). A critical/scholarly edition includes a commentary that explains the editorial decisions that have been made, and how the editorial emendations deviate from the original source. A critical/scholarly edition is seen as an authoritative, credible source because of the standing of the editor in the community of scholars.

Ürtext and critical/scholarly editions compared: At the heart of both Ürtext and critical/scholarly editions is a scholarly intention: that of being faithful to the original notation of the composer. Through its overlay of editorial emendation and commentary, however, a critical/scholarly edition can be distinguished from its Ürtext cousin, which seeks only to replicate a composer's holograph.

Collected edition (also referred to as a complete works edition): An edited compilation of the complete works of a composer. A collected edition does not necessarily include every work written by a composer; it may, for example, include a subset of compositions.[31] Like a critical/scholarly edition, a collected edition is based on original and/or early sources and includes a critical commentary that explains the sources that have been drawn upon and the editorial decisions that have been made. Collected editions are also referred to as *Werke*, *Sämtliche Werke*, or *Gesamtausgabe* (German); *Opere* (Italian); or *Oeuvres* (French). They are seen as authoritative, credible sources.

Monumental edition: A multi-volume series unified by a particular focus, such as the music of a country, time period, or genre. Examples include *Musica Britannica*, *Recent Researches in the Music of the Middle Ages*, and *Women Composers*. Monumental editions are also referred to as historical sets, monuments, or *Denkmäler* (German). They contain a scholarly introduction and editorial notes, and are seen as authoritative, credible sources.

Performance edition: This is typically prepared by a performer known for his/her interpretation of a particular repertoire. It contains interpretative suggestions regarding dynamics, phrase markings, articulation, tempi, fingerings, and so on. A performance edition is notably different from an Ürtext edition or a critical/scholarly edition.

Anthology: A collection of musical works taken from various sources and linked by a common focus, for example an anthology of piano music, an anthology of brass band music, or an anthology of music for analysis. Anthologies can also be historical in nature, for example *The London Pianoforte School 1766–1860*.[32] An anthology may comprise a single volume or multiple volumes.

Finding Scores, Editions, and Collections

Scores, editions, and collections can be found in a number of ways. University libraries and major public libraries are key repositories of printed music, including collected, monumental, and facsimile editions. A further resources is the International Music Score Library Project (IMSLP, also known as the Petrucci Music Library; https://imslp.org), which provides online access to digitized scores and recordings free of charge (or, for a small annual subscription, with enhanced functionality). The IMSLP database includes holographs, different editions of works, and many collected editions.

There are two useful, though somewhat dated, printed sources that can be used to locate collected and monumental editions: Anna Harriet Heyer's *Historical Sets, Collected Editions, and Monuments of Music: A Guide to Their Contents*; and George R. Hill and Norris L. Stephens' *Historical Sets, Collected Editions, and Monuments of Music: A Bibliography*.[33] Information that is more up-to-date can be found in the RILM Index to Printed Music (IPM), an online database that includes collected and monumental editions, as well as anthologies and individual musical works. The IPM can be accessed through library subscription.

Collected editions are also listed in *The New Grove Dictionary of Music and Musicians*; up-to-date listings can be found in *Grove Music Online*. *Grove* provides two avenues for locating collected editions: first, the comprehensive, composer-by-composer guide that is included in the article entitled "Editions, Historical"[34]; and second, listings in the individual composer articles. Figure 2.3 shows how this information is presented in the individual composer articles, using Anton Bruckner as an example. Four collected editions are listed, each of which is assigned a code—respectively A, B, C, and GA. The series within the collected editions are indicated by Roman numerals; volumes within the series are denoted by Arabic numerals.

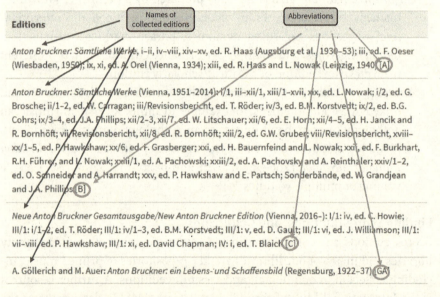

Figure 2.3. *Grove Music Online*'s listing of collected editions for the music of Anton Bruckner

A listing of individual works follows the index of collected editions. Figure 2.4 shows how individual works can be located, again using the orchestral works of Bruckner as an example. The right-hand column ("edition") includes a capital letter that refers to the collected edition in which a work can be found (abbreviated as A, B, C, or GA); this is followed by a Roman numeral and an Arabic numeral (respectively the series and volume). The first composition listed in figure 2.4 (no. 96 in the list of works by Bruckner) can therefore be found in collected edition B, series xii, volume 4.

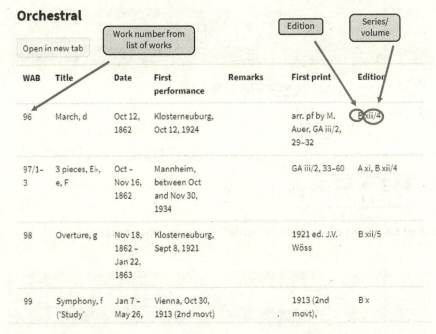

Figure 2.4. Extract from *Grove Music Online*'s listing of Anton Bruckner's works

Finding Musical Sources

A key tool for locating extant musical sources is the *Répertoire international des sources musicales*—International Inventory of Musical Sources (RISM; www.rism.info).[35] RISM is an international organization whose goal is to document primary musical sources held in archival collections around the world. RISM focuses mainly on the period 1600–1800. It documents the locations of holographs, printed editions, writings on music theory, and libretti; it also includes information about publishers, scoring and parts, incipits (opening notes) of key themes, and, in the online version, the functionality to create searchable incipits.

Much of the content of RISM's printed volumes is available through its online catalogue, which can be accessed free of charge at https://rism.info. The catalogue includes both basic and advanced search options, with a range of source types and search fields in the advanced option (see figures 2.5 and 2.6; see also chapter 3 for a discussion of basic and advanced searches).

Thematic Catalogues

A thematic catalogue is an index of a composer's works, or (less commonly) an index of a particular collection of music.[36] The term "thematic" refers to an

32 Postgraduate Research in Music

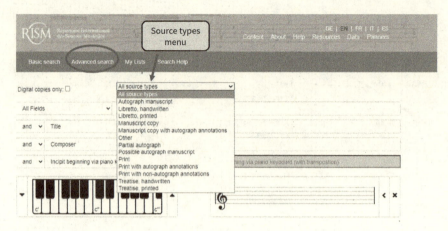

Figure 2.5. RISM's advanced search screen with source types menu

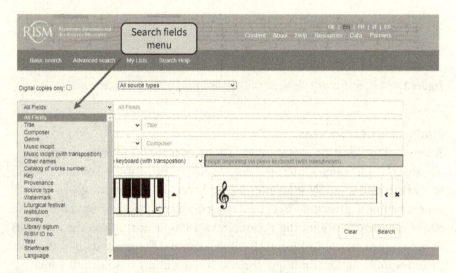

Figure 2.6. RISM's advanced search screen with search fields menu

incipit of the opening theme, which is included as a way of identifying a composition. Thematic catalogues are organized in various ways: chronologically, by opus number, by type of composition, or by performance medium.

A thematic catalogue assigns an Arabic number to each work within the catalogue. The number is preceded by one or more letters that usually denote the name of the person who compiled the catalogue, for example, K. for Köchel (for the works of Mozart), and Hob. for Hoboken (for the works of Haydn). In some cases, the acronym WV (*Werkeverzeichnis*, or works catalogue) is used; examples include thematic catalogues for the music of Bach (BWV), Buxtehude (BuxWV), Handel (HWV), and Mendelssohn (MWV).

The thematic catalogue number becomes part of the descriptive title of a work (for example, Mozart, Symphony No. 40 in G minor, K. 550).

The amount of information that is included for each composition varies from catalogue to catalogue. A typical catalogue entry includes all or most of the following information, as appropriate for individual works:

- Thematic catalogue number.
- Title of composition.
- Genre and work number (for example, Symphony No. 2).
- Key.
- Opus number.
- Librettist or author of the text (for vocal works).
- Popular name of the work.
- Number of movements.
- Instrumentation/performance resources.
- An incipit of the opening theme (or incipits of two or more movements).
- Information about, and location of, the autograph score and any significant copies.
- Information about, and location of, the first edition and other significant editions (including the date/s of publication).
- Date and place of composition.
- Bibliography.

Thematic catalogues are an important source for the preparation of critical editions, and for historical, analytic, and performance-based research. They are meticulously compiled and are considered to be authoritative and reliable sources. Notwithstanding this, as Sampsel notes, they are not always complete, up-to-date, or entirely accurate, particularly those that are less recent.[37]

Thematic catalogues have been compiled for hundreds of composers and collections; for some composers, there is more than one catalogue. To locate a thematic catalogue, check the composer entry in *Grove Music Online* (or the print version, *The New Grove Dictionary of Music and Musicians*). Thematic catalogues can also be located through library catalogues, and through Barry S. Brook and Richard J. Viano's *Thematic Catalogues in Music: An Annotated Bibliography*.[38]

Music Iconography

Music iconography is concerned with the study and interpretation of musical images that appear in works of art. Some researchers use these images to supply historical facts about instruments and performance; others consider the works of art in their own right.[39] Musical images are a rich source of information about such matters as instruments and their construction, instrumental technique, performance ensembles, the gendered distribution of performers, performance venues, and the social context of music making.

There is a substantial body of source material in which musical images are documented. These resources are set out in chapter 11 of Sampsel's *Music Research: A Handbook*. There are also brief discussions in chapter 5 of Gottlieb's *Music Library and Research Skills*, and in chapter 17 of Bayne and Komara's *A Guide to Library Research in Music*.

A further resource is the *Répertoire internationale d'iconographie musicale*—International Inventory of Music Iconography (RIdIM, https://ridim.org). RIdIM is an international index of visual sources relating to music, dance, theater, and opera; its brief is to catalogue the sources, and to provide a framework for their interpretation.[40] RIdIM's web-based database provides free, online access to more than 5,000 records (see figure 2.7).

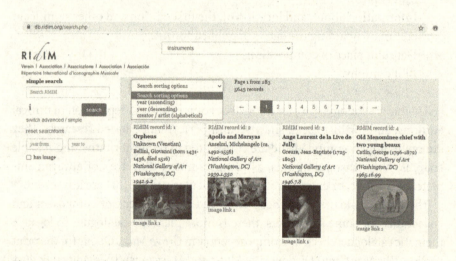

Figure 2.7. RIdIM database search page

Sound Recordings, Films, and Videos

Most music research draws upon sound recordings in some way. Historical recordings reissued in modern formats inform such matters as past repertoire, changing aesthetic taste, and historical performance styles. A recording of Debussy playing Debussy, for example, sheds a great deal of light upon Debussy's conception of his music and the performance style of his time. Research in the area of jazz often involves the analysis of the performance style of a particular artist, as documented in recordings; and ethnomusicological research draws upon recorded repositories of world music.

There are four main ways in which recordings can be located:

- Library catalogues, which include recordings within the library's own holdings and beyond it as well through WorldCat. Useful hints for searching library catalogues for this purpose can be found in Bayne and Komara's *A Guide to Library Research in Music*.[41]
- Discographies (catalogues of recordings). The major discographies are documented in chapter 10 of Sampsel's *Music Research: A Handbook*, and chapter 7 of Gottlieb's *Music Library and Research Skills*.
- Streaming services such as YouTube, Classical Music Library, Music and Dance Online, and Naxos Music Library. Naxos Music Library, for example, contains well over two million classical music tracks, with multiple recordings of individual works and options for searching by work, composer, artist, period, year of composition, instrument, genre, and so on. There are also several Naxos "companion" series, including Naxos Historical, Naxos Music Library Jazz, Naxos Rock Legends, and Naxos Music Library World (music from around the world, including the Smithsonian Folkways Recordings).[42] Both Sampsel and Gottlieb provide lists of streaming services, respectively in chapters 10 and 7. Streaming services are generally available through individual or institutional subscription.
- Projects worldwide for the preservation and digitization of historic recordings (often with free online access). One of the more extensive of these projects is the Internet Archive's 78rpms and Cylinder Recordings (https://archive.org/details/78rpm). Digital preservation projects are typically found through web searches, secondary sources, and research networks.

Films and videos are also significant sources for music research. A study of the music of Erich Korngold (1897–1957), for example, would be likely to draw not only upon the scores he wrote for films, but also upon the films themselves. Films and videos can be located in a number of ways, including online searches, Naxos Video Library, Music and Dance Online, WorldCat, and secondary sources and their bibliographies.

Search Engines and Websites

Search engines and websites may seem, at first thought, to have little to do with academic enquiry, but they are in fact integral to research. A search engine is software that looks for information on the internet, basing a search on information keyed in by the user.[43] A website is a collection of related web pages (or electronic documents) located through a search engine.

Search engines need to be used with care. Google, Bing, Yahoo, and Ask—the search engines of everyday life—locate public web content rather than specifically academic content. Public web content is not refereed and cannot be assumed to be scholarly; opinion can easily masquerade as fact, and the information may not be based in reliable sources. Wikipedia, for example—a website commonly presented through a Google search—is an un-refereed encyclopedia that can be contributed to, or updated, by anyone. Wikipedia therefore cannot be assumed to be a reliable source. Notwithstanding this, search engines such as Google should not be discounted in the search for sources, for they also locate websites that are reliable and authoritative—sites such as the BBC Proms Archive (http://www.bbc.co.uk/proms/archive), and official composer websites such as that of the Ralph Vaughan Williams Society (https://rvwsociety.com). Web searches that use everyday search engines therefore have a role to play in academic research, but they must be used with discrimination.

There are also search engines that have been designed specifically for academic research; they include Google Scholar (https://scholar.google.com), CORE (https://core.ac.uk), Microsoft Academic (https://academic.microsoft.com/home), and RefSeek (https://www.refseek.com). These search engines locate journal articles, books, theses, book reviews, conference papers, and unpublished articles.

Just as the pedigree of a search engine is an important consideration, so too is the pedigree of a website. Websites that are appropriate for academic research fall into a number of categories:

- An official website of a significant organization, for example that of the Ralph Vaughan Williams Society (https://rvwsociety.com).
- An artist's own website, for example that of the composer Cat Hope (https://www.cathope.com).
- A website hosting well-researched content, for example *Colonial Film: Moving Images of the British Empire* (http://www.colonialfilm.org.uk).
- A website hosting content that is substantial in content, stylistically appropriate in an academic context, cogently argued, and well written—preferably by an authority in the field.

- A website whose content includes appropriate scholarly citations, and accurate formatting of the citations.

Social Media, Blogs, and Podcasts

Like other online content, social media, blogs, and podcasts should not be discounted as sources of information. These are un-refereed sources, however, and the information they contain must be carefully evaluated. The following questions provide a foundation for making this assessment:

- What is the academic standing, and the authority, of the person providing the information?
- Are the ideas based in research or opinion?
- Are the ideas presented in a scholarly, analytical way? Are they substantiated by evidence? The style can be informal, but the content must be substantial.
- Do the ideas tie in with the views of other scholars? Do they challenge other views?
- Are the ideas persuasive? Why or why not?

Coda

This chapter has discussed the nature of sources as primary, secondary, and tertiary, and outlined the key resources and resource portals that are available for music research. With this foundation in place, the next task is to identify strategies for accessing information in an efficient and effective manner. This will be addressed in chapter 3.

Exercises

The exercises for chapter 2 are integrated into those included in chapter 3.

Reading List

"A Brief Introduction." RIPM. Accessed July 8, 2021. https://ripm.org/?page=About.
"About Association RIdIM—Mission Statement." RIdIM. Accessed July 12, 2021. https://ridim.org/association-ridim/about-ridim.
"About JStor." JStor. Accessed July 8, 2021. https://about.jstor.org.

38   Postgraduate Research in Music

"All Newspapers." Google News. Accessed September 26, 2021. https://news.google.com/newspapers.

"Archival Research." CUNY Graduate Center, Mina Rees Library. Accessed October 3, 2021. https://libguides.gc.cuny.edu/archivalresearch/archives.

"Archival Research." Dalhouse University: Dalhousie Libraries. Accessed October 3, 2021. https://dal.ca.libguides.com/c.php?g=257178&p=1718238.

"Archive Finder." ProQuest. Accessed September 29, 2021. https://about.proquest.com/en/products-services/archives_usa.

"Autograph." In *The New Harvard Dictionary of Music*, edited by Don Michael Randel. Cambridge, Massachusetts: The Belknap Press of Harvard University Press, 1999.

Bayne, Pauline Shaw, and Edward M. Komara. *A Guide to Library Research in Music*. 2nd ed. Lanham, Maryland: Rowman & Littlefield, 2020.

Boorman, Stanley. "Holograph." In *Grove Music Online*. Oxford University Press, 2001. https://doi-org.ezproxy.ecu.edu.au/10.1093/gmo/9781561592630.article.13248.

Boorman, Stanley. "Urtext (Ger.: 'original text')." In *Grove Music Online*. Oxford University Press, 2001. https://doi-org.ezproxy.ecu.edu.au/10.1093/gmo/9781561592630.article.28851.

Brook, Barry S. "Thematic Catalogue." In *Grove Music Online*. Oxford University Press, 2001. https://doi-org.ezproxy.ecu.edu.au/10.1093/gmo/9781561592630.article.27785.

Brook, Barry S., and Richard J. Viano. *Thematic Catalogues in Music: An Annotated Bibliography*. 2nd ed. Stuyvesant, NY: Pendragon, 1997.

"Cat Hope: Artist, Scholar." Accessed August 4, 2021. http://www.cathope.com.

Charles, Sydney Robinson, George R. Hill, Norris L. Stephens, and Julie Woodward. "Editions, Historical." In *Grove Music Online*. Oxford University Press, 2001. https://doi-org.ezproxy.ecu.edu.au/10.1093/gmo/9781561592630.article.08552.

"Classical Music Cataloging Systems Explained." Accessed July 3, 2021. http://electricka.com/etaf/muses/music/classical_music/composer_catalog_systems/composer_catalog_systems_popups/about_these_catalog_systems.htm.

"Critical Editions, Collected Editions, Urtext, Facsimile Scores: What Are the Differences?" Indiana University Bloomington. Accessed July 10, 2021. https://guides.libraries.indiana.edu/scores.

Dean, Jeffrey. "Editions, Historical and Critical." In *The Oxford Companion to Music*. Oxford University Press, 2011. https://www-oxfordreference-com.ezproxy.ecu.edu.au/view/10.1093/acref/9780199579037.001.0001/acref-9780199579037-e-2188.

"FAQ: About JURN." Accessed October 25, 2021. https://jurnsearch.wordpress.com/about/#mix.

Finsche, Ludwig, ed. *Die Musik in Geschichte und Gegenwart*. 2nd ed. Kassel: Bärenreiter, 1994–2008.

"Gale Historical Newspapers." Gale. Accessed September 26, 2021. https://www.gale.com/intl/primary-sources/historical-newspapers.

Gottlieb, Jane. *Music Library and Research Skills*. 2nd ed. New York: Oxford University Press, 2017.

H.E.S. "Thematic Catalog (Index)." In *The New Harvard Dictionary of Music*, edited by Don Michael Randel. Cambridge, Massachusetts: The Belknap Press of Harvard University Press, 1999.

Heyer, Anna Harriet. *Historical Sets, Collected Editions, and Monuments of Music: A Guide to Their Contents*. 3rd ed. Chicago: American Library Association, 1980.

Hill, George Robert, and Norris L. Stephens. *Collected Editions, Historical Series & Sets & Monuments of Music: A Bibliography*. Berkeley, California: Fallen Leaf Press, 1997.

"How to Use a Finding Aid for Researching in Archives." Simmons University, Simmons College Library and Information Sciences. Accessed October 3, 2021. https://simmonslis.libguides.com/using_finding_aids/home.

Immel, Steven. "Facsimile." In *Grove Music Online*. Oxford University Press, 2001. https://doi-org.ezproxy.ecu.edu.au/10.1093/gmo/9781561592630.article.40475.

"Introduction to Archive Research." University of Wisconsin. Accessed October 3, 2021. https://library.uwsuper.edu/c.php?g=224382&p=1487309.

"Is a Journal Peer-Reviewed?" University of Queensland. Accessed October 25, 2021. https://guides.library.uq.edu.au/how-to-find/peer-reviewed-articles/check.

Kennedy, Joyce, Michael Kennedy, and Tim Rutherford-Johnson, eds. *The Oxford Dictionary of Music*. 6th ed. Oxford: Oxford University Press, 2012.

Maple, Amanda, Beth Christenssen, and Kathleen A. Abromeit. "Information Literacy for Undergraduate Music Students: A Conceptual Framework." *Music Library Association Notes* 52, no. 3 (1996): 744.

Marston, Nicholas. "Autograph." In *Grove Music Online*. Oxford University Press, 2001. https://doi-org.ezproxy.ecu.edu.au/10.1093/gmo/9781561592630.article.01567.

"MGG Online." RILM: Répertoire International de Littérature Musicale. Accessed August 4, 2021. https://www.rilm.org/mgg-online.

"Music Index." EBSCO. Accessed 8 July 2021. www.ebsco.com/products/research-databases/music-index.

"Music Index with Full Text." EBSCO. Accessed October 26, 2021. https://www.ebsco.com/products/research-databases/music-index-full-text.

"Music Online: Smithsonian Global Sound for Libraries." Alexander Street. Accessed October 27, 2021. https://search.alexanderstreet.com/glmu.

"Music Periodicals Database." ProQuest LibGuides. Accessed July 8, 2021. https://proquest.libguides.com/musicdatabase.

"National Digital Newspaper Program." Library of Congress. Accessed September 26, 2021. https://www.loc.gov/ndnp.

Nettl, Bruno, Ruth M. Stone, James Porter, and Timothy Rice, eds. *The Garland Encyclopedia of World Music*. New York: Garland, 1998–2002.

"News and Newspapers." ProQuest. Accessed September 26, 2021. https://about.proquest.com/en/content-solutions/news.

Nichols, Cindi. "What's the Difference Between Periodicals, Journals, Magazines and Newspapers?" University of Memphis Library. Accessed September 24, 2021. https://libanswers.memphis.edu/faq/34544.

"Performing Arts Periodicals Database." ProQuest LibGuides. Accessed October 25, 2021. https://proquest.libguides.com/performingarts/content.

Powell, Kimberly. "How to Search the Google News Archive." Accessed September 26, 2021. https://www.thoughtco.com/search-tips-for-google-news-archive-1422213.

"ProQuest Historical Newspapers." ProQuest. Accessed September 26, 2021. https://about.proquest.com/en/products-services/pq-hist-news.

Randel, Don Michael, ed. *Harvard Dictionary of Music*. 4th ed. Cambridge, Massachusetts: Belknap Press of Harvard University Press, 2003.

"RILM Abstracts of Music Literature with Full Text." RILM: Répertoire International de Littérature Musicale. Accessed July 8, 2021. www.rilm.org/abstracts.

"RISM Catalogue of Musical Sources." RISM: Répertoire International des Sources Musicale. Accessed July 10, 2021. https://rism.info/index.html.

Root, Deane, ed. *Grove Music Online*. Oxford University Press, 2001. http://www.oxfordmusiconline.com.

Sadie, Stanley, and John Tyrrell, eds. *New Grove Dictionary of Music and Musicians*. London: Macmillan, 2001.

Sampsel, Laurie J. *Music Research: A Handbook*. 3rd ed. New York: Oxford University Press, 2019.

40   Postgraduate Research in Music

Scholes, Percy, and John Wagstaff. "Dictionaries of Music." In *The Oxford Companion to Music*. Oxford University Press, 2011. https://www-oxfordreference-com.ezproxy.ecu.edu.au/view/10.1093/acref/9780199579037.001.0001/acref-9780199579037-e-1939.

Scott, Allen. *Sourcebook for Research in Music*. 3rd ed. Bloomington: Indiana University Press, 2015.

"Search Engines." BBC. Accessed July 29, 2021. https://www.bbc.co.uk/bitesize/guides/zpkhpv4/revision/1.

Seebass, Tilman. "Iconography." In *Grove Music Online*. Oxford University Press, 2001. https://doi-org.ezproxy.ecu.edu.au/10.1093/gmo/9781561592630.article.13698.

"Smithsonian Folkways Recordings." Smithsonian. Accessed October 4, 2021. https://folkways.si.edu.

Streby, Paul. "What's the Difference Between a Periodical, a Scholarly Journal, and a Magazine?" University of Michigan-Flint, Frances Willson Thompson Library. Accessed September 24, 2021. https://libanswers.umflint.edu/faq/86816.

Temperley, Nicholas, ed. *The London Pianoforte School 1766–1860*. 20 vols. London: Garland, 1984–1986.

"The Alan Hovanhess Website." Accessed August 4, 2021. http://www.hovhaness.com/Hovhaness.html.

"What are Archives?" Society of American Archivists. Accessed October 4, 2021. https://www2.archivists.org/about-archives.

"What are Search Engines?" Edith Cowan University. Accessed October 26, 2021. https://ecu.au.libguides.com/search-engines/what.

"What is a Finding Aid?" Ball State University Archives and Special Collections, Finding Aid Tutorial Part 1. Accessed October 3, 2021. https://bsu.libguides.com/c.php?g=1039276&p=7544214.

"What is a Finding Aid?" CSUDH University Library. Accessed October 3, 2021. https://libguides.csudh.edu/finding_aid.

"What's the Big Deal about Editions?" Butler University: Libraries and Center for Academic Technology. Accessed July 10, 2021. https://libguides.butler.edu/c.php?g=717690&p=5255553.

"Why Can't I Just Google?" La Trobe University Library. Accessed September 21, 2018. https://www.youtube.com/watch?v=N39mnu1Pkgw.

3

Searching for Sources Part 2

Strategies for Locating Information

Knowing *where* to look for information, as discussed in chapter 2, is only part of the challenge. Knowing *how* to look is equally important. This chapter addresses the "how" of searching for sources. It sets out strategies for locating information through electronic databases, then provides systematic steps and checklists for planning and executing a search in an efficient and effective manner.

Searching Databases

A database is, in essence, an organized collection of information, usually, and for the purposes of this chapter, in digital (electronic) form. Most sources of information are located through a database of some kind, for example a library catalogue, or a repository of academic research such as RILM (*Répertoire international de la littérature musicale*). Database searching is an essential skill for music research, for crucial sources of information will be missed if a search is not conducted in a proficient manner.

Databases can be searched in a number of different ways, and although they vary in design and appearance, they are underpinned by a shared set of operating principles. These principles are encapsulated in the following strategies.

Strategy 1: Basic and Advanced Searches, and the Use of Filters

Databases include two search options, basic and advanced, which are incorporated as tabs (or options) on the database home page. A basic search using a broad, undifferentiated search term is helpful in the early stages of a research

Postgraduate Research in Music. Victoria Rogers, Oxford University Press. © Oxford University Press 2024.
DOI: 10.1093/oso/9780197616031.003.0004

project because it presents a wide range of results. Some of these results will be useful, some will be redundant, and some will offer new avenues of enquiry. The limitation of a basic search, however, is that it often produces too much information; clearly it is inefficient to check hundreds, or even thousands, of individual search results.

In such cases, an advanced search is needed. This is a more refined process, narrowing the results through specific parameters, or filters, that are selected by the user. These filters include such things as the document type (for example, article or book), date range (for example, 1980–2000), linked full text (the search only returns full-text articles), scholarly (peer-reviewed) journals, and major topic (for example, performance practice). Different databases include different filters. The same operating principles apply, however: the option of basic or advanced searches, and the choice of search modes and filters that delimit a search to specific parameters selected by the user.

The search modes and filters included in the RILM database are shown in figure 3.1 (as noted in chapter 2, RILM is one of the key databases for music research). Some of the search options that are available in a typical library catalogue are shown in figure 3.2.

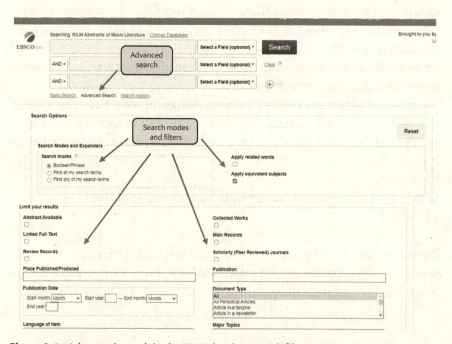

Figure 3.1. Advanced search in the RILM database, with filters

Searching for Sources Part 2   43

Figure 3.2. Search filters in a typical library catalogue

Strategy 2: Selecting a Search Field

The advanced search option opens to a screen that presents two or more search fields with pull-down menus, each of which offers a number of options such as author, title, subject, or abstract (see figures 3.3 and 3.4). Alternatively, all fields can be searched simultaneously through the default keyword setting. Limiting a search to a specific field, however, is likely to yield a more focused set of results. Both the content and number of search fields vary from database to database; this is evident in the search fields shown in figures 3.3 and 3.4,

Figure 3.3. Search fields in RILM, a typical database of academic research

Figure 3.4. Search fields in a typical library catalogue

which are included in (respectively) a typical database of academic research, and a typical library catalogue.

Amongst the most frequently used fields are those that search by keyword, subject, phrase, author, and title. These will now be discussed in turn.

Searching by Keyword

A keyword search, which appears as the default option in both the basic and advanced search options, uses words or concepts that encapsulate what a topic is about. The database searches for these words in various places within the individual records, for example in the title, and in the abstract. A keyword search can be used in a number of contexts:

- When there are synonymous, or related, terms.
- When multiple concepts are involved.
- When the subject classification is not known (see below, subject search).
- When a subject search produces little or no information.

A keyword search is a relatively undifferentiated process; as such it often presents too many, and/or irrelevant, results. On the other hand, it may also present results that point to new avenues of enquiry, including subject headings that can then be applied in a subject search. A keyword search is therefore a useful starting point in the search for sources.

Searching by Subject

A subject search, which is selected from the pull-down menu in the search field box, is more precise than a keyword search as it narrows the search results and largely eliminates superfluous or irrelevant results. Each item in a database or library catalogue is assigned one or more subject headings that describe its essential content. These subject headings, which are applied consistently across the database or catalogue, can be used as search terms to locate relevant sources.

The subject terms themselves, however, are not always intuitive or self-evident. Some databases therefore include a thesaurus, or listing, of subject headings, referred to variously as "subjects," "thesaurus," "topics," or "descriptors." The RILM database, for example, includes, in the top menu, a thesaurus that is labeled "subjects." As shown in figure 3.5, a search for "performance practice" in this thesaurus presents a range of subject sub-headings that include "performance practice—historical, by instrument/voice," "performance practice—historical, by period," "performance practice—historical, by topic," "performance practice—by composer," and so on. Each of these subject sub-headings can then be used in searches that focus on a particular aspect of a topic.

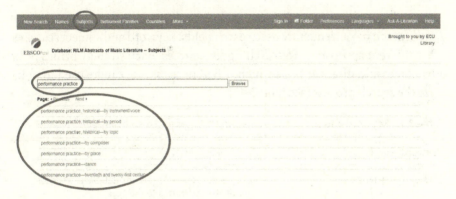

Figure 3.5. Subjects listed within "performance practice" in the RILM thesaurus

Subject information is also embedded in library catalogue entries. It is therefore important not to take library catalogue entries at face value, but rather to drill into them to see whether the subject information might lead to further areas of enquiry. Embedded in the catalogue entry for John Blacking's edited book, *The Anthropology of the Body*, for example, are a number of subject headings which, when opened, lead to listings of related sources (see figure 3.6). Subject headings in library catalogues are generally derived from the Library of Congress Subject Headings (LCSH), which are used by libraries worldwide to create thesauri, or "controlled vocabularies," of subjects within bibliographic records. The subject headings comprise either single words or brief phrases, each of which embodies a concept that is related to the search term.

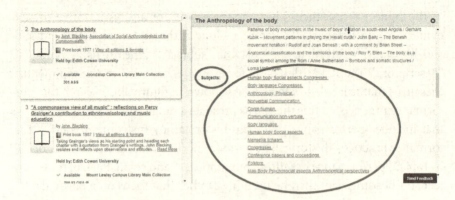

Figure 3.6. Subjects information embedded in a typical library catalogue entry

Comparing Keyword and Subject Searches

As two of the most frequently used search fields, keyword and subject searches offer different approaches to searching for sources. Each strategy brings both advantages and disadvantages which, when understood, can be used to optimize the search process (see table 3.1[1]).

Table 3.1. Keyword and subject searches: Advantages and disadvantages

Keyword search	Subject search
Uses everyday language	Uses the vocabulary of the database, which is not always known to the user
Flexible; the database searches for keywords anywhere in a record	Less flexible; the database only searches subject headings in the catalogue entries
Often produces too many results	Can only produce results if the search term corresponds to a subject heading in the database
Often produces irrelevant results	Results are usually focused and relevant

Searching by Phrase

Searching for a complete phrase is an effective strategy when a particular combination of words is likely to have been used by a number of authors (for example, "performance practice"). A phrase search can be undertaken simply by typing the search phrase into the keyword search box, at the same time enclosing it in double quotation marks. The use of double quotation marks switches the search from keyword to phrase; the database will then search for the words together, and in the specified order.

It should be noted, however, that not all databases search in the same way. Some automatically search adjacent words as a phrase, even when the search term is not enclosed by quotation marks. Others automatically insert the

Boolean operator **AND** between each word, thus undertaking a separate search on each word (see strategy 3 below for a discussion of Boolean operators); and in some databases, a phrase search is an option that can be actively selected from the search fields menu. If phrase searching is to be undertaken, and if the modus operandi of a particular database is not clear, the database settings may need to be checked. These settings are included in a "Help" link (sometimes called "search instructions") on the home page of the database.

Searching by Author

An author search, which is activated by a pull-down menu in the search field box, locates results relating not only to authors but also to composers, arrangers, performers, conductors, translators, and editors. An author search may also retrieve publications by organizations and government bodies, as well as conference and symposium proceedings. An author search is particularly useful when writings *by* a particular author or creator need to be distinguished from writings *about* him/her. Writings by the British ethnomusicologist John Blacking, for example, can be distinguished from the body of writings about him through the selection of "author" in the search fields box.

Searching by author also needs to take into account different spellings of an author's name, for example Beethoven and van Beethoven. It is sometimes necessary to undertake multiple searches using different spellings because cataloguers may have entered the information in different ways. Diacritics (accents written above or below a letter to signify pronunciation) are a further consideration. When diacritics are included in a name, searches should be undertaken both with and without them. Sometimes this is an automated function in a database; at other times it is not.

Searching by Title

Searching by title is a further option that can be selected from a pull-down menu in the search field box. This option is used when searching for items that are already known, including books and e-books, journals, scores, and video and sound recordings. A title search can be further refined through the selection of the source type, which is located in another pull-down menu. The source type is typically described in databases of academic content as "item type" or "document type," and in library catalogues as "format." Punctuation and capital letters do not need to be included in a title search, and articles can be omitted, regardless of the language that is used (a, an, the, un, une, le, la, l', les, ein, der, die, das, etc).

Uniform Titles

More than any other discipline, music presents special challenges for a researcher undertaking a title search. Titles appear in different editions and in different versions (for example, a piano arrangement of a string quartet); they may use diminutive or abbreviated forms, such as cello vs. violoncello; and they may be in English, French, German, Italian, Russian, or some other language. Haydn, for example, did not write a work called *The Seasons*; he named it *Die Jahreszeiten*. This places demands on a researcher to think laterally, and to be aware that an item might be found in another language, or a different version, or with the title formatted in different ways.

Libraries circumvent this problem by using a set of cataloguing conventions that are shared worldwide, creating "uniform" (or "preferred") titles for works, regardless of the language or word order that appears in the titles of individual editions. This is a critical concept for music scholars, particularly when searching for scores and recordings. Uniform titles gather together, under a single title and in the language of the original score, all editions and recordings of a work. Rather than undertaking a number of separate searches and "second guessing" how a work might be catalogued, all that is needed is a single search using the uniform title. This ensures that all of the catalogue records are retrieved.

Beethoven's "Moonlight Sonata" serves as a useful example. Beethoven himself did not name the "Moonlight Sonata" as "Moonlight"; it was given this title by someone else after it was composed. A library would not catalogue the work as the "Moonlight Sonata", or *Mondscheinsonate*, or as Klaviersonate Op.27, no. 2, but would apply uniform cataloguing conventions that include the following information, and in the following order: genre or form (in plural), instrument, number of composition, thematic catalogue or opus number, and key. The uniform title for Beethoven's "Moonlight Sonata" is therefore Sonatas, piano, no. 14, op. 27, no. 2, C# minor. A search using the uniform title presents recordings and scores published in both English and German; it also presents editions of the sonata in complete collections of Beethoven's piano sonatas, and in editions of the complete works of Beethoven. Just two of many manifestations of the title page for this work are given in the following examples, together with the uniform title.

Beethoven, Ludwig van, 1770–1827
Uniform title | Sonatas, piano, no. 14, op. 27, no. 2, C# minor
Title in Wiener Ürtext edition | Klaviersonate op. 27/2 Piano sonata op. 27/2: Sonata quasi una Fantasia

Beethoven, Ludwig van, 1770–1827
Uniform title | Sonatas, piano, no. 14, op. 27, no. 2, C# minor
Title in ABRSM edition | Sonata in C# minor sonata quasi una Fantasia: op. 27, no. 2

Uniform title catalogue entries also include, when appropriate, the format and language in which particular editions are presented. This can be seen in the following example, which sets out two versions of the title of Verdi's opera, *The Force of Destiny*: first, the uniform title (which is in the original language, Italian), then the translated title that appears in Ricordi's 1962 vocal score (in English). It should be noted that the uniform title itself is *Forza del destino*, to which details of format and language have been added. Only the uniform title, *Forza del destino*, needs to be keyed into a search.

Verdi, Giuseppe, 1813–1901
Uniform title   Forza del destino. Vocal score. English.
Title in 1962 Ricordi vocal score   The force of destiny melodrama in 4 acts

Sometimes the uniform title for a work is immediately evident because it takes the form of the distinctive, or individual, title set in the original language. Verdi's *Forza del destino* is one such example. At other times, the uniform title needs to be found through a related search.

Strategy 3: Boolean Operators and Nesting Terms

Boolean operators are a special command relating specifically to the search terms that are used, as compared with other parameters such as the source type and date range. In the RILM database, Boolean operators appear as a pull-down menu to the left of the search field box in the advanced search page (see figure 3.7).

The term "Boolean" originated in a system of logical thought developed by the English mathematician George Boole (1815–1864). Through using the conjunctions **AND, OR,** and **NOT**—referred to as Boolean operators— search terms can be connected, broadened, or narrowed to produce more focused results. Boolean operators are used when a search contains more than one term and the relationships between the terms need to be defined.

The first of the Boolean operators, **AND**, is used (counter-intuitively) to narrow the search results by instructing the database to include all of the search terms in the records that are presented; records containing only some, but not all, of the search terms will not appear in the search results. A search for performance practice in early music, for example, can be conducted by entering the two components ("performance practice" and "early music") into two separate search fields, connected by the Boolean operator **AND**. This instructs the database to search for records that contain both search terms,

Figure 3.7. Boolean operators in the RILM database

rather than one of them. Differing numbers of search results are generated if the search terms either are, or are not, enclosed by double quotation marks. Sometimes the numerical difference is considerable; at other times it is not. Both possibilities therefore need to be explored.

Again using the RILM database as an example, a search for the two search terms "performance practice" **AND** "early music" (without the use of double quotation marks, and without any further filters) produces almost 3,500 results (see figure 3.8).[2] In this particular database and in this particular search, the number of search results is not markedly different when the terms are enclosed by double quotation marks (a disparity of around 200 results). There are too many results to process, however. Further delimiters need to be applied.

One possibility is to narrow the search by adding ornamentation (or some other term). The search then contains three terms: "performance practice" **AND** "early music" **AND** "ornamentation." The greater the number of **AND** search terms included, the fewer the results presented—in this search, a reduction to the manageable number of 146. These results can be further reduced by selecting filters from the "refine results" menu to the left of the search results. If, for example, English is selected as the language, and if the document type is limited to academic journals, the search results are reduced to sixty-five (see figure 3.9).

The second Boolean operator, **OR**, broadens a search to include two or more similar search terms or concepts. The instruction given to the database is to search for either or both of the search terms. Each record that is presented will therefore contain at least one of the terms. The greater the number of **OR**

Searching for Sources Part 2   51

Figure 3.8. A search for two terms connected by the Boolean operator **AND**

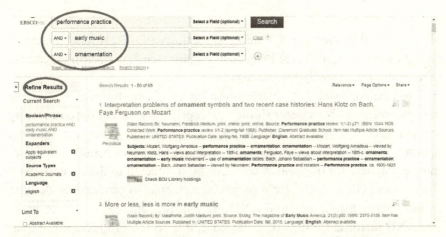

Figure 3.9. Narrowing the search results by adding search terms and applying filters

terms included in a search, the greater the number of results presented. This is a useful strategy when searching for information on a topic that might be clothed in different terminology, such as "early music performance practice" and "historic performance practice."

A search for these two terms can be conducted in a number of ways. One approach is to enter the terms in two text boxes, respectively "early music performance practice" **OR** "historic performance practice." This search in the RILM database, with no filters applied and without quotation marks, yields over 1,300 results. Some refinement of the search is therefore necessary. This can be done by selecting filters from the menu to the left of the search results. The number of results can be reduced to over 400 by choosing three (hypothetical)

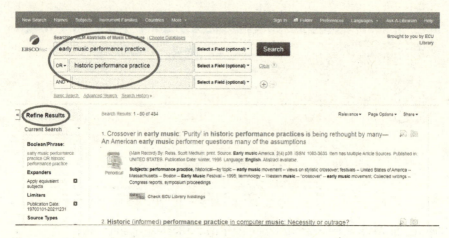

Figure 3.10. A search using the Boolean operator **OR**

filters from this menu: (1) Publication date: 1970–2021; (2) Document type: Academic journals; (3) Language: English (see figure 3.10). Of course, other filters would yield different results.

A second approach is to incorporate "nesting" into the search. Nesting uses parentheses ( ) to cluster similar concepts, at the same time connecting the parenthetical variants to the rest of the search through a Boolean operator—in this case, **AND**. Again using the above example, "performance practice" (in one search box) can be connected to the parenthetical "early music **OR** historic" (in a second search box) to produce results that include performance practice **AND** early music, and performance practice **AND** historic. In the RILM database, this search produces more than 3,600 results—too many to process. The results can then be reduced to sixty-five by applying four hypothetical filters: (1) Publication date: 1970–2021; (2) Document type: Academic journals; (3) Subject: Performance practice historical by instrument/voice; and (4) Language: English (see figures 3.11 and 3.12, which show the search in two ways: diagrammatically, then in the RILM database[3]).

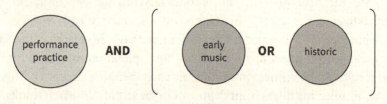

Figure 3.11. Search using nesting and Boolean operators

Searching for Sources Part 2   53

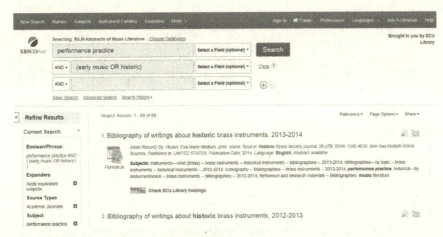

Figure 3.12. Search using nesting and Boolean operators in RILM

The nesting strategy can be further expanded. The topic of performance practice in early music, for example, can be broadened to include terms that are frequently encountered in this context: "historically informed" and "authentic." Again using the strategy of nesting, search box 2 is now expanded to include the following parenthetical variants: (early music **OR** historic **OR** historically informed **OR** authentic). With the same four filters that were applied in the previous example (Publication date: 1970–2021; Document type: Academic journals; Subject: Performance practice historical by instrument/voice; Language: English), and either with or without double quotation marks, this search identifies a further seven search results—seventy-two in all (see figures 3.13 and 3.14).

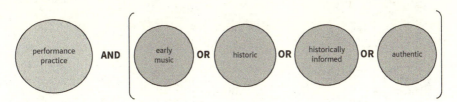

Figure 3.13. An expanded search using additional search terms, nesting, and Boolean operators

54 Postgraduate Research in Music

Figure 3.14. An expanded search using nesting, additional search terms, and Boolean operators in RILM

The third Boolean operator, **NOT**, excludes specified terms or concepts that are irrelevant to a search. This operator narrows the parameters of a search and is used when there is a need to focus on a particular aspect of a topic. Again using the RILM database as an example, a search on "early music" could be narrowed to omit results relating to, for example, "ornamentation." This search produces almost 14,000 results, which can be reduced to a manageable number by applying four filters from the left-hand menu: (1) Publication date: 1970–2021; (2) Document type: Academic journals; (3) Subject: Performance practice historical by topic; (4) Language: English (see figure 3.15). These filters reduce the results to 531. With the additional subject options now appearing in the left-hand menu, and with the selection of "early music movement," the search reduces to twenty-seven results that focus on the movement itself.

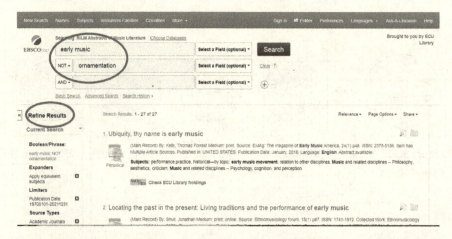

Figure 3.15. A search on "early music," NOT "ornamentation," with further filters applied

Strategy 4: Truncation

Truncation instructs a database to look for different forms of the same word, for example "historic" and "historical." Through the addition of a truncation symbol (usually an asterisk*) immediately after the root of a word and without a space, a database will search for all permutations of the root term. This enables a search to be set up quickly and efficiently because each variant of a word need not be entered as a separate search term. It also ensures that closely related terms are not inadvertently by-passed in the search for sources. Some databases use other truncation symbols, for example ?, !, or #; this information can be found in the "Help" or "Search Tips" section of a database.

The second of the two earlier nesting examples (set out in figures 3.13 and 3.14) can be used to explore how truncation works in practice. In these examples, "historic" and "historically informed" were entered as separate terms in search box 2, separated by the Boolean operator OR. A more efficient approach is to use the truncated historic* as a single root term. Again using the RILM database as an example, this search will locate records that include any of three related terms: "historic," "historically," and "historical." This strategy can also be applied to the term "authentic," which, when entered as a root term (authentic*), instructs the database to search, in addition, for results containing the words "authenticity" and "authentically." "Performance practice" could also be truncated to "perform* practice" to capture results that use the synonymous term, "performing practice" (see figures 3.16 and 3.17).

Truncation is ineffective, however, if the stem of a word is truncated too soon, resulting in a search for superfluous or irrelevant terms. A search on the

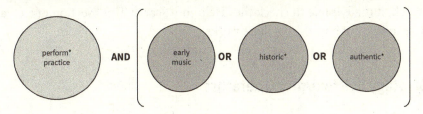

Figure 3.16. A search using Boolean operators, nesting, and truncation

Figure 3.17. A search using Boolean operators, nesting, and truncation in RILM

truncated root "mus*", for example, would include irrelevant words such as muscle and museum, as well as words relating to music. Extending the root term to "music*" expands the search to include a more relevant set of terms, including musical, musicality, musician, and musicianship.

Strategy 5: Wildcard Symbols

The wildcard is similar to truncation in that it uses a symbol (for example, #) to search for different permutations of a word. Where truncation adds a symbol at the end of a root term and retrieves words related to the root, wildcard symbols replace a letter or letters within a word, searching for such things as different spellings. Alternatively, all variants can be typed into separate search boxes, or the nesting strategy can be employed. It is more efficient, however, to use a wildcard symbol when undertaking such searches.

Different databases have different ways of searching for alternative spellings. In EBSCOhost databases such as RILM, a hash sign is placed "where an alternate spelling might contain an extra character."[4] EBSCO cites two examples: "colo#r" to present records containing color or colour; and "p#ediatric" to locate records that are spelled as pediatric or paediatric.[5] On the other hand, ProQuest databases (such as the Music Periodicals Database) are programmed "to look for US/UK spelling variants (color, colour), and English language form variants such as comparatives (smaller, bigger), superlatives (smallest, biggest), and plurals (tree, trees)."[6] By default, then, a ProQuest database searches for both the exact search term and its variants.

If alternative spellings need to be taken into account when conducting a search, it is advisable to check the "Help" or "Search Tips" section of a database to find out how the database works.

Strategy 6: Proximity Operators

Some databases include the function of a proximity search, which enables a database to search for two or more words that are present within a specified number of words. This is useful when a concept might be expressed in different ways, and/or with a different ordering of words. A search for sources on "aural testing," for example, would miss a number of largely synonymous terms such as "testing of aural skill," "aural skill and testing," "testing of aural ability," and "testing and measurement of aural capacity." It would also miss the synonymous term "ear testing," which would need to be factored into the search—perhaps most efficiently through the use of the Boolean operator OR.

Again using the RILM database as an example, two operators are used in proximity searches: **N (Near)**; and **W (Within)**. The N operator, together with a specified numeral to designate the proximity of the words, locates the search words within a specified distance of each other, regardless of the order in which they appear in the document.[7] Thus a search on **aural N6 testing**, with the proximity operator placed between the two words and with a space on both sides, locates results in which the words appear no more than six words apart, and in any order. All of the synonymous terms enumerated above would therefore be included in the search results.

The **W (Within)** operator, together with a numeral, also locates the words within a specified numerical distance, but only in the order given in the search term.[8] A search on **aural W6 testing** would therefore omit records that include three of the above synonymous terms: "testing of aural skill", "testing of aural ability", and "testing and measurement of aural capacity".

There is a clear resonance between proximity operators and phrase searching, the latter of which was discussed in Strategy 2. In phrase searching, however, the words enclosed by quotation marks are treated as a complete search entity, and in the given order. By contrast, proximity operators are less literal and more flexible, allowing variable distances and orderings of the search words. This is an advanced search technique that is employed less frequently than the other strategies. There are, however, circumstances in which a proximity search is an appropriate and effective strategy—although not all databases include the proximity function. This information can be found in the Help section of a database.

Strategy 7: Explore All Possibilities

If a search does not produce any results, this does not necessarily mean that there are no sources of information on a particular topic. Database searching needs flexible and lateral thinking. Persevere. Explore. Experiment. Use different search terms. Use different filters. Use uniform titles and subject headings. Check the information provided in the Help section of a database. Find online library guides and YouTube clips. Ask a librarian for help. And include a range of different databases, for search results vary from database to database. Only then is it likely that all relevant sources will be located.

Concluding Thoughts on Strategies

The importance of these search strategies cannot be overstated. Understanding what they are and when they should be used, and developing the skill to apply

58   Postgraduate Research in Music

them, are not optional extras in the toolkit of research skills. These are essential tools of trade, and they need to be understood and applied appropriately. They also underpin the important task of planning a search. This task, which draws together all of the knowledge, skills, and strategies that have been set out in chapters 2 and 3, will now be discussed.

Planning a Search

No single source captures everything relating to a particular topic. Different repositories store different information, and content that appears in one source might not appear in another—even when databases share a common purpose. Some journal articles and books, for example, might be located through one academic database but not another. Library catalogues, academic databases, and Google Scholar will all locate different aggregations of information when the same search term is applied. The search net therefore needs to be cast far and wide both within and across different source types; duplication of content cannot be assumed.

A carefully considered plan is needed, for without this any search for sources is unlikely to be optimal. Important sources may be missed, and valuable time can easily be wasted in duplicating searches whose parameters have not been recorded. Planning takes time but it saves time in the long run; it also leads to better outcomes. It is therefore wise to spend time devising a plan that sets out which resources will be accessed, and how. The following guidelines provide steps and checklists for this task.

Step A: Which Sources Will Be Accessed?

With the need to draw upon a wide range of sources, it is important to think carefully about the information that is sought and where it might be found. It is helpful to compile a checklist that sets out the full range of possibilities, and to tick those that will be used. The following list can be used for this purpose.

Writings about Music
☐   Books and e-books
☐   Journal articles
☐   Historical treatises and documents
☐   Encyclopedias and dictionaries of music
☐   Theses and dissertations
☐   Conference proceedings

Searching for Sources Part 2   59

- ☐ Album notes, liner notes, accompanying notes, and program notes
- ☐ Newspapers, periodicals, and magazines
- ☐ Official records and reports

Finding Writings about Music
- ☐ Library catalogues
- ☐ Academic databases
- ☐ Google Books
- ☐ Google Scholar
- ☐ Internet Archive
- ☐ Hathi Trust Digital Library
- ☐ Music Index (or Music Index with Full Text)
- ☐ Music Periodicals Database
- ☐ RILM Abstracts of Music Literature (or RILM Abstracts of Music Literature with Full Text) (*Répertoire international de littérature musicale*)
- ☐ Performing Arts Periodicals Database
- ☐ JStor
- ☐ JURN
- ☐ DOAJ (Directory of Open Access Journals)
- ☐ Journals of music organizations and associations
- ☐ Archives for historical treatises and documents
- ☐ *The New Grove Dictionary of Music and Musicians* (or *Grove Music Online*)
- ☐ MGG (*Die Musik in Geschichte und Gegenwart*) (or *MGG Online*)
- ☐ *The Garland Encyclopedia of World Music* (or *Music Online: The Garland Encyclopedia of World Music*)
- ☐ *Oxford Companion to Music*
- ☐ *Oxford Dictionary of Music*
- ☐ *Harvard Dictionary of Music*
- ☐ Other encyclopedias and dictionaries of music
- ☐ ProQuest Dissertations & Theses Global
- ☐ DDM (Doctoral Dissertations in Musicology)
- ☐ EThOS (E-Theses Online Service)
- ☐ NDLTD (Networked Digital Library of Theses and Dissertations)
- ☐ EBSCO Open Dissertations
- ☐ Album notes, liner notes, accompanying notes, and program notes
- ☐ RIPM (*Répertoire international de la presse musicale*)
- ☐ ProQuest Historical Newspapers
- ☐ Gale Historical Newspapers
- ☐ Google News Archive
- ☐ Other digital repositories
- ☐ ICON (International Coalition on Newspapers)

60 Postgraduate Research in Music

☐ Wikipedia listing of online newspaper archives
☐ Federal records offices or legal deposit for official records and reports

Archival Sources
☐ Online searches
☐ Secondary sources and their bibliographies
☐ Research networks
☐ WorldCat
☐ Archive Finder

Scores, Editions, and Collections
☐ Holograph
☐ Autograph
☐ Manuscript
☐ Copy
☐ Facsimile
☐ Ürtext edition
☐ Critical/scholarly edition
☐ Collected edition
☐ Monumental edition
☐ Performance edition
☐ Anthology

Finding Scores, Editions, and Collections
☐ University and public libraries
☐ IMSLP Petrucci Music Library (International Music Score Library Project)
☐ Heyer's *Historical Sets, Collected Editions, and Monuments of Music*
☐ Hill and Stephens' *Historical Sets, Collected Editions, and Monuments of Music*
☐ RILM Index to Printed Music (IPM)
☐ *The New Grove Dictionary of Music and Musicians* (or *Grove Music Online*)

Musical Sources
☐ RISM (*Répertoire international des sources musicales*)

Thematic Catalogues
☐ *The New Grove Dictionary of Music and Musicians* (or *Grove Music Online*)
☐ Library catalogues
☐ Brook and Viano's *Thematic Catalogues in Music*

Music Iconography
- ☐ Sampsel's *Music Research: A Handbook* (chapter 11)
- ☐ Gottlieb's *Music Library and Research Skills* (chapter 5)
- ☐ Bayne and Komara's *A Guide to Library Research in Music* (chapter 17)
- ☐ RIdIM (*Répertoire internationale d'iconographie musicale*)

Sound Recordings, Films, and Videos
- ☐ Libraries and WorldCat
- ☐ Discographies
- ☐ YouTube
- ☐ Classical Music Library
- ☐ Music and Dance Online
- ☐ Naxos Music Library
- ☐ Smithsonian Folkways Recordings
- ☐ Other streaming services
- ☐ Internet Archive's 78rpms and Cylinder Recordings
- ☐ Other Digital preservation projects for historic recordings
- ☐ Naxos Video Library

Search Engines and Websites
- ☐ Google
- ☐ Bing
- ☐ Yahoo
- ☐ Ask
- ☐ Google Scholar
- ☐ CORE
- ☐ Microsoft Academic
- ☐ RefSeek
- ☐ Websites

Social Media, Blogs, and Podcasts
- ☐ Social media
- ☐ Blogs
- ☐ Podcasts

Step B: Which Search Terms Will Be Used?

A search can only be as good as the search terms that are used. Poorly conceived terms are unlikely to shed much light on a topic and will inevitably miss vital information. It is therefore important to spend time constructing key concepts and search terms that capture the essential content of a topic, and which take into account synonymous terms and closely related research areas.

First write down the proposed topic, then formulate the key concepts and any synonymous or related terms that will be used in the search. These concepts and terms can be combined in various ways, using the search strategies set out earlier in this chapter (such as Boolean operators).

Topic: _____

_____

Concept	Synonymous or related terms
Concept 1:	
Concept 2:	
Concept 3:	
Concept 4:	

Step C: Which Search Strategies Will Be Used?

The next step in planning a search is to consider which search strategies will be used. Here, too, it is helpful to compile a checklist that sets out the full range of possibilities, and to tick those that will be used—at the same time noting, where appropriate, the search terms that will accompany them.

Basic and Advanced Searches, and the Use of Filters

☐ Will a basic search be undertaken? If so, which search term/s will be used?

_____

_____

Will an advanced search be undertaken? If so, which search term/s will be used? Which filter/s will be applied (e.g. document type, date range)?

_____

_____

_____

_____

Selecting a Search Field

☐ Will the search utilize the default keyword option?

☐ Will the search use a specific search field or fields? If so, which one/s? And which search term/s will be used within each field?

☐ Keyword

_____

☐ Subject

_____

☐ Phrase

_____

☐ Author

_____

☐ Title

_____

☐ Uniform title

_____

☐ Other

_____

Boolean Operators and Nesting Terms

☐ Will the search utilize Boolean operators? If so, which one(s), and in conjunction with which search terms?

☐ **AND**

_____

64 Postgraduate Research in Music

☐ OR

_____

☐ NOT

_____

☐ Is nesting an appropriate strategy? If so, which terms will be nested, and how?

_____

_____

Truncation
☐ Will truncation be used to search for different permutations of a word? If so, which word/s will be truncated, and how?

_____

_____

Wildcard Symbols
☐ Will wildcard symbols be used to search for different permutations of a word? If so, which word(s) will be searched, which symbol will be used, and where will the symbol appear in the word(s)?

_____

_____

Proximity Operators
☐ Will proximity operators be used to search for two or more words that are present within a specified proximity? If so, which term or concept will be searched, which proximity operator will be used, and where will the operator appear in the term or concept?

_____

_____

Step D: How Will the Search Results Be Saved?

An important step in planning a search is to establish a mechanism for saving the search results. Even a slight change in a search term or filters can produce a different set of results. For this reason, it is essential to keep a record of all of the search parameters, and to apply the same parameters consistently across all databases. This practice also ensures that a search is not duplicated, and that it can be replicated at a later date, should it be necessary.

The search parameters can be stored electronically through the "save" function that is included in most databases. Exactly how this works varies from database to database; time therefore needs to be spent in becoming familiar with the databases that will be accessed. Alternatively, a table can be constructed to record the search parameters (see table 3.2).

How Will the Search Results Be Saved?
☐ Utilizing the "save searches" function in the database?
☐ Utilizing the template set out in table 3.2?

Table 3.2. Record of search terms and filters

Search term	Filters	Date	Notes/outcomes
1.			
2.			
3.			
4.			

Step E: Searching for Sources as an Ongoing Process

Planning and executing a search is not a matter of "set and forget." New information is constantly coming to light, including newly published research and newly catalogued archival sources. Searching for sources must therefore be an ongoing process through the entirety of a research project.

Step F: Managing Anxiety and Other Emotions

The final factor that needs to be taken into account is dealing with anxiety and other emotions. There is sure to be uncertainty at the beginning of a project, and anxiety as to whether a search might miss vital sources. These emotions can best be dealt with through careful planning. A systematic search is certain to uncover key sources in a given area of research, alleviating the need for anxiety. If few sources are located, there is also no need for anxiety; indeed, this may be a positive outcome as it would indicate a gap in the existing research. The confidence that this is so can only arise, however, if a search has been well planned and systematically executed.

A further uncomfortable emotion is the feeling of being overwhelmed, not least by the number of sources that may be presented in a search. There are steps that can be taken to deal with this. Filters can be applied so that irrelevant results are omitted; and abstracts, tables of contents, and headings can be scanned so that irrelevant writings can be discounted.

The third uncomfortable emotion is the confusion that can easily arise when contradictory information is found; one authority says one thing and another says something quite different. Rather than being anxious about such contradictions or ignoring them altogether, the contradictions can be put to good use as a basis for discussion, or even used to inform the direction of the thesis.

Perhaps the best way of managing unhelpful emotions is the understanding that searching for sources is a skill that needs to be learned. It takes time, perseverance, practice, and patience. This need not be a solitary journey, however. Help is always at hand from music librarians, who have specialized skills and knowledge that can be drawn upon. They are an important resource for the music scholar.

Coda

The three foundation stones of music research are now in place: finding a topic; knowing where to look for sources of information; and knowing how to look. A search strategy can now be prepared. Before doing so, however, exercises 1, 2, and 3 should be completed to ensure that the requisite knowledge has been assimilated and key skills developed. These exercises vary in difficulty. Some are included simply to cultivate familiarity with the content and/or functionality of the resources; others are more challenging. Once exercises 1–3 have been completed, exercise 4 (preparing a search strategy) can be undertaken.

Exercises

Exercise 1

Retrace the search on performance practice and early music, as set out earlier in this chapter. Begin with the RILM database, then apply the search to the Music Periodicals Database. Compare the functionality of the databases, and the search results. What conclusions can be drawn?

Exercise 2

Find the uniform titles for the following works:

- Beethoven's Symphony No. 5
- Mozart's Piano Concerto K. 595
- Stravinsky's *Rite of Spring*
- Brahms's Second Cello Sonata
- Handel's *Messiah*
- Richard Strauss's *Thus Spake Zarathustra*

Exercise 3

This exercise provides practice in accessing many of the key resources and resource portals that are used in music research.

1. Using Online Databases

a) Using the RILM Abstracts of Music Literature and the Music Periodicals Database, locate two articles, in English, on each of the following topics. Ensure that each article for each topic is from a different database. Do not include reviews. Provide a full citation for each article and download the abstract. Use either the Chicago Notes and Bibliography or the APA referencing style (for a discussion of referencing styles see chapter 5; for referencing models of the various source types, see appendices A and B).

 (i) Benjamin Britten's settings of poetry.

 (ii) The Orpheus legend/myth in opera.

b) Using RISM as your source, locate a library that holds a manuscript of each of the following works. Provide the full name of the library and the identifying shelfmark.

68   Postgraduate Research in Music

     (i) Rondo in C major, by Charles Neate (holograph score)

     (ii) 24 Caprices for Violin, Op. 3, by Pietro Locatelli (autograph score)

c) Using ProQuest Dissertations & Theses Global, find two doctoral dissertations on the subject of Australian Aboriginal music. Provide a full citation for each dissertation, using either Chicago or APA referencing.

d) One of your colleagues has told you about an article entitled "Loyalty and Longevity in Audience Listening," by Stephanie Pitts. Find an on-line copy of the article and print out the first page. Include this page as part of your answer; also provide a full citation of the article, using either Chicago or APA referencing.

2. Comparing Results from Different Sources

Locate all of the monographs that have been written about the composer Peggy Glanville-Hicks, searching four different sources: RILM; Music Periodicals Database; JStor; and Google Scholar. Provide a full citation for each of the monographs, using either Chicago or APA referencing. List the source through which each monograph was located and compare the search results. Does each source present the same set of writings? What can be learned from this exercise?

3. Browsing International Library Catalogues

a) Find the following book in the British Library's online catalogue: E. Walker, *A History of Music in England* (1907). Provide a full citation, using either Chicago or APA referencing. Also provide the British Library's shelfmark for the book.

b) Again browsing the online catalogue of the British Library, find two recordings of gamelan music that are not commercial recordings. As your answer to this question, copy and paste the British Library's catalogue details for each recording.

c) Search the WorldCat online catalogue for Michael Nyman's chamber opera *The Man Who Mistook His Wife for a Hat.* In which formats is this work listed in the catalogue?

4. Collected and Monumental Editions

a) Using the online database Index to Printed Music (IPM), locate the scores of the following works, both of which are included in monumental editions. Provide the name of the series or set, together with the volume and page numbers.

     (i) Samuel Sebastian Wesley: *O Give Thanks Unto The Lord*

(ii) Michel de La Barre: Suite No. 2 in G major for Flute and Continuo, from *Pièces pour la flûte traversière avec la basse continue, livre 1.*

b) Using the online version of the *Neue Mozart-Ausgabe* as your source, cite the series, volume, and page numbers for Mozart's Adagio and Fugue in C Minor, K. 546.

5. IMSLP Petrucci Music Library

a) Find your way to the "Instrumentation/Genre" section of IMSLP. Locate a work scored for three players with continuo and provide a complete citation for this work.

b) Find IMSLP's listing of scores for Bach's Cantata BWV 61.
   (i) Where is the holograph housed?
   (ii) Name the major editions of this work that have been scanned into IMSLP, the publisher of each, and the century in which each was compiled.

c) Imagine you are a performance student specializing in early keyboard music, in particular the fortepiano. You are interested in locating historic, English-language writings about fortepiano technique. You suspect there might be some useful material in IMSLP.
   (i) Document the search strategy that leads you to this material.
   (ii) Name two nineteenth-century English writings on the subject, and the date of each.

6. Composers' Digitized Archives

Find a digitized copy of the holograph (referred to online as the autograph) of the Piano Sonata No. 30 in E major, op.109 by Beethoven. In which archive is the holograph housed? Now locate the first edition of this work. Print off the title page and the first page. Include the printouts as your answer to the question, and in a few sentences explain how and where you located this source.

7. Digitized Archival Collections

a) Using Trove, a digital repository based in the National Library of Australia, locate a review of an opera performance given by the Cagli-Pompei Opera Company in South Australia on Tuesday March 19, 1872. Which opera was performed? Who performed the title role?

b) On Tuesday October 16, 1923, the *Kalgoorlie Miner* published a letter written by a visiting examiner from the Trinity College of Music, London. The letter was entitled "Musical Prodigy in Kalgoorlie." Using Trove as your source, answer the following questions.

70 Postgraduate Research in Music

    (i) What was the name of the examiner?

    (ii) What was the name of the young artist to whom he was referring?

8. Locating Sound Recordings Online

  a) Find a recording of the *Five Bagatelles* Op. 23a, by Gerald Finzi, in the online database *Naxos Music Library*. Who are the performers?

  b) In the online database *Naxos Music Library*, locate a recording of Pablo Casals playing Bach's six unaccompanied suites for cello. Name the record label and catalogue number.

  c) The complete recordings of the singer Enrico Caruso are available on *Naxos Historical*. How many volumes are there? What are the years of the first and last recordings?

  d) Eric Korngold wrote one cello concerto. Find the recordings of this work in the *Naxos Music Library* and address the following questions: (i) In which year was the concerto composed? (ii) How many recordings are listed here? (iii) How many movements does the concerto contain? (iv) What are Korngold's dates of birth and death?

Exercise 4

Part A: Using the guidelines set out in steps A, B, C, and D of the "planning a search" section of this chapter, formulate a plan for locating sources relevant to your thesis topic.

Part B: Test the plan, making adjustments to the plan if and as necessary.

Part C: Select five of the search results, ensuring that each has been located through a different resource portal. Briefly evaluate the usefulness of each of these portals in locating relevant references for your thesis. Include at least two different databases in your answer; other resource portals may include, but are not limited to, the Internet Archive, IMSLP, and RISM.

Part D: Critically, and briefly, evaluate your overall success or failure in finding appropriate sources for your research.

Reading List

Bayne, Pauline Shaw, and Edward M. Komara. *A Guide to Library Research in Music*. 2nd ed. Lanham, Maryland: Rowman & Littlefield, 2020.

"Boolean Operators: A Cheat Sheet." University of Minnesota Libraries. Accessed September 7, 2018. https://libguides.umn.edu/BooleanOperators.

"CLIO Help." Columbia University Libraries. Accessed September 7, 2018. http://www.colum bia.edu/cu/lweb/help/clio7/searchBasic.html.

"Database Search Tips: Keywords vs. Subjects." Massachusetts Institute of Technology, MIT Libraries. Accessed October 9, 2018. https://libguides.mit.edu/c.php?g=175963&p=1160804.

"Effective Database Searching: Planning Your Search." University of Reading. Accessed 21 September, 2018. https://libguides.reading.ac.uk/database-searching/planning.

Gottlieb, Jane. *Music Library and Research Skills*. 2nd ed. New York: Oxford University Press, 2017.

"Proximity Searches." EBSCOhost. Accessed October 28, 2021. https://support-ebsco-com. ezproxy.ecu.edu.au/help/index.php?help_id=55.

Sampsel, Laurie J. *Music Research: A Handbook*. 3rd ed. New York: Oxford University Press, 2019.

"Searching with Wildcards and Truncation Symbols." EBSCOhost. Accessed October 28, 2021. https://support-ebsco-com.ezproxy.ecu.edu.au/help/index.php?help_id=137.

"Top Ten Search Tips." Northeastern University Library. Accessed July 3, 2021. https://libr ary.northeastern.edu/get-help/research-tutorials/effective-database-searches/top-ten-sea rch-tips.

"Uniform Titles: A Guide." Manhattan School of Music, Peter Jay Sharp Library. Accessed July 31, 2021. https://msmnyc.libguides.com/uniformtitles.

"Variant Forms or Spellings." ProQuest Help. Accessed October 28, 2021. https://www.proqu est.com/help/academic/webframe.html?Search_Results.html#Search_Results.html.

"What are Truncation Symbols and Wildcards?" University of Notre Dame Australia. Accessed September 7, 2018. https://askus.library.nd.edu.au/faq/204648.

"Why Use Uniform Titles?" University of Nebraska-Lincoln. Accessed August 2, 2021. https:// libraries.unl.edu/music/tutorial/04.

4
Writing a Literature Review

Chapter 4 explores the next step in the research process: writing a literature review. This is a section within a research proposal or thesis that reports on existing research which is related, or relevant, to the thesis topic. A literature review is both process and product—a process of reviewing the existing body of relevant research, together with its documentation in a research proposal or thesis.[1]

In the context of music research, and particularly in the area of practice-based research, the term "literature" takes on a broader meaning. Here, the background literature can be defined as the expert and scholarly material to which a project responds, and upon which it builds.[2] Recordings, performances, and scores can therefore be seen as legitimate inclusions in a literature review, in addition to written sources. In practice-based research, then, the literature is not necessarily restricted to words when the examinable material can include more than words.[3]

Chapter 4 begins by discussing the purpose of a literature review, the sources it includes, and the skills it employs. The remainder of the chapter sets out guidelines for writing a literature review, and guidelines for writing an annotated bibliography—an exercise that is often undertaken as preparation for the literature review itself.

It takes time, thought, and skill to write a good literature review; this is something that cannot be left until the last minute. Indeed, the importance of undertaking a comprehensive review of the existing literature will become abundantly clear in the next section.

Why Write a Literature Review?

There are many reasons for undertaking a review of the existing literature. First, and perhaps most importantly, it ensures that the thesis is original and does not duplicate work that has already been done. This is better established at the beginning of a research project, rather than months into it. Better it is by far to avoid a major crisis, and the necessity of finding a new topic!

Postgraduate Research in Music. Victoria Rogers, Oxford University Press. © Oxford University Press 2024.
DOI: 10.1093/oso/9780197616031.003.0005

A literature review also contextualizes the thesis within the existing body of knowledge. This is important because scholarship operates on the principle of building upon, or contradicting, other research. New research needs to relate to what has come before, and to be seen to relate to it.

Gaps or misunderstandings in the existing literature also become apparent, and ideas for new research directions almost inevitably emerge. How a thesis might be designed may also become evident, and theoretical and methodological approaches used by other scholars can sometimes be adopted or adapted.

Finally, a literature review lends credibility to a thesis. Engagement with key writings, familiarity with leading scholars, an understanding of significant issues, and an awareness of recent developments in a field of study, all add authority to a thesis.

Which Sources Belong in a Literature Review?

As noted in chapter 2, sources of information are generally divided into three categories: primary, secondary, and tertiary. These categories signal not only where source material may be found, but also whether the sources should be included in a literature review.

Many primary sources do not belong in a literature review—such things as archival documents, and holograph and facsimile scores. These are original, primary sources of information that inform *how* the research will be done. They should therefore be included in the methodology section of a thesis, not in the literature review.

There are other times, however, when primary sources do in fact belong in a literature review. Take, as an example, a study of the pedagogical application of post-tonal piano techniques, as exemplified in the three-volume set, *Century*, by the composer Larry Sitsky. This study would include, in its review of relevant literature, a survey of other post-tonal pedagogical resources such as Béla Bartók's *Mikrokosmos*, Ross Lee Finney's *32 Piano Games*, and György Kurtág's *Játékok*—all of which are primary sources.[4] Whether a primary source belongs in a literature review or in the methodology section of a thesis is, then, determined by its role in the research.

Secondary sources generally belong in a literature review because this is where the existing writings on or around a subject are discussed. If secondary sources were to be used as methodological models, however, they would be located in the methodology section—for example, an existing method for the analysis of historic recordings. If, on the other hand, a project were to devise a new way of analyzing historic recordings, a survey of the existing approaches would form part of the literature review.

74 Postgraduate Research in Music

Tertiary sources sometimes belong in a literature review, for example, an encyclopedia entry that provides significant contextual background to a study. A dictionary definition, on the other hand, simply needs to be acknowledged in a footnote, endnote, or in-text citation.

The following example illustrates how scores and recordings can be incorporated into a literature review. This fictitious study comprises two components: the preparation of an historically informed performance edition of the flute sonatas of Giovanni Battista Sammartini (1700–1775), together with an extended critical commentary; and the performative realization of this edition as a final recital. The recital is also recorded and submitted for examination along with the performance edition and its critical commentary. These two components of the study are reflected in the literature review, which includes three sections:

1. Other editions of Sammartini's flute sonatas, both historical and modern.
2. Recordings of Sammartini's flute sonatas, both historically informed and modern.
3. Secondary sources about Sammartini: (a) his life and musical style; and (b) the broader musical and historical context of the study, including the transition from the late Baroque to the early Classical period.

There are two notable omissions from the preceding enumeration: the holograph and the historical treatises on which the critical edition would be based. These sources inform *how* the study would be undertaken. They therefore form part of the methodology section, and do not belong in the literature review.

The key point to be taken from the preceding discussion is that things are not always clear cut. To determine which sources belong in a literature review, a useful rule of thumb is as follows. If the sources form part of the existing research or scholarly material on or around a thesis topic, regardless of their classification as primary, secondary, or tertiary, they should be included in a literature review. If they do not form part of the existing research or scholarly material on or around the topic, they do not belong in a literature review and should be located elsewhere in the thesis.

How Recent Should the Sources Be?

A literature review must be up-to-date. It should include recent advances and trends in an area of research, as well as significant, less recent research. Older research is sometimes highly significant, even decades after its publication.

Indeed, it often precipitates further research, creating a lineage of scholarship that can be traced in a literature review.

The Skills Needed for Reviewing Sources

Three key skills are needed if sources are to be reviewed efficiently and effectively: critical thinking skills; note taking skills; and writing skills. They will now be discussed in turn.

Critical Thinking: The Foundation of Good Scholarship

Critical thinking lies at the heart of good scholarship. It is closely related to literary and artistic criticism, which involves "the analysis and judgment of the merits and faults of a literary or artistic work."[5] In a scholarly context, criticism is expanded into a more broadly based process that is often referred to as critical thinking. Analysis and judgment remain central to its operation, but its base is expanded to include the examination of data, ideas, theories, methods, and artistic outputs.

Critical thinking is a multi-faceted process that incorporates three interrelated activities:

- **Critical analysis** uses logic and reasoning to break information down into its constituent parts. It deepens understanding and uncovers relationships that may not be apparent at first sight.
- **Critical evaluation** assesses the merit, or truth, of facts, data, theories, and other objects of investigation. Its role is to question, never taking things at face value.
- **Critical synthesis** draws the threads of thought together, teasing out points in common and points of difference. It takes the individual pieces of an analytic puzzle and looks at them as a whole, making correlations and moving from the particular to a broader perspective.

These three aspects of the critical process provide a foundation for reflective and independent thinking, and for the rigor that underpins all good research. Nothing should be immune from the critical process, both the work of others and one's own work and ideas. How crucial it is, then, to develop the mind of a detective, forensically examining the evidence that is presented, analyzing, evaluating, and synthesizing. From this, further aspects of the research process emerge: interpretation, discussion, and the formulation of new knowledge. The role of critical thinking should be neither overlooked nor taken for granted. It underpins the entirety of the research process and its importance cannot be overstated.

Guidelines for Critical Thinking

The skill of critical thinking is one that needs to be cultivated. The following questions, set out in a table that includes four rubrics (or categories of critical engagement), incorporate the three aspects of critical thinking discussed above (see table 4.1). These questions should be directed systematically to each source that is being reviewed. It should be noted that matters of style and presentation (rubric 4) do not, strictly speaking, fall within the usual ambit of critical thinking. These elements are, however, intrinsic to good scholarship and should not be consigned to the back burner of optional extras. Sound argument (and indeed poor argument) can easily be lost in poorly constructed prose; the reader should not need to forage in dense textual undergrowth to locate elusive meaning! The evaluation of style and presentation is included, then, to draw attention to a central, though too often neglected, element of scholarship. It should also be noted that a critical reading does not necessarily debunk the ideas of earlier scholars. It can also acknowledge the strength and value of those ideas.

Expanded Critical Skills for the Music Scholar

The music scholar needs to develop an expanded set of critical skills because critical thinking in music goes beyond the printed word.[6] It also extends to the critical consideration of score types, different editions of music, and the editorial decisions that underpin critical editions. Critical thinking also informs interpretation, nowhere more so than in the study and performance of early music. In the context of recordings, a whole new set of critical considerations comes into play, including the interpretative comparisons of such parameters as tempo, articulation, and ornamentation, and when and how a recording was produced. The technological limitations of early recordings, for example, often had a direct a bearing upon the tempo of a recorded performance, and whether repeats were included. For the music scholar, a critical mindset is essential in all contexts, both research and performative.

Note Taking

Note taking is the second skill that is needed for writing a literature review. This skill is often taken for granted. It should not be. One of the most frustrating aspects of academic research is having to revisit a source to check the

Writing a Literature Review   77

Table 4.1. Guidelines for critical thinking

1. Context

- What is the time period, and the context, within which each writing emerged?
- In which philosophical and/or social & cultural and/or intellectual environment did each writing emerge? Are there historical perspectives that need to be taken into account?
- Is there a particular theoretical framework underpinning the ideas and arguments set out in each of the writings? If so, what is it? Is it implicit or explicit?

Ancillary question

- Are there assumptions, attitudes, values, or beliefs held by you, the student scholar, that might influence your interpretation of the texts?

2. Strengths, weaknesses, limitations, omissions

- Are the aims of the writing set out at the beginning? Does the writer address the aims?
- What are the strengths of the ideas and arguments that are presented?
- What are the weaknesses and/or limitations of the ideas and arguments?
- Is the position put forward by the writer supported by evidence, and by a well-developed argument?
- Is the argument presented in a logical sequence and built up progressively over the course of the writing? Are there any logical inconsistencies?
- Has the writer failed to consider issues which, through omission, undermine the strength of the argument?
- Is there either deliberate or unintentional bias? If so, how does this manifest itself?
- Are there any implicit assumptions in the writing?
- Are the conclusions consistent with the aims and with the evidence that is presented? Are the conclusions compelling?
- What, if anything, does each writing add to the existing body of knowledge?

3. Critical synthesis

- What do the writings as a whole have in common?
- Are the viewpoints of different scholars contradictory? Complementary?
- Which writings offer the more compelling arguments? Why?
- How do the perspectives presented in each writing relate to other research, if at all?
- What, if anything, do the writings as a whole add to the existing body of knowledge?
- What broad conclusions, if any, can be drawn?

4. Style and presentation

- For whom is the writing intended? What impact, if any, does this have on content and style?
- Is the language usage clear and efficient? Accessible? Unnecessarily complex? Impenetrable?
- What about the sentence structure? Are the sentences easily comprehended, or are they unwieldy and difficult to "unpick"?
- Is the writing cohesive? Is there continuity from sentence to sentence, from paragraph to paragraph and from section to section?

citation details, or the accuracy of a paraphrase or direct quotation, because they were not documented accurately in the note-taking phase. Whilst this is less of a problem for sources in e-format because word or phrase searches can be done at a later date, it can be difficult, and sometimes impossible, to revisit other sources. Imagine, for example, the case of material that is held in an archive in another country. It may be impossible to travel to the archive again, but academic integrity demands accuracy. This is a dilemma to be avoided.

78   Postgraduate Research in Music

By observing a few basic guidelines, note taking can be done in a way that minimizes the likelihood of such dilemmas. These guidelines also streamline the note-taking process and reduce the amount of time that is needed, for reviewing sources is one of the more time-consuming aspects of a research project.

Begin by Noting the Full Publication Details for Each Source
The full publication details of each source must be documented at the beginning of the notes, including the page range of book chapters and journal articles, the address and date accessed for web sources, and the filing details of archival sources (series, box, and file numbers).

Note the Page Numbers of Each Documented Segment
It is important to note the page number(s) of every segment of information that is documented in the notes. This information will be needed when citing both paraphrased material and direct quotations. It sounds obvious, but it can easily be overlooked.

Direct Quotes and Paraphrasing
Direct quotations and paraphrases must be clearly differentiated in the notes. To avoid any possibility of confusion later on, enclose direct quotations in quotation marks or set them as indented quotations. Be sure, too, to differentiate between paraphrased material and any accompanying thoughts or commentary by you, the note taker.

What to Record, and How Much?
A constant tension that needs to be managed is how much information should be recorded. As noted above, revisiting sources is sometimes impossible, so enough detail has to be recorded in the note-taking phase of the research. On the other hand, a lot of time can be wasted through excessive documentation. It is helpful to remain grounded in such questions as: What is my research question? What are the aims of my research? How and where might this information slot into the thesis? How significant is this information in the context of my topic? Clearly too much detail is better than too little, but excessive transcription can rob a project of time that will be needed for other phases of the research. What is needed is a distillation of the essential, significant, and relevant information from each source—nothing more.

The Habit of Critical Reading and Critical Note Taking
Whilst the critical evaluation of sources appears in the literature review, the groundwork for this is laid in the note-taking phase of the research. For

each source that is reviewed, the critical thinking guidelines (as set out in table 4.1) should be kept in mind, and any critical observations recorded as they arise. These observations, which might otherwise be lost, can later be incorporated into the literature review. There must be no mistaking, however, as to whose ideas they are—those of the note taker, or those of the author of the source. Such confusion can lead to inadvertent plagiarism—and plagiarism, whether deliberate or inadvertent, is the worst academic crime and punishable by failure of the thesis (see chapter 7 for a discussion of plagiarism).

Filing Information

Filing information is another aspect of note taking that can easily be neglected. Efficient filing, however, lies at the heart of data management. A chaotic approach at best makes it difficult to retrieve information later on; at worst it completely loses track of things. A good filing system therefore needs to be set in place at the beginning of a research project.

Filing is based on the idea of differentiated levels of content. The uppermost level divides a project into a number of broad, overarching subject categories. Each of these is broken down into smaller sub-categories, each of which is broken down into further sub-categories until no further reduction of content is needed. Each sub-category represents a different level of content, rather like the doll within a doll principle of Russian dolls.

Filing systems can be constructed in either digital format or hard copy; the same principles apply to both. An overarching subject category therefore appears as a folder in e-format, or as a lever-arch file (or other material file type) in hard-copy. Each e-folder contains other e-folders (a folder within a folder), the hard-copy analogy for which might be cardboard file dividers within a lever-arch file. At the lowest level of classification are word, pdf or excel files, or, in hard copy, individual documents or segments that might be differentiated by such things as adhesive labels. Filing systems for research are generally created in both formats, with varying degrees of duplication.

A filing system can be designed either as a series of headings, sub-headings, and bullet points, or as a flow chart; this is a matter of individual preference. A fictitious thesis on the music of the imaginary Peruvian composer, Diego Ferrera (1910–1985), which will be referred to again in chapters 5 and 6, provides a useful case study in applying the principles of systematic filing. This project includes seven upper-level categories, each of which contains a number of sub-levels (see figure 4.1). Some of the sub-levels are broken down further to create a third level of content.

80 Postgraduate Research in Music

1. Writings by Ferrera
   o Concert reviews
      ▪ New York Times
      ▪ Other newspapers
   o About music and composition
2. Writings about Ferrera
   o Journal articles
   o Newspaper and magazine articles
3. Radio and film programs
   o Tape
   o Video
4. Secondary sources
   o Peruvian folk music
   o European art music
5. Archival research
   o New York Public Library for the Performing Arts
      ▪ Communications with the archive
      ▪ Notes from archival research
   o National Library of Peru
      ▪ Communications with the archive
      ▪ Notes from archival research
6. Thesis chapters
   o Chapter 1
   o Chapter 2 (etc.)
7. Administration
   o Enrolment records
   o Scholarship records
   o Research proposal
   o Travel records
   o Notes from supervision meetings

Figure 4.1. Filing system for the fictitious research project on the music of Diego Ferrera

A filing system is not a fixed object. It evolves as the research unfolds, for additional folders and files will inevitably be needed. A well-designed system, however, should remain largely intact through the entirety of a research project.

Legitimate Shortcuts

There are legitimate shortcuts that can be taken to evaluate the relevance of a source. There is no shame in taking these shortcuts; they are an important aspect of good time management.

- If there is an abstract, read it to see if the source is relevant.
- Check the chapter outline of a book, or skim through the headings of a book chapter or journal article, to get an idea of its content. This determines which sections, if any, need to be read in detail.
- Top and tail each source—in other words, read the introduction and the conclusion. These two sections contain the essential content of a source and indicate whether it needs to be read in its entirety.
- Use the index of a book (or use the "find" function for e-sources) if a specific term or concept is sought.

These shortcuts streamline the reviewing process. They enable irrelevant sources to be weeded out early on; moreover, the headings and sub-headings often provide a useful framework for summarizing the content of a source.

Writing Skills

Polished writing skills are also needed if sources are to be reviewed efficiently and effectively. How a literature review is presented is as important as its content; even the most incisive review will fail to make its mark if it is clothed in poorly written prose.

Writing skills are discussed in two places in this book: in the following guidelines, and in chapter 7, "Writing a Thesis Part 2: Style in Academic Writing." Both sections should be studied before writing a literature review.

Guidelines for Writing a Literature Review

Once the relevant sources of information have been identified, summarized, and critically considered, work can begin on writing the literature review. The following factors need to be taken into account when embarking upon this task.

Location of the Literature Review

The first question that arises is where to locate the literature review. There are three possibilities. If the review is not extensive, it can be incorporated into the introduction. Alternatively, a long review may follow the introduction as

82 Postgraduate Research in Music

a stand-alone section (in a research proposal) or as a separate chapter (in a thesis). In both cases, the review of literature should emerge seamlessly from the introduction, and the aims and methodology should follow on seamlessly from the literature review. This ordering of content is the one most commonly adopted in a thesis: introduction, literature review, aims and methodology. A third, less usual, possibility is to locate the review immediately *after* the aims and methodology; this may be appropriate in some studies.

How Many References?

There can be no definitive guide as to the number of references that should be included in a literature review. More can reasonably be expected in a thesis than in a research proposal because a proposal is a preparatory document. The length of a thesis is also a factor. A literature review for a 20,000-word honors thesis, for example, would generally not be as extensive as one for a doctoral thesis of 80,000–100,000 words. A further variable is the amount of existing scholarship in an area of research; clearly if there is little existing research, the review of literature will be correspondingly thin. In such cases, it is important to note this at the beginning of the review, lest the reader mistake a paucity of sources for a paucity of effort!

Notwithstanding these variables, the guidelines in table 4.2 provide a starting point for considering the number of references to include in a thesis. These guidelines are not a rigid prescription, but rather a general indication amidst a sea of variables.

Table 4.2. The number of references included in a literature review

Word count of thesis	No. of references in a research proposal	No. of references in a thesis
15,000–20,000	15–20	20–30
20,000–40,000	15–25	25–35
40,000–100,000	25–35	35–60

Clustering the References

After considering where the literature review will be located, the next step is to cluster the references into appropriate groups. The optimal groupings may be thematic and reflect key issues within an area of research. They may be historical or chronological (for example, writings 1950–1970; writings 1971–present); or organized by subject matter (for example, writings about Aaron Copland; writings about American music); or grouped by source type (for example, books, journal articles, newspaper reports). Each project will, by its very nature, suggest how the references can be clustered.

When there is a substantial number of references, headings can be used to identify the clusters, thereby adding clarity to the review. Other reviews can be structured effectively as a continuous narrative, with the clusters demarcated by paragraph divisions—particularly in projects for which there are few sources.

Organizing the References within Each Cluster

Thought also needs to be given to how the references will be organized within each cluster. A chronological survey may be the most appropriate ordering, showing the development of thought over time. Alternatively, the references might be grouped according to positions taken by the authors. An alphabetical listing, however, is not appropriate—although it *is* appropriate in an annotated bibliography.

How to Begin

A literature review should begin with a broad overview of the research that has already been undertaken on or around the topic. This is followed by an outline of how the review will proceed—what it will include, and in which order. All that is needed is a single, succinct paragraph to orient the reader to what is to follow—and to orient the writer as to what should follow! Such signposting is an important aspect of good writing; it will be discussed further in chapter 7.

Reviewing the Sources

The next part of a literature review comprises summaries, or précis, of the sources that are being reviewed. As a general rule, each précis should be somewhere between fifty and 300 words in length. Some references can be mentioned in a sentence or two, for example those that largely replicate other sources; more significant references should be discussed in greater

84 Postgraduate Research in Music

detail. Each précis should include some or all of the following information, depending upon the content of the source and its significance:

- A brief introduction to the source.
- The aims, methodology, and scope of the source.
- A summary of its contents.
- Its conclusions.
- A brief evaluation of its strengths, weaknesses, omissions, and limitations.
- Contextualization: what does this writing mean in a broader context? How does it relate to other writings and perspectives?
- The relevance of the source for the thesis.

Providing a Citation for Each Reference

A citation must be provided at the first mention of each reference—a full citation in a footnote or endnote if notes and bibliography referencing is used, or an abbreviated, parenthetical reference if author-date referencing is used (with full citation details provided subsequently in the reference list) (see chapter 5 for a discussion of referencing).

The Style of a Review

A number of elements hold the key to writing a compelling and effective literature review: precision and concision; building a case through critical engagement; creating a cohesive narrative; using the appropriate person, tense, and voice; and distinguishing clearly between the voice of the source and the voice of the reviewer.

Precision and Concision
It takes considerable skill to reduce a substantial writing to a brief summary. Precision and concision are of the essence. Words must not be wasted; only the essential content should be included. At the same time, complete sentences must be used. Incomplete sentences and bullet points are inappropriate in this context.

Building a Case through Critical Engagement
By its very nature, a literature review not only describes but also critically engages with the sources. As noted earlier in this chapter, the critical mind never takes things at face value. It analyzes, evaluates, and synthesizes.

Writing a Literature Review **85**

This critical stance requires a particular stylistic approach, for a case needs to be built up progressively over the course of a review. A key element in this is identifying the strengths, weaknesses, omissions, and limitations of each source. This leads to the gap that will be addressed by the thesis. This approach is illustrated in the following example, which concludes a discussion of Jones's hypothetical research by acknowledging its strengths as well as its limitations:

> Jones's study pointed the discipline in new and significant directions, and its importance cannot be overstated. What it failed to investigate, however, was . . .

The critical reviewing of sources should be informed by the guidelines for critical thinking that were set out earlier in this chapter. These guidelines, and the questions they contain, provide a systematic framework for reviewing each source.

Creating a Cohesive Narrative

If a case is to be built up effectively, a literature review needs to read as a narrative and not as a litany of disconnected summaries. This is achieved through the use of linking phrases and sentences to connect ideas, or to signal a change of direction. These phrases and sentences take time to craft, but they are worth the effort; without them, the text can easily become disjointed. This approach is exemplified in the following example, which creates a bridge between hypothetical studies by Smith and Jones:

> Building on the work done by Smith in his ground-breaking study, Jones embarked upon a new, although related, direction . . .

A useful strategy is to compile a list of words or phrases that can be used to connect one idea to another. Table 4.3 sets out some of the words and phrases that can be used for this purpose.

Which Person to Use

In the context of this discussion, the term "person" refers to which pronoun to use: I/we (first person); you (second person); or he/she/it/they (third person). Clearly the first person (I/we) is inappropriate in a literature review because this is the voice that is used when we refer to ourselves. A literature review, on the other hand, reports on research undertaken by other people. The second person (you) is also inappropriate because it is used to address people (for example, "You need to consider which person to use."). This leaves the third person (he/she/it/they), which is the appropriate person to use in a literature

86　Postgraduate Research in Music

Table 4.3. Connecting words and phrases

Connecting by contradiction	Connecting by continuity
• Although	• Accordingly
• By contrast	• Adding to
• Contrary to	• Also
• Conversely	• Also of great significance
• Directly contradicting	• As
• However	• As a result of
• Notwithstanding this	• Building on
• On the contrary	• Consequently
• On the other hand	• For example
• Running counter to	• Further
• Whilst	• Furthermore
	• Further to
	• Hence
	• Indeed
	• It might also be suggested that
	• Just as
	• Likewise
	• Moreover
	• More specifically
	• Not only . . . but also
	• Therefore
	• Thus

review. The third person expresses the viewpoint of the writer whose research is being discussed.

Which Tense to Use

Tenses are concerned with the temporal (or time) aspect of an action—in other words, whether the action takes place in the past, present, or future. Of the three tenses, two predominate in a literature review: the past and the present.

The past tense is used to report and describe the research findings—actions that took place before the present time, and which have already been concluded:

> Smith's interview data revealed a strong correlation between perfect pitch and perfectionism.

The present tense is used when sources are discussed and evaluated. It projects the discussion as a present-moment event and as an ongoing process:

> The implications of these findings are profound, suggesting that . . .

The present tense is also used when research findings are accepted as being universally true:

Studies from around the world show perfect pitch to be a universal phenomenon.

Whilst the past and present tenses predominate, the future tense occasionally has a role to play in the discussion and evaluation of sources:

Jones's study is ground-breaking in its findings and will have a significant impact on the future treatment of Parkinson's Disease.

Each tense (past, present, and future) can also take a number of different forms, each of which has the capacity to convey a subtle inflection of meaning. These subtleties can be put to good use in a literature review. The following examples illustrate just a few of the possibilities that are inherent in tenses.

The present perfect tense (present past) describes an action that has happened once or many times in the past, and may continue into the present. It combines the present form of the verb "to have" (has/have) with a past participle (for example, "used"):

Following Smith's ground-breaking study, other researchers have used a similar methodology.

If the past tense were to be used instead in this example (the verb "used"), the meaning would be slightly different. The continuation that is implied by the present perfect tense ("have used") would be replaced by the reporting of an action that has already been concluded ("used"), with no implication of continuation:

Following Smith's ground-breaking study, other researchers used a similar methodology.

The conditional form of a verb can also communicate nuances of meaning. This tense signals what would, could, should, might, or will happen, depending upon a condition of some kind. It can be valuable, for example, when commenting upon the limitations of a study:

If Jones had included a larger sample of respondents in his research, the findings would be more credible.

88   Postgraduate Research in Music

This example could be adjusted to carry a slightly different meaning. In the following variation, the conditional and present perfect tenses are combined ("might have been"):

If Jones had included a larger sample of respondents in his research, the findings might have been more credible.

These are just a few of the many inflections of meaning that can be invoked through the sophisticated and sensitive use of tenses. Whilst the simple past and present tenses predominate in a literature review, other forms of the tenses can be used to add both clarity and subtle nuances of meaning. The key is to be aware of which tense is being used, and for what purpose.

Which Voice to Use

A further consideration is whether to write a literature review in the active or passive voice. Consider the following pairs of sentences and analyze the changes that occur in each pair.

Pair 1:
Smith and Brown discuss ornamentation in considerable detail.
Ornamentation is discussed in considerable detail by Smith and Brown.

Pair 2:
Broadwood manufactured English square pianos in the late eighteenth century.
English square pianos were manufactured by Broadwood in the late eighteenth century.

The same information is being conveyed in each of the paired examples. There is, however, a different emphasis in the second sentence of each pair. The content has been re-ordered, and the form of the verb has changed. What has happened is that the voice has changed from active to passive.

In the active voice, the subject of a sentence is the "doer"—in other words, the one performing the action (for example, Smith and Brown). With the reordering of content in the passive voice, the subject is the recipient of the action (for example, ornamentation). The verb is also different in the passive voice, which always combines some form of the verb "to be" (for example, "is") with a past participle (for example, "discussed"). These two elements—the (re) ordering of content, and the form of the verb—are the defining elements of the passive voice.

Pair 1:
Active voice: Smith and Brown discuss ornamentation in considerable detail.
Passive voice: Ornamentation is discussed in considerable detail by Smith and Brown.

Pair 2:
Active voice: Broadwood manufactured English square pianos in the late eighteenth century.
Passive voice: English square pianos were manufactured by Broadwood in the late eighteenth century.

In general in academic writing, the active voice is preferred because it is clear and direct. The passive voice also has a role to play. It is useful for changing the emphasis of a sentence, and for providing syntactical variation.

Distinguishing between the Voice of the Source and the Voice of the Reviewer

The term "voice" has a further meaning. It also refers to whose voice is speaking: that of the source being discussed, or that of the reviewer. It is easy to confuse the two voices—and it is so important not to do so. Without due care, paraphrases of a source can appear to be attributable to the reviewer; conversely, comments by a reviewer can appear to be attributable to the source. Such inaccuracies can be avoided by ensuring that a citation is meticulously provided for each quoted or paraphrased sentence from another source, thereby placing authorship completely beyond doubt—and avoiding the risk of inadvertent plagiarism.

How to End a Literature Review

A literature review should not come to an abrupt end after the final source has been reviewed. A concluding paragraph is needed, drawing the threads of thought together, evaluating the sources as a whole, and identifying any gaps in the existing research. The gaps then become a springboard for the statement of aims.

Six Common Pitfalls in Writing a Literature Review

A literature review should be just that: a review of literature. Yet so often things are included that should not be there. The following six pitfalls should be avoided:

1. Some primary source material belongs in a literature review, and some does not. Be mindful as to which sources belong and which do not (see the discussion earlier in this chapter).
2. Do not include information that belongs in the introduction. A literature review should begin with a broad overview of the research that has already been undertaken on or around the topic, followed by an outline of how the review will proceed. This is different from the contextual background that is included in the introduction.
3. Do not include material that belongs in the methodology. It may be appropriate to note the methodology used in a particular source. It is *not* appropriate to include the methodology for the thesis in the literature review.
4. Do not deviate into the aims of the research. Whilst the research question or hypothesis may be included at the very end of the literature review, the aims do not belong here. They should be set out in a separate section.
5. Never confuse the voice of the reviewer with the voice of the source being reviewed.
6. Do not discuss how the findings of your own research confirm, contradict, or add to the existing writings. It makes no sense to do this before the data have been presented. This discussion belongs in the concluding chapter of the thesis; it has no place in the literature review.

Guidelines for Writing an Annotated Bibliography

An annotated bibliography is a preparatory exercise that can be undertaken before writing a literature review. It is a hybrid form that lies somewhere between a bibliography and a literature review. Like a bibliography, an annotated bibliography comprises an alphabetical list of references. It also shares common ground with a literature review by providing a description, or annotation, of each of the references. In function, however, an annotated bibliography can be differentiated from a literature review. It is an autonomous, self-contained document that serves as an antecedent to a literature review.[7]

A literature review, on the other hand, forms part of a research proposal or thesis and generally functions as a springboard to the aims of the research. In the detail of its content, too, and in its manner of presentation, an annotated bibliography differs from a literature review. The following guidelines provide a systematic approach to writing an annotated bibliography, at the same time drawing out points in common and points of difference between these two related, though different, ways of reviewing the literature.

Cluster the References

Like a literature review, an annotated bibliography clusters the references into appropriate groups, for example by theme, or by chronology. Headings are generally included. Within each heading, the sources are listed alphabetically by author—a practice that is not followed in a literature review, where the references may, for example, be sequenced to show the development of thought over time, or the positions taken by the authors.

How to Begin

As noted earlier, a literature review begins with a broad overview of the existing research and a plan for how the review will proceed. An annotated bibliography begins differently. This is a stand-alone exercise for which a broader context needs to be set in place—context which, in a research proposal or a thesis, is provided in the introduction. An annotated bibliography therefore begins with a brief overview of the research topic and its context, the aims of the research (in broad terms), and an outline of how the annotated bibliography will proceed. This information is typically contained within a single paragraph.

Reviewing the Sources

Annotated bibliographies come in varying levels of detail. Some simply provide brief summaries, or descriptive overviews, of each source. Others not only summarize but also evaluate the sources. A third approach goes further again, not only summarizing and evaluating but also correlating the sources with the topic of the thesis. Whilst any of these approaches may be used, the ensuing guidelines follow the third method because it offers a more comprehensive preparation for the literature review.

92 Postgraduate Research in Music

- Begin each précis with a complete citation of the source, formatted in the appropriate referencing style for the research area (see chapter 5 for a discussion of referencing styles). Set the citation in bold to distinguish it from the précis that follows.
- Beginning on a new line, provide a summary of the source in no more than 200 words. The summary should comprise a single paragraph and include the following information:
  - An introduction to the source (a single sentence should suffice).
  - Its aims and scope.
  - A summary of its content.
  - An evaluation.
  - A brief reflection on the reason(s) for including the source in the annotated bibliography—in other words, its value and how it relates to the topic of the thesis.

Nothing further is needed—no critical comparison of the sources, no linking sentences from one précis to the next. This is simply a preparatory exercise for the literature review.

Style

With no more than 200 words in which to summarize each source, the efficient use of language is essential. Each précis must be concentrated and minimal. At the same time, complete sentences must be used; incomplete sentences and bullet points are not acceptable. The third person should predominate; the first person should only be used when reflecting upon the reason(s) for including a source in the annotated bibliography. The past and present tenses are prioritized—the past tense for reporting research findings, and the present tense for evaluating the sources. The future tense may also be used in the evaluation, and when reflecting upon the reasons for including a source in the bibliography. The active voice is predominant, although the passive voice may be used when appropriate.

How to End an Annotated Bibliography

Where a literature review ends with a concluding paragraph that evaluates the sources as a whole and identifies the gap(s) in the existing research, an annotated bibliography does not. In this it is more like a bibliography, which, like an annotated bibliography, ends when the listing of sources is complete.

A Literature Review and an Annotated Bibliography in Summary

A literature review and an annotated bibliography are similar but different. Both begin with an introduction of some kind; both provide summaries of the references that will be included in the thesis; and both cluster the references into appropriate groupings. A literature review, however, goes further. In addition, it critically engages with the sources and builds a case over the course of the review. It creates a cohesive narrative through summative and linking sentences, and includes a concluding paragraph that summarizes the key points, critically drawing the threads together and identifying gaps and/or misunderstandings in the existing literature. A literature review is, then, a more sophisticated piece of writing, and more expansive in both content and critical engagement.

Coda

A literature review is a process that continues throughout a research project. It appears first in the research proposal and remains as work-in-progress until its final iteration in the thesis. Further sources inevitably come to light as the research unfolds. It is therefore important to see a literature review not only as a written document, but also as an ongoing process that continues to shape and inform the thesis through the entirety of the project.

Exercises

Exercise 1: Critical Thinking

Exercise 1 is designed to sharpen the skill of critical thinking. It draws upon a group of writings that engage in various ways with the topic, "Music and Meaning." These writings represent some of the key approaches that have emerged since the mid-nineteenth century. They are not proposed as a comprehensive survey of writings on the subject; rather, they embody some of the significant strands of thought from the past 150 years or so. In the context of

94 Postgraduate Research in Music

this book, the writings present a rich opportunity for developing the skill of critical thinking. Exercise 1 comprises two parts: (1) seminar preparation and discussion, in which the writings are critically evaluated and discussed (Part A); and (2) review essay in which the critical observations are embedded in a scholarly narrative (Part B).

Part A: Seminar Preparation and Discussion
Seminar Preparation

1. Read the five writings listed below, each of which explores the topic of "Music and Meaning" in a different way. Keep in mind the tenets of critical thinking that were discussed earlier in this chapter, together with the guidelines set out in table 4.1.
2. Briefly summarize the main content and arguments put forward in each writing, at the same time providing a critical analysis and critical evaluation of the sources. These summaries may be formulated in bullet points.
3. Critically synthesize the ideas set out in the five writings, first identifying the points in common and points of difference then offering a broader evaluation of the writings as a whole. The critical synthesis may be formulated in bullet points.

The Five Writings

Hanslick, Eduard. *The Beautiful in Music: A Contribution to the Revisal of Musical Aesthetics.* Translated by Gustav Cohen. 7th ed. London: Novello, 1891. [First published in 1854.]

Chapter I: "Aesthetics as Founded on Feelings" (pp. 15–31).

Chapter II: "The Representation of Feelings is not the Subject of Music" (pp. 32–33).

Chapter III: "The Beautiful in Music" (pp. 66–67 only).

Chapter VII: "Form and Substance (Subject) as Applied to Music" (pp. 160–163).

Meyer, Leonard B. *Emotion and Meaning in Music.* Chicago: University of Chicago Press, 1956. Chapter 1: "Theory" (pp. 1–42).

Cooke, Deryck. *The Language of Music.* London: Oxford University Press, 1959.

Chapter 2: "The Elements of Musical Expression" (pp. 34–112).

Chapter 3: "Some Basic Terms of Musical Vocabulary" (pp. 113–167).

Blacking, John. *How Musical is Man?* London: Faber and Faber, 1976.

Chapter 4: "Soundly Organised Humanity" (pp. 89–116).

McClary, Susan. *Feminine Endings: Music, Gender and Sexuality.* Minnesota: University of Minnesota Press, 1991.
Chapter 3: "Sexual Politics in Classical Music" (pp. 53–79).

Seminar Discussion

The questions set out in the four rubrics of enquiry in table 4.1 can be used as a framework for the seminar discussion. Rubrics 1, 2, and 4 inform the critical analysis and critical evaluation of each of the five writings; rubric 3 is concerned with the critical synthesis of the writings as a whole.

Part B: Review Essay

Critically analyze and evaluate the ideas on the subject of "Music and Meaning," as set forth in the above writings. Then, in drawing the threads of thought together, tease out points in common and points of difference between the writings, moving from the particular to a broader perspective.

Word length: 2,500 words.

The guidelines set out in tables 4.1 and 4.4 can be used as a framework for the essay. Like all writing at postgraduate level, the essay should have as its goal a sophistication of thought and an elegance of expression that take time to formulate. The first thoughts, and the first sentences, are not necessarily the best ones; it takes time and effort to chisel a sculpture in words.

Exercise 2: Critical Evaluation of a Literature Review

Study the guidelines in this chapter on how to write a literature review. Then, using the library search skills set out in chapters 2 and 3 of this book, locate a masters or doctoral thesis on a topic relevant to your area of research. The thesis should be at least 20,000 words in length. Critically evaluate the literature review that is included in the thesis, using the following questions as the foundation of your evaluation. Restrict the evaluation to no more than 1,000 words. Complete sentences must be used throughout the review; bullet points are not acceptable.

Questions

- How does the literature review begin? Does it include an introductory paragraph? If so, is it effective? Why or why not? If there is no introductory paragraph, what impact (if any) does this have on your apprehension of the review?

96 Postgraduate Research in Music

Table 4.4. Guidelines for the review essay

1. Planning

- Review the writings, summaries of the writings, and any additional notes taken at the seminar.
- Formulate a plan for the review essay. Which content will be included and in which order? Will the writings be dealt with consecutively? Thematically? In some other way?
- Be mindful that plans often change as the writing unfolds. Without a plan, however, chaos and confusion can easily take hold.

3. Style and presentation

- Present the content in a logical sequencing of ideas; the thread of thought needs to be clear at all times.
- There must be continuity from sentence to sentence, from paragraph to paragraph, and from section to section. Strategies for this include the use of summative and connecting sentences (see discussion of the academic style in chapter 7).
- Use language in a clear and efficient way, avoiding unnecessary complexity and sentences that are unduly long and unwieldy. Concision and precision are of the essence.
- Headings may be used to elucidate the structure of the essay.
- Be meticulous with the referencing of sources. Choose an appropriate referencing style and apply it consistently and accurately.

2. Structure and content

The essay should include three main sections:
- Introduction, which includes a brief contextual background, the aims of the essay, and an outline of how it will proceed.
- Middle section, which presents a summary of the key ideas in the writings, together with critical analyses and critical evaluations of those ideas.
- Conclusion, which provides a brief summary then a critical synthesis of the writings as a whole. Be sure to address the "So what?" question. What does all of this *mean*? This broadening of the discussion may bring in other ideas on the subject, for example those of Igor Stravinsky and Glenn Gould, both of whom had interesting thoughts on the subject of music and meaning.* The "So what?" question is a key aspect of good scholarship. It probes beneath the surface to explore the implications of the information that is presented.

---

* Igor Stravinsky, *Chronicle of My Life* (London: Victor Gollancz Ltd, 1936), 91–93; and Kevin Bazzana, *Glenn Gould: The Performer in the Work: A Study in Performance Practice* (Oxford: Oxford University Press, 1997), 11–35.

- How is the literature review organized (for example, thematically, chronologically, or by source type)? Is the organization appropriate? Why or why not? Are headings used? If so, are they effective? Why or why not?
- Observe the précis of the sources. Do they capture the essential content of each source? Why or why not?
- Comment on the style of the review. Does the review engage critically with the sources? Does it consider the strengths as well as the weaknesses and limitations of the sources? Is the appropriate person used? Are the appropriate tenses used? The appropriate voice(s)?

Writing a Literature Review **97**

- Does the review read as a cohesive narrative? If so, identify three sentences that fulfil this function. If not, identify three sentence that create bumps, or discontinuities, in the text.
- Is a case built up systematically over the course of the review? If so, how is this done?
- Observe the referencing. Which referencing style is used? Is it appropriate for the sub-discipline of the research? Is the referencing consistent and accurate?
- How does the review end? Does it summarize the preceding content? Does it identify a gap in the existing research? Does it include a research question or hypothesis? Does it provide a link to the aims?

Exercise 3: Annotated Bibliography

Prepare an annotated bibliography on the topic of your thesis, following the guidelines set out earlier in this chapter. At least fifteen references should be included for a thesis of 15,000–40,000 words; at least twenty-five should be included for a thesis of 40,000–100,000 words.

Reading List

Bazzana, Kevin. *Glenn Gould: The Performer in the Work: A Study in Performance Practice.* Oxford: Oxford University Press, 1997.

Blacking, John. *How Musical is Man?* London: Faber and Faber, 1976.

Cooke, Deryck. *The Language of Music.* London: Oxford University Press, 1959.

Cryer, Pat. "Reading Round the Subject: Working Procedures." In *The Research Student's Guide to Success,* 56–64. Buckingham: McGraw-Hill Education, 2006.

Cryer, Pat. "Reading Round the Subject: Evaluating Quality." In *The Research Student's Guide to Success,* 65–82. Buckingham: McGraw-Hill Education, 2006.

Efron, Sara Efrat, and Ruth Ravid. *Writing the Literature Review: A Practical Guide.* New York: Guilford Publications, 2019.

Galvan, Hose L., and Melisa Galvan. *Writing Literature Reviews: A Guide for Students of the Social and Behavioural Sciences.* 7th ed. London: Routledge, 2017.

Hanslick, Eduard. *The Beautiful in Music: A Contribution to the Revisal of Musical Aesthetics.* Translated by Gustav Cohen. 7th ed. London: Novello, 1891.

Hart, Chris. *Doing a Literature Review: Releasing the Research Imagination.* 2nd ed. London: Sage, 2018.

Kumar, Ranjit. "Reviewing the Literature." In *Research Methodology: A Step-by-Step Guide for Beginners.* 5th ed., 55–72. Los Angeles: Sage, 2019.

Machi, Lawrence A., and Brenda T. McEvoy. *The Literature Review: Six Steps to Success.* 4th ed. Thousand Oaks, California: Sage, 2022.

98 Postgraduate Research in Music

McClary, Susan. *Feminine Endings: Music, Gender and Sexuality*. Minnesota: University of Minnesota Press, 1991.

Meyer, Leonard B. *Emotion and Meaning in Music*. Chicago: University of Chicago Press, 1956.

Orna, Elizabeth, and Graham Stevens. *Managing Information for Research: Practical Help in Researching, Writing and Designing Dissertations*. 2nd ed. Maidenhead: Open University Press, 2009.

Potter, Stephen. "Undertaking a Literature Review." In *Doing Postgraduate Research*. 2nd ed., edited by Stephen Potter, 152–179. London: Sage, 2006.

Ridley, Diana. *The Literature Review: A Step-by-Step Guide for Students*. 2nd ed. London: Sage, 2012.

Stravinsky, Igor. *Chronicle of My Life*. London: Victor Gollancz Ltd, 1936.

5
Writing a Research Proposal

With the review of literature now under way, it is time to consider a further milestone in the research process: writing a research proposal. This is a document that sets out the context of the proposed research, what has been written on or around the topic, what the research aims to do, why it is being undertaken, and how and when it will be done.

A research proposal is about planning—careful, considered planning, for there is undoubtedly a close correlation between a good research proposal and a good thesis. It is a task that takes sustained effort and deep reflection over several months; a research project needs to put down roots before it can grow. This crucial step should not be left until the last minute. Thorough planning, as noted already in chapter 3, is one of the keys to good academic research.

A research proposal is not only a plan; it is also a feasibility study. It ensures that:

- The topic is clearly defined and worth investigating.
- The proposed research is original and viable.
- What is being proposed is neither too broad nor too narrow.
- The project can be completed within the specified word count and timeframe.
- The methodology is appropriate and has the potential to yield a meaningful outcome.

A research proposal is therefore not an optional extra, a prefix that has to be appended to the research process to get it under way. It is central to the success of a project, and this is why it is mandatory in programs of postgraduate study throughout the world. Without a feasibility survey and a clear plan, a good research outcome is unlikely. Things need to be thought through and navigation systems need to be set in place.

All research proposals include a number of key elements. There are also several optional elements whose inclusion is determined by the nature of the research or by institutional policies; many faculties and departments have

Postgraduate Research in Music. Victoria Rogers, Oxford University Press. © Oxford University Press 2024.
DOI: 10.1093/oso/9780197616031.003.0006

100 Postgraduate Research in Music

their own requirements. In the following list, the key elements are highlighted in bold to distinguish them from the optional inclusions.

- **Title page**
- **Project title**
- Table of contents
- List of tables, list of figures, list of musical examples
- Abstract
- **Introduction**
- **Hypothesis or research question**
- **Literature review**
- **Aims and rationale**
- **Anticipated outcomes**
- **Significance**
- **Methodology**
- **Structure of the thesis**
- **Timeline**
- Ethics clearance
- Budget
- **Bibliography/reference list**
- Footnotes and endnotes
- Appendices

The following guidelines set out the what, the why, and the how of each of these elements. These guidelines should not be seen as a rigid prescription from which no deviation is possible. Some flexibility may be needed in both content and ordering to accommodate the requirements of a particular project, or those of a particular institution.

Title Page

The exact content and ordering of a title page vary from institution to institution, and from degree to degree; individual institutions often have their own templates. The following list captures all of the information that may be included, and the order in which it may be set out. The essential elements are set in bold to differentiate them from those that are optional.

- **Title of the proposed research**
- **Research Proposal**

- **Degree for which the proposal is presented**
- **Student Name**
- Student number, email address and phone number
- Supervisor/s (including title/s—Professor, Associate Professor, Dr., Ms., Mr., as appropriate)
- **Department and university**
- **Date**

The formatting of a title page is illustrated in figures 5.1 and 5.2, which set out, in respectively shorter and longer versions, the title page for a fictitious doctoral study of the musical language of the imaginary Peruvian composer, Diego Ferrera (1910–1985).

**The Musical Language of Diego Ferrera:
A Sign of Things to Come?**

Research Proposal
DOCTOR OF PHILOSOPHY

MARY SMITH

Faculty of Music
University of the Antipodes

2022

Figure 5.1. Content and ordering of a title page

102 Postgraduate Research in Music

The Musical Language of Diego Ferrera:

A Sign of Things to Come?

Research Proposal

DOCTOR OF PHILOSOPHY

MARY SMITH

Student number: 12345678 | Email: m.smith@uoa.edu | Ph. 0123 456 789

SUPERVISORS

Professor Matthew Mars and Dr Jane Jupiter

Faculty of Music
University of the Antipodes

2022

Figure 5.2. Content and ordering of a title page: Alternative version with additional information

Project Title

The project title should describe, in a few words, what the research is about. Phrases such as "an investigation into" and "a study of" are unnecessary and should be avoided, for it is self-evident that research involves investigation and study.[1] A good title can take time to formulate but it is time well spent.

This is the portal, the entry point, to the proposal, the first thing a reader encounters. First impressions count!

Consider the following examples. The first version is, in each case, too wordy and rather clumsy. The second version is a more succinct way of indicating what the research is about.

Example A
The compositions of John Blacking and how they relate to his work as an ethnomusicologist (15 words)

Better is:
John Blacking: composer and ethnomusicologist (5 words)

Example B
Differences in the *Lieder* settings by Wenzel Johann Tomášek and Franz Peter Schubert of the same texts by Johann Wolfgang von Goethe—a comparative analysis (25 words)

Better is:
Settings of Goethe by Tomášek and Schubert: a comparative analysis (10 words)
OR
Goethe, *Lieder*, Tomášek, and Schubert (5 words)

The unedited version of example B is particularly verbose. The reworkings omit unnecessary repetition ("differences" and "comparative analysis"), as well as detail that can be left for the methodology section ("the same texts"). First and middle names have also been omitted from the reworkings; they are not included in a title, but they should be added, together with a composer's dates, at first mention in the body of the proposal (and at first mention in the abstract, and in the thesis as well). The revised versions also employ the colon, which is often used in titles as a neat way of linking two elements.

If a good title does not spring immediately to mind, jot down significant words and concepts then let the ideas rest and allow the subconscious mind to work its magic. When an idea comes to mind, write it down immediately lest it be lost. Remember: the subconscious mind is one of a scholar's best friends.

Table of Contents

A table of contents, referred to simply as "contents," is an optional inclusion in a research proposal. It can be a useful navigation tool if a proposal is long or complex; in shorter, straightforward proposals it can be left out, provided the headings and sub-headings are clear in the body of the proposal.

If a table of contents is included, it should list the sections in the ensuing pages (not the preceding ones), together with the starting page number of each section. For neatness, the page numbers are justified right. The listing may be brief and refer only to the major sections, or be more detailed and include both the major sections and the sub-sections within them.

To add clarity, a contents page may use indentation and capitalization/non-capitalization to differentiate the headings (see also the discussion of headings in chapter 6, "Writing a Thesis Part 1"). The further an indentation sits to the right, the lower the section sits within the structural hierarchy of the proposal; put another way, indentation to the right denotes a section within a section. This hierarchy is also reflected in the capitalization/non-capitalization of headings, with capitalization often used for non-indented headings and lower case for indented sub-headings.

Corresponding numerical and/or alphabetical labeling may also be applied, although this, too, is optional. If such labeling is used, there is a hierarchy of upper- and lower-case numerals and letters that should be followed. It would be inappropriate, for example, to denote a major section with a lower-case roman numeral or lower-case letter (i or a) and the sub-sections within it with Arabic numerals or upper-case letters (1 or A); convention decrees the opposite. As to the matter of whether numerals have priority over letters or vice versa, there are no hard and fast rules. A table of contents may, for example, employ heading levels as follows (assuming that four levels are needed): 1 A (i) (a); or it may prioritize letters over numbers, as follows: A 1 (a) (i). A further option is to apply labeling that is often associated with report writing—thus delineating three levels as 1, 1.1, and 1.1.1 (and so on). Different faculties and different disciplines have their preferred approaches. The main thing is to be consistent and to ensure that the same numerical/alphabetical hierarchy—if it is used at all—is applied throughout.

It can be seen, then, that if a table of contents is included in a proposal, it may extend beyond a straightforward listing of sections and sub-sections. These three elements—indentation, the capitalization/non-capitalization of headings, and numerical/alphabetical labeling—work together to add clarity to the listing of content in multi-layered proposals. Of course, any numerical or alphabetical signification that is used, together with any capitalization/non-capitalization of headings, needs to carry through to the body of the proposal.

Figure 5.3 sets out a table of contents for the fictitious doctoral study referred to in figures 5.1 and 5.2.

CONTENTS	
ABSTRACT	1
LIST OF TABLES	2
INTRODUCTION	
Contextual and biographical overview	3
Ferrera's ideas about music and composition	5
Overview of Ferrera's compositions	6
Research question	7
LITERATURE REVIEW	
Writings about Ferrera	8
Writings about Peruvian folk music	10
Writings about twentieth-century composition	13
Summary, synthesis, identification of the gap in current research	16
AIMS AND RATIONALE	17
ANTICIPATED OUTCOMES AND SIGNFICANCE OF THE STUDY	18
METHODOLOGY	
Archival research	19
Interviews	20
Works to be analyzed	21
Analytic methods	22
TIMELINE	24
ETHICAL CONSIDERATIONS	25
BUDGET	25
LIST OF REFERENCES	26

Figure 5.3. Table of contents for the fictitious study of the musical language of Diego Ferrera

List of Tables, List of Figures, List of Musical Examples

It is not essential to list the illustrations in a research proposal, although they must be listed in a thesis. If a list is included in the proposal, it is set on a new page immediately after the table of contents. The list includes a descriptive title for each illustration, together with a corresponding page number. For neatness, the page numbers are justified right. Each category of illustration is generally set on a separate page (tables on one page, figures on the next, and so on). If there are only a few illustrations, they may be listed together on a single page.

Abstract

An abstract is a précis, or summary, of the contents of a document. It is typically 300–400 words in length. Part of the challenge of writing an abstract is knowing what to leave out. It should focus clearly on the key points and avoid any information and/or viewpoints that are not included in the original source.

Abstracts are encountered in various contexts. As a scholarly convention, an abstract precedes a piece of academic writing such as a thesis or a journal article. Abstracts of conference papers are included in conference programs; they are also incorporated into library catalogues and other databases; and they are an optional inclusion in research proposals.

There are two approaches to abstract writing: the traditional approach, and the one sometimes followed in contemporary scholarship. In the traditional approach, an abstract comprises a single paragraph (one paragraph, one idea—the idea in this case being the research proposal). The opening sentence is not indented. Only complete sentences are used; bullet points and other abbreviations are not appropriate. The present and past tenses predominate, although an abstract for a research proposal may sometimes employ the future tense as well. The third person (he/she/it/they) is used; the first person (I/we) is avoided because an abstract implicitly objectifies the research and distances the writer from his/her own work. The active voice is generally preferred over the passive voice (see chapters 4 and 7 for discussions of the active and passive voices).

In some contemporary scholarship, two of these stylistic conventions have been loosened. An abstract is sometimes seen as a constellation of ideas rather than a single idea and is accordingly divided into more than one paragraph. The first person singular is also used, corresponding to the use of the first person more broadly in contemporary scholarship. The idea of objectifying the research and distancing the writer from his/her own work has less currency because the relationship between the researcher and the object of research is seen differently. The use of the first person, then, acknowledges the subjectivity that is seen as an implicit part of the research process.

These more recent practices, which are by no means universal, may be seen to be sidestepping the underlying reasons for the traditional approach. They may also be seen as a matter of style and individual preference. Remember, too, that four of the six elements are common to both approaches: non-indentation of the first paragraph; the use of complete sentences; the predominance of present and past tenses; and a preference for the active voice. The two styles of abstract writing are summarized in table 5.1.

Just as there are stylistic conventions that must be considered when writing an abstract, so, too, are there conventions that govern its content. Most or all of the following information should be included; administrative detail such as the timeline, budget, and ethical considerations should be omitted from the abstract—but not, of course, from the proposal itself.

- A contextual overview of the research area.
- An indication of research already undertaken, and identification of the gap in the existing research.
- A description of the proposed research—the issue it will address, what it aims to do, the outcomes that may be anticipated, and the significance of the research.
- The methodology that will be employed.

Table 5.1. Two approaches to abstract writing

The traditional approach	The approach in some contemporary practice
One paragraph	More than one paragraph
First sentence not indented	First sentence of opening paragraph not indented
Complete sentences only	Complete sentences only
Present and past tenses predominate	Present and past tenses predominate
Use of third person	Use of third person and first person
Active voice preferred	Active voice preferred

108 Postgraduate Research in Music

> **ABSTRACT**
>
> The Peruvian composer Diego Ferrera (1910–85) studied in Paris with Lucia Boucher and in Vienna with Gustav Waschenwasser before moving to the USA, where he spent fifteen years as a high-profile figure in the musical life of New York. In the early 1960s he moved to Greece, where he wrote many of his major works. He returned to Peru in 1975 and spent his final years in Lima in relative obscurity. Ferrera left a legacy of 157 works, including twelve operas, fourteen ballets, and many vocal and instrumental works. After his return to Peru, several brief, largely biographical newspaper articles were written about him, and a number of film and radio programmes were made. There has been some study of his music—mostly student dissertations—but no comprehensive investigation of his musical language, its development over five decades, or its significance in twentieth-century composition. This thesis addresses this gap by examining Ferrera's musical language, tracing the changes that occur from the early works of the 1930s through to the late works of the 1970s. The analysis provides a springboard for evaluating Ferrera's significance in twentieth-century composition, and for exploring the relationship between his musical aesthetic and the development of postmodern thought later in the century.

Figure 5.4. Abstract for the fictitious study of the musical language of Diego Ferrera

The principles of abstract writing are illustrated in figure 5.4, which sets out an abstract for the fictitious doctoral study referred to earlier in this chapter.[2]

Introduction

An introduction is, in a sense, the front door to a research proposal. It acquaints the reader with what the research is about, where the research sits in the broader scheme of things, and—again in broad terms—why it is being undertaken.

Context is a crucial aspect of an introduction, outlining the surrounding issues or circumstances from which the proposed research arises (for example, musical, artistic, historical, social, or cultural), and through which it can be better understood. Schoenberg's Expressionist compositions, for example, can be better understood in the context of late nineteenth-century Romanticism, and in relation to the philosophical and artistic movements of the early twentieth century. Contextualization should be a priority at the outset of a research project and should carry through to the thesis itself.

An important principle in writing the introduction is to proceed from the broad to the narrow—that is, to begin with a broad contextual overview and to narrow down progressively to a general statement of what the research is about. The following four steps can be used as a framework for this.[3]

1. Provide a broad overview of the area of research, including any biographical, musical, historical, social, cultural, and/or other contexts.

Writing a Research Proposal **109**

2. Identify the main issues in the broad area of research. Key research and researchers may be mentioned here, but this is not a literature review; that follows later.
3. Through a process of narrowing and delimitation, gradually move to a general statement of what the study is about and why it is being undertaken. This can be formulated either as a hypothesis or as a research question (see discussion below). It leads directly to either the literature review or the aims.
4. Provide a link to the next section of the proposal; one or two sentences will suffice.

These guidelines provide a useful starting point for writing an introduction. Every research project is unique, however, and the nature of each project determines the content of the introduction, its ordering, and the section that follows. Even the heading itself ("Introduction") can be varied. "Setting of the Study," "Background," or some other heading may be used instead.

Hypothesis or Research Question

A research project can be set up as a hypothesis that is stated and tested (also referred to as a thesis statement), or as a research question that is asked. This is determined by the subject of the research, or by the way in which the researcher chooses to approach it. As a general rule, a hypothesis is used when a specific answer is sought for a clearly defined question (for example, the hypothesis that the quality, rather than the quantity, of practice yields better results). A project set up as a hypothesis may sometimes yield a negative result—although this in itself can be a meaningful and significant outcome. A project designed around a research question, on the other hand, is open ended; it offers the possibility of a range of research findings, including unexpected ones. A hypothesis is commonly employed in quantitative research; a research question is typically used in qualitative research (see below for discussion of qualitative and quantitative research methods).

The following examples show two different approaches to studying the compositions of the ethnomusicologist, John Blacking.

As a hypothesis:
John Blacking's compositional style was informed by his ideas on the role of music as an expression of cultural meaning and social processes.

As a research question:
What might a study of John Blacking's ethnomusicology tell us about his compositions, and what might his compositions tell us about his ethnomusicology?

Both examples imply a link between Blacking's compositions and his ethnomusicology. The first approach (stated as a hypothesis) explores just one possibility—that Blacking's compositional style was informed by his ethnomusicology. The second approach (stated as a research question) enables the study to explore the possibility of reciprocal influences; there is also no expectation of a particular finding (What *might* a study . . .).

The hypothesis or research question is a critical aspect of a research project. It encapsulates what the research is about and functions as a springboard to the aims of the study. Most research proposals and theses include a hypothesis or research question, although some proceed directly from the introduction or literature review to the aims and rationale.

It can take many iterations before a hypothesis or research question is clarified and expressed succinctly and precisely. The following questions address the key issues that need to be taken into account when designing this part of a research proposal.

- Does the hypothesis or research question address a meaningful problem or issue?
- Does it capture the essence of what the research is about?
- Is the wording precise and concise? Does it include key words and/or concepts?
- Will it lead to analytical rather than descriptive findings?

Literature Review

The literature review has already been discussed in chapter 4. As noted in the earlier chapter, a literature review identifies, summarizes, and critically evaluates the existing research within a field of study. It establishes who wrote what and when, and discusses how the various writings relate to each other. The literature review is a pivotal part of a research project, locating the proposed research within the context of the existing writings, identifying the gap that leads to the aims of the study, and ensuring that the research does not duplicate work that has already been done. It is an essential inclusion in a research proposal, and in a thesis as well.

The guidelines set out in chapter 4 need not be replicated here. They should be referred to when writing the literature review for both a research proposal and a thesis.

Aims and Rationale

The aims and rationale set out exactly what will be done in the research—in other words, the specific steps, or actions, that will be taken to address the hypothesis or research question. They typically follow the literature review; in some projects, they are more appropriately located after the introduction.

There are conventions that need to be observed, as set out in the following guidelines.

- Begin with one or two sentences that provide a broad statement of intention, the rationale, and any demarcations around the topic. This brief statement ends with a sentence that leads into the specific aims.
- Ensure that each aim is specific and applies to a particular aspect of the research. If necessary, include sub-aims.
- Consider listing the aims numerically if more than one is included.
- If the aims are listed numerically, begin each one with an infinitive (the base form of a verb), for example "to ascertain," "to investigate," "to conduct," "to explore."
- State the aims in incomplete sentences if they are listed numerically. Alternatively, the aims may be set in a paragraph and stated in complete sentences.
- Be systematic, precise, and concise in stating the aims.

Figure 5.5 sets out the aims and rationale for a fictitious, 20,000-word, masters-level study entitled *John Blacking: Composer and Ethnomusicologist*.[4] These aims assume the study to be based on the following research question: "What might a study of John Blacking's ethnomusicology tell us about his compositions, and what might his compositions tell us about his ethnomusicology?"

112 Postgraduate Research in Music

> **Aims and rationale**
>
> The broad aim of this study is to explore possible links between John Blacking's musical compositions and his work as an ethnomusicologist and social anthropologist. Of necessity this will be a selective investigation, it being beyond the scope of the study to explore the entirety of Blacking's compositional output.
> The specific aims are as follows:
>
> 1. To explore Blacking's musical background and training.
> 2. To examine the nature of Blacking's musical language through the analysis of three representative compositions: *Pahoom: A Characteristic Study in Rhythm for Violin and Piano* (1954); *Incidental Music for Midsummer Night's Dream* (1956); and *Te Deum* for SATB (1963, revised 1965).
> 3. To study Blacking's ethnomusicological writings on the role of music in culture and society.
> 4. To determine whether there are contradictions or continuities between the musical language of Blacking's compositions and his work as an ethnomusicologist, in particular his conceptualisation of music as an expression of cultural and social processes.

Figure 5.5. Aims and rationale for a masters-level study entitled *John Blacking: Composer and Ethnomusicologist*

Aims Compared With Hypothesis or Research Question

The aims should not be confused with the hypothesis or research question. Where the role of the hypothesis or research question is to provide a broad statement, or a question, that governs the entire thesis, the aims set out specific actions that will be taken to address the hypothesis or research question. Both are generally included in a research proposal, and each is related to the other. At the same time, they have different roles and should not be confused.

Anticipated Outcomes

There can be no definitive prediction of the outcomes before the research has been undertaken. It is therefore wise to express the anticipated outcomes in general terms. A study of Blacking's compositions within the context of his ethnomusicology, for example, might be anticipated to shed new light upon both his ethnomusicology and his compositions, and to lead to greater awareness of his hitherto neglected activities as a composer (assuming that the study were to be set up as a research question). The anticipated outcomes are important because they implicitly address the "So what?" question. They ensure that the study will address a meaningful issue, and that it will add something of value to the existing body of knowledge.

Significance

The significance of a study is an extension of the anticipated outcomes. It may be set in a separate section or subsumed within a single section entitled "anticipated outcomes and significance." The significance is, in effect, the justification for the study; if a project does not hold the promise of a significant outcome, there is little point in undertaking it.

The significance should not be exaggerated. All that is needed is a brief, clear indication as to why the proposed research is significant, and what it will add to the existing body of knowledge. The preparation of an historically informed guide for the performance of Buxtehude's *Membra Jesu Nostri*, for example, may, through its aim of resolving issues of pitch and ornamentation, provide a significant resource for the historically informed performance of Buxtehude's vocal music.

Methodology

Where the aims set out exactly *what* will be done in a research project, the methodology sets out *how* it will be done. In essence, the methodology considers three issues:

- Which data will be gathered.
- How the data will be gathered.
- How the data will be analyzed.

The methodology therefore includes such things as procedures for the collection and analysis of survey and interview data; techniques for the analysis of scores, electro-acoustic music, and recordings; the archival resources that will be accessed; and the theoretical framework that will be employed. The methodology follows on directly from the aims, addressing the "what" of each aim with how it will be done.

With the broadening of music research in recent decades and the emergence of new sub-disciplines, there is now a multiplicity of research methods to draw upon, ranging from the traditional historical and analytic methods to those that have been drawn from the social and political sciences, cultural studies, linguistics, gender and sexuality studies, and practice-based research. This subject is so vast as to require an entire book, for each sub-discipline has its own methodological approaches. The following discussion will therefore be limited to an overview of some of the key methodologies used in some of the more commonly encountered areas of music research. The discussion is by no means exhaustive in scope or content, and readers are referred to the large body of methodological literature that can be accessed for individual projects (see the reading list at the end of this chapter).

Music as Artifact and Music as Activity

In general terms, music can be viewed in two ways: as an artifact, or as an activity.[5] Seen as an artifact, or object, music can be studied historically, analytically, theoretically, semiotically, cognitively, aesthetically, acoustically, as an expression of gender or ethnicity, and so on. Seen as an activity, music can be investigated as a social and cultural process (music as a social science), as therapeutic intervention (music therapy), in terms of performance health and well-being, as artistic practice, and so on.

These two broad categories—artifact and activity—offer a useful starting point for considering the methodological approaches that may be employed in music research. The categories should not be seen as mutually exclusive; in practice they often overlap. Music research that focuses on gender and sexuality, for example, might draw upon methods from both analytical musicology and the social sciences.

Music as Artifact

Digital Musicology

In recent years, the multi-disciplinary field of digital humanities has led to new approaches in music research. Referred to as "digital musicology," this methodological umbrella uses a number of software tools (digital technologies) to facilitate research across a range of music sub-disciplines. In historical musicology, digital technologies can be used to create digital scores that are searchable for musical elements such as melodic and/or rhythmic patterns (see, for example, The Josquin Research Project, https://josquin.stanford.edu/). Digital technology can also be used to superimpose and compare different early music editions, facilitating the creation of critical editions (see Aruspix, http://www.aruspix.net/index.html). Software can be used to generate interactive digital archives (see, for example, Schenker Documents Online, http://schenkerdocumentsonline.org/index.html), and to explore the intersections of space, time and sound through interactive musical maps (see The Musical Geography Project, https://musicalgeography.org/).

In the area of performance research, software tools are now used to study historical recordings, measuring such parameters as tempo and rubato, which, when expressed as visual (graphic) representations, enable researchers to compare recordings from different historical periods, and to examine differing performative interpretations (see the Centre for the History and Analysis of Recorded Music, https://charm.rhul.ac.uk/index.html).

Historical Musicology

The term "historical musicology" covers a broad range of research areas, all of which have an historical focus of some kind. These areas include the study of composers, compositions, and contexts; reception history; past performance practices; historical instruments; and historical recordings.

Many different methods are used within historical musicology, sometimes more than one in a given project. A study of historically informed performance practice, for example, might draw upon a critical reading of historical treatises together with reflective practice; and a project in the area of organology might, in addition to the detailed measurement of historical instruments, utilize archival material such as correspondence and treatises.

Music Analysis

The term "music analysis" refers to a wide range of analytic parameters that include not only the critical reading of scores, but also such areas as sketch studies, musico-poetic design in vocal music, and the rhythmic dimension in music.

Different methods of analysis are often combined to shed light on different aspects of a composition. Formal analysis combined with pitch class set theory, for example, provides both a broad structural analysis of a work and a detailed understanding of its pitch organization. The study of music as gendered language might combine music analysis with feminist theory; and an interview with a composer could be used to supplement the analysis of the music.

Notwithstanding the recent expansion of analytic methods in music research, the analysis of scores continues to be a central methodology. The following list captures the main approaches that are used in this area, and the musical styles to which they apply.

Basic shape analysis: Identifies the musical shape/s (motives) that underpin the thematic material of some or all movements of a composition. Is applied to music from the Baroque era to the present, although it is not appropriate for all music.

Formal analysis: Examines a work in terms of its broader structure, the functions of the various musical elements, and the correlations between those elements. Can be applied to pre-tonal, tonal, and post-tonal compositions.

Harmonic analysis: Analyses the chordal (vertical) dimension of the musical structure, typically in the functional analysis of tonal music. Harmonic analysis is also applied to the vertical dimension of post-tonal music, although the analytic paradigm is different.

Neo-Riemannian analysis: A method applied to music that is both triadic and chromatic (typically music of the mid-late nineteenth century, for example Wagner and Liszt), but not based in a referential triad or tonal area. Neo-Riemannian analysis focuses on the relationships between chords and tonal areas without the conceptual framework of functional harmony and unifying diatonic collections.

Pitch class set theory: A method developed for the analysis of post-tonal music to describe recurrent patterns of notes as groups of integers (numbers). The groupings ("pitch class sets") occur in different permutations: "normal" form (the most intervallically condensed form), inversion, and transposition.

Schenkerian analysis: A method applied to tonal works to distil the underlying structure as a descending scalar melodic line ("Urlinie" or "fundamental line"), supported by a harmonic skeleton ("bass arpeggiation") of I–V–I in a two-part contrapuntal framework known as the "Ursatz" (or "fundamental structure").

Semiotic analysis: A system of signs developed from literary theory which, when applied to music, seeks to define musical meaning by dividing a musical composition into significant units to discover the principles that govern how the units are distributed.[6] Can be applied to all kinds of music, including music from different cultures.

Music as Activity

Research that explores music as an activity applies two main approaches to the collection of data: qualitative, and quantitative. Qualitative research investigates the social world of individuals, groups, and cultures from the perspective of the participants, with the aim of understanding the nature and meaning of social and cultural processes. Quantitative research is concerned with the measurement, or quantification, of phenomena or behavior, leading to generalization and explanation. Where qualitative research draws upon individual experiences and interpretations of social situations, quantitative research is concerned with statistics that provide objective, measurable proof. Qualitative research is diverse in its methodological and theoretical approaches. Quantitative research, on the other hand, is relatively one-dimensional in its approach. Whether to employ qualitative or quantitative methods, or a mix of the two, is determined by the questions for which answers are sought. The main methods employed in each of these approaches are set out below.

Key Methods in Qualitative Research

Action research: Research that involves interaction and collaboration between researchers and participants with the aim of increasing the awareness of participants and helping them to make changes within an organizational setting.

Auto-ethnography: Is concerned with a researcher's subjective experience, using self-reflection and autobiography as a way of understanding a broader cultural experience.

Case study research: In-depth examination of one or a few cases of a social phenomenon (an individual, a group, an organization, or an event) with the aim of developing a theory that explains the phenomenon.

Ethnography (a term often used interchangeably with "participant observation"): Field-based research in which a researcher is immersed for an extended period of time in the phenomenon being studied, such as a group or a community—observing, listening, interviewing, and developing an understanding of the group culture.

Feminist research: Examines gender as it applies to such things as power, and workplace organization and interactions.

Focus group (also referred to as "group interview"): A group interview conducted by a researcher/facilitator to elicit views that may not emerge in one-to-one interviews.

Grounded theory: Theory that is based, or grounded, in research data. The collection and analysis of the data, and the development of the theory, emerge not consecutively but interactively through a feedback loop that coalesces, after a number of iterations, into a final theory.

118   Postgraduate Research in Music

Hermeneutic research: "Hermeneutics is the study of interpretation. . . . Hermeneutics thus treats interpretation itself as its subject matter and not as an auxiliary to the study of something else."[7]

Interviews: A dialogue in which an interviewer seeks facts, opinions, and other information from one or more respondents with the aim of understanding or explaining a phenomenon of some kind.

Phenomenological research: A method of enquiry in which the researcher seeks "to understand and explain how an individual or a group of individuals experience a particular phenomenon from the individual's or individuals' perspective(s)."[8] Uses in-depth interviews to gather data.

Reflective practice: A process of deliberate (rather than incidental), sustained reflection upon, and (importantly) documentation of, an action or situation, questioning assumptions and critically examining the issue from different perspectives with the aim of bringing about change.

Key Methods in Quantitative Research

Quantitative research, which is concerned with numerical quantification, is conducted through surveys that can be administered in four ways:

Interview survey: Questions put to respondents in face-to-face interviews rather than through the distribution of a questionnaire. The interview is less flexible in quantitative (as compared with qualitative) research because it is concerned with consistent, reliable measurement. In qualitative research, on the other hand, the interview gathers perceptions and opinions.

Online survey: A questionnaire administered electronically through survey software.

Self-administered questionnaire survey: A questionnaire designed to be completed by the respondents without feedback or intervention by the researcher/interviewer. Was traditionally delivered by mail or in person to large groups but is now increasingly administered online.[9]

Telephone survey: Essentially the same as an interview survey but conducted by phone.

Practice-Based Research

With the influence of postmodern thought in recent decades and the assimilation of conservatories into universities, practice-based research has emerged as a significant area of music scholarship. It is one that requires particular discussion.

Practice-based research is one of a number of terms that link artistic practice with research; other terms that fall under this conceptual umbrella are "research-led practice," "practice-led research," "practice research," "practice as research," "artistic practice as research," "artistic research," and "creative research." These terms refer to three things:

- Artistic practice that is treated as the object of research, including the analysis and documentation of the creative process.
- Artistic practice that is informed by research—an activity that is more closely aligned with the traditional research model.
- The artistic product itself.

Some writers make distinctions between similar terms such as "practice-based" and "practice-led." Such distinctions are not universally applied, however, and a clear consensus on practice-based terminology has not been reached.

Practice-based research is undertaken in many different areas, including instrumental technique and composition. This diversity is reflected in a corresponding multiplicity of research methods. Indeed, in this relatively new area of research, the practice-based scholar needs to be nimble in devising appropriate methodologies, because each project is different and there are sometimes no existing models to follow. Some of the methods outlined earlier in this section can be employed in practice-based research, such as reflective practice.

The marriage of practice and research has not been an easy one, for it challenges the idea of what research is and the traditional models of knowledge and knowledge formulation. With its basic premise of a different form of knowledge—knowledge that can be embedded in both the creative process and the creative output—practice-based research has been a contentious addition to the academic world. The conventions of the academy require a clear research question, an identifiable methodology, objectivity, evidence, argumentation, and outcomes. These things do not always sit comfortably with artistic practice, which is subjective in nature and which often generates outcomes that sit outside the existing knowledge paradigms. These tensions need to be understood by students undertaking practice-based research, for a project must fulfill not only its artistic raison d'être but also the research requirements of the academy. As noted in the introduction to this book, however, there are certain principles, practices and standards that underpin all

120 Postgraduate Research in Music

good scholarship, regardless of the area within which it is conducted. In this context, Henk Borgdorff's observation bears repeating:

> Even if one accepts that the knowledge embodied in art is of a different order than the more "conventional" forms of academic or scientific knowledge, that does not mean the methods for accessing, retrieving, and disseminating such knowledge are also different.[10]

As part of the work of designing a project in the area of practice-based research, students would be well advised to read around this subject and to consider the following questions:

- What is knowledge?
- Can knowledge be embedded in the creative process and in creative outputs?
- In which ways and at what point might a project cross over from practice to research?
- Where is the boundary between practice and research? *Is* there a boundary? Can practice in itself, or even a completed artistic product, be considered to be research?
- Can the documentation of artistic decisions be considered to be research, or is such reflection simply an aspect of good practice?
- Is there an implicit misfit between practice-based research and the research paradigm of the academy? Or do definitions of research and knowledge, and the methodological conventions of the academy, need to broaden to accommodate practice-based research?

These are important questions. Research in the area of creative practice needs to comply with academic imperatives; it must also fulfill the creative impulse that lies at its heart, and be substantial enough to generate a meaningful outcome. The relationship between practice and research is not necessarily a straightforward one. Creative activity which in the past would have been seen as distinct from research is now seen as a form of research, necessitating conceptual rethinking by both the academy and scholar/performers.

Concluding Thoughts on Methodology

Academic research works on the principle of providing evidence that makes a convincing case and leads to conclusions that are beyond question.

How much evidence is enough? What is a representative sample? What is needed for convincing deductions to be made? Such questions underpin the credibility of the research data and the conclusions that can be drawn. Patterns need to be replicated in a meaningful way and in a meaningful number of cases, regardless of the sub-discipline of the research. These issues need to be taken into account when the methodology is planned.

One final point for consideration is how long the methodology section should be, and the level of detail it should include. A methodology that is carefully thought through, and which contains a generous level of detail, can provide a valuable map for the research process. In a project drawing upon archival resources, for example, such planning might list the folders and files that will be accessed, and the specific information that is sought. With this worked out in advance, travel time can be minimized and time spent in the archive optimized. Methodology sections may therefore expand beyond a straightforward listing of methods and approaches, offering, in addition, a breakdown of tasks and a level of detail that can lead to great efficiency in the conduct of the research.

Structure of the Thesis

The anticipated structure of the thesis is an essential inclusion in a research proposal, for it provides further opportunity to reflect upon the direction, content, and scope of the study. Figure 5.6 sets out the structure for the previously mentioned doctoral thesis on the music of Diego Ferrera. It can be adapted for individual projects.

Timeline

A timeline divides a project into segments, organizes the segments into a logical sequence, and allocates a plausible amount of time for each. A timeline is an essential inclusion in a research proposal.

Clearly there are unknown factors here. Nonetheless, it is important to make a best possible estimate of tasks, sequencing, and time, knowing, at the same time, that adjustments will probably be needed as the research proceeds. Some tasks will take longer than expected; unanticipated events, such as illness, or delays in procuring essential research material, can also put a project behind

122 Postgraduate Research in Music

THESIS STRUCTURE

CHAPTER 1: INTRODUCTION
Contextual background
Biographical overview
Literature review and research question
Aims, rationale, anticipated outcomes, and significance
Methodology

CHAPTER 2: FORMATIVE MUSICAL INFLUENCES
Peruvian folk music
European art music

CHAPTER 3: THE EARLY WORKS
Four Folk Songs for Voice and Piano
Choral Suite
Sonatina for Flute, Panpipe and Piano

CHAPTER 4: THE NEOCLASSICAL WORKS
Pre-Columbian Prelude and Presto
Inca Concerto
Musica Antiqua

CHAPTER 5: EL CONDOR PASA (opera in two acts)

CHAPTER 6: TUPAC AMARA (opera in three acts)

CHAPTER 7: CONCLUSION

LIST OF REFERENCES
APPENDIX: COMPOSITIONS BY FERRERA

Figure 5.6. Thesis structure for the fictitious study of the musical language of Diego Ferrera

schedule. Contingency time should therefore be built into each stage of the research process to avert the frantic, last-minute rush that is all too often the hallmark of a student research project—and which leads to a disappointing outcome that does little justice to a student's ability. It is especially important to allow enough time for the analysis of data, writing, and final editing.

A key aspect of an effective timeline is the level of detail that is included. Vague headings such as "collect data" over a twenty-week period, and "write thesis" over a twelve-week period, are largely useless as planning tools. Tasks need to be broken down into smaller components, and specific goals need to be set. These goals also need to be achievable to ensure that there is a constant sense of progress, rather than one of frustration at targets not met.

A timeline can be devised around five headings:

- Further review of literature (if necessary).
- Data acquisition.
- Data analysis.
- Writing the thesis.
- Supervisor feedback and editing of drafts.

With this framework in place, a number of questions can then be addressed:

- Is additional reading necessary?
- Which segments of data will be gathered, and in which order? How much time will be needed for each one?
- How much time will be needed for the analysis of data?
- Will the chapters be drafted one by one as the data are analyzed, or collectively once the findings have been assembled? How much time will be allocated for each chapter? Will some chapters take longer to write than others?
- When will the introduction be written? At the beginning or the end of the project?
- How much time will be allocated for the front matter (preliminary content such as the abstract, table of contents, and preface) and back matter (content following the main text, including the bibliography, endnotes, and appendices)?
- How much time will be needed for supervisors to read the penultimate and final drafts? Are there tasks that can be done while this is happening, such as the formatting of references and the setting of musical examples?
- How much time will be needed for final formatting, editing, and finessing, and for printing and binding the thesis?

Table 5.2 sets out a timeline that can be adjusted for individual projects. It includes the major project segments (LH column); the breakdown of segments into smaller components, together with a target date range (middle columns); and the deadline for each segment (RH column).

124   Postgraduate Research in Music

Table 5.2. Timeline template

Major tasks	Breakdown into smaller tasks	Deadline
Further review of literature (if necessary)		
Data acquisition: • Fieldwork • Archival research • Score analysis • Practicing repertoire • Other		
Data analysis		
Writing the thesis • Introduction • Chapters • Conclusion • Front matter • Back matter		
Full draft to supervisors		
Editing of draft (with supervisors' feedback)		
Revised full draft to supervisors		
Final editing of draft (with supervisors' feedback)		
Contingency time		
Submission of thesis		

Ethics Clearance

Research projects that involve human or animal participants, or that use people's personal data, are governed by an ethical code of conduct that is set out in a university's ethics guidelines. These guidelines are designed to protect the participants in the study, the researcher, the university, and the community by ensuring that appropriate ethical standards are met, particularly in matters of informed consent and confidentiality.

A considerable amount of music research does not need ethics clearance (for example, archival research, and the analysis of scores). For projects in the area of music as an activity, however, with the qualitative and quantitative methods that these projects entail, ethics clearance is required. Each university has its own ethics processes, which need to be ascertained when the research proposal is being written.

It is important to allow enough time for seeking ethics clearance. How frustrating it is when, through poor planning, the gathering of research data begins behind schedule because ethics clearance has not been obtained. It takes time to prepare an ethics application and time for it to be considered by a university's ethics committee.

Budget

Universities generally provide an allocation of funds for each postgraduate student for such things as research travel, the dissemination of questionnaires, and the purchase of scores. A budget is therefore essential, for students are accountable for the expenditure that is proposed.

Table 5.3 sets out a budget for hypothetical archival research in and around London. It can be adapted for individual projects.

Table 5.3. Hypothetical budget for archival research

Item		Cost
Airfares, New York to London and return		$1,200
Accommodation (30 days x $150 per day)		$4,500
Food (30 days x $50 per day)		$1,500
Local travel:		$ 432
Underground, Central London (20 days, $8.60 per day)	$172.00	
BBC Archives in Reading (5 days—train + bus, $44 per day)	$220.00	
EMI Archives (1 day, train)	$40.00	
TOTAL		$7,632

126 Postgraduate Research in Music

Bibliography/Reference List

A bibliography, also referred to as a "reference list," is the final element in a research proposal (or the penultimate element if appendices are included). These two terms (bibliography and reference list) denote essentially the same thing: an alphabetical list of the sources referred to in a research proposal, thesis, book, or other document. The specific term, and the way in which the sources are formatted, is contingent upon the referencing style that is used.

Referencing Styles

There are many different referencing styles, each of which has its own formatting conventions. Within this plethora of styles, there are two distinct approaches: notes and bibliography, sometimes referred to as the Oxford style; and author-date, also referred to as in-text, or the Harvard style. In both approaches, sources of information are acknowledged in two places: in the text itself, and in the list of sources at the end of the document.

Notes and Bibliography Referencing

In notes and bibliography referencing, the sources referred to in the text are cited in footnotes (at the bottom of each page), or endnotes (clustered at the end of each chapter, or chapter-by-chapter at the end of the document). The notes are generated by the "insert footnote" (or endnote) pull-down menu, which inserts a superscript number into the text (for example[1]), together with a corresponding footnote (or endnote) in which the citation can be documented. The superscript number is located at the end of a sentence if it relates to the entire sentence, or following a specific clause or segment within a sentence if the remainder of the sentence is not attributable to that source. The sources cited in the footnotes/endnotes are subsequently aggregated in a list at the end of the document. This list is referred to as a bibliography in the notes and bibliography referencing style.

A bibliography may also include significant works that have been consulted but not cited in the footnotes/endnotes. These additional sources may either be integrated into the list of sources, or grouped in a second list entitled "additional sources consulted." Personal communication (for example, email correspondence) is not included in a bibliography because it is, by definition, personal to the author and therefore not accessible to readers. It is cited only in the footnotes/endnotes.

Notes and bibliography referencing is used in humanities-based music research. It provides the flexibility that is needed for the irregular and less common sources that are often encountered in this area of research. The notes and bibliography style that is typically used in music research is the Chicago style, as set out in *The Chicago Manual of Style: The Essential Guide for Writers, Editors, and Publishers*, 17th ed.[11] It will be referred to throughout this book as the Chicago style.

The referencing conventions in the Chicago style are outlined in appendix A.

Author-Date Referencing

In author-date referencing, an abbreviated, parenthetical citation is given immediately after the source referred to in the text. The citation includes the surname of the author and the publication date of the research—for example (Smith 2019). The specific part of a source may also be included—for example, (Smith 2019, p. 12), or (Smith 2019, Chapter 2), or (Smith 2019, Table 2). The formatting of in-text referencing varies in different referencing styles, for example (Smith 2019: 12).

A parenthetical author-date reference is a signpost to the full citation that is provided in the aggregated list of sources at the end of the document. In the referencing style set out in the *Publication Manual of the American Psychological Association*[12] (referred to throughout this book as the APA style), the list of sources is called a "reference list." As noted in the APA Manual, all sources cited in the reference list must appear in the text, and all sources cited in the text must appear in the reference list; the only exception to this is personal communication, which is referred to parenthetically in the text but omitted from the list of references.[13] If significant additional sources have been consulted but not cited, they may be included in a second list entitled "additional sources consulted."

APA author-date referencing is commonly used in the social sciences, and in music research referred to in this chapter as "music as an activity." The referencing conventions in the APA style are outlined in appendix B.

The Importance of Accurate Referencing

Ensuring that the referencing details are absolutely correct is painstaking and time-consuming work. Accurate referencing is essential, however, because it enables other scholars to locate the sources that have been cited. Inaccurate referencing can make it difficult, or even impossible, for scholars to do this. It also diminishes the credibility of the research.

Accuracy takes on even greater significance in the context of music research, where there are often multiple editions of scores and treatises. Imagine, for example, the difficulties that could arise if a thesis failed to cite the correct edition of Quantz's *On Playing the Flute*, or that incorrect page numbers were given in a footnote citation. How frustrating this would be for a reader wishing to follow up on a source.

The matter of accuracy extends beyond content; it is equally important in the formatting of citations. A comma or a period; single or double quotation marks; italics or non-italics; capitalization or non-capitalization; the ordering of information . . . any sloppiness or inconsistency in the formatting of citations reflects poorly upon the research.

Information That Must Be Referenced

There are four types of information that must be referenced:

- A direct quotation from another source (book, score, archival document, website, etc.).
- Paraphrased material from another source.
- An idea or concept from another source.
- Mention of another source.

Information from a source that is not acknowledged (referenced) is plagiarized—in other words, it is stolen. This is a serious academic offence and can lead to automatic failure of a thesis. Guidelines on avoiding plagiarism, and on incorporating quoted and paraphrased material into the text, are set out in chapter 7.

Information That Does Not Need to Be Referenced

There are four types of information that do not need to be referenced:

- Contextual background that draws upon other writings in a general, non-specific way.
- Common knowledge within an area of research: that chords I, IV, and V are primary triads, for example, is common knowledge within the discipline of music; there is no need to cite a source for this information. For a discussion of common knowledge, see the section on plagiarism in chapter 7.
- Quotations from interview or survey content: the source of this content is simply indicated in the text that introduces the quotation.
- A quotation within a quotation when APA referencing is used. In such cases, only the secondary source is given. The Chicago style is different,

with both sources cited in both the footnote and bibliography. For a discussion of this issue, see the section entitled "Referencing Quotations within Quotations" in chapter 7 of this book.

If there is any doubt as to whether to cite a source, it is better to err on the side of caution, thereby avoiding any possibility of plagiarism.

How to Approach Referencing

Each referencing style has its own formatting conventions. The same information is included, however, regardless of the referencing style that is used. The issue is what appears where, and how the information is formatted.

Referencing is best approached by working from a model such as those provided in appendices A and B of this book. There are further models that can be drawn upon. Of particular value are Sampsel's *Music Research: A Handbook*, which provides music-specific examples in both the Chicago and APA styles, as well as the Modern Language Association (MLA) style; and Turabian's *A Manual for Writers of Research Papers, Theses and Dissertation*, which provides a wide range of examples in both Chicago styles (notes and bibliography and author-date) and includes sources in the visual and performing arts.[14] The *Chicago Manual of Style* and the *Publication Manual of the American Psychological Association* are both comprehensive in their coverage, although they scarcely engage with music.

Another way to approach referencing is to draw upon citation management software that formats the sources in a style selected by the user. Endnote is often available for download through university libraries; similar software such as Mendeley (https://www.mendeley.com/) and Zotero (https://www.zotero.org/) can be downloaded from the web free of charge. It should be noted, however, that citation management software does not always render citations with complete accuracy. If these tools are used, the citations need to be checked individually to ensure that they are correct. It should also be noted that citations generated in this way can only be as good as the information that is fed into the software. Any gaps or inaccuracies in the inputting of data will appear as gaps or inaccuracies in the citations.

Clustering Sources

Music research is unique in the diversity of sources it draws upon. Researchers sometimes deal with this by creating bibliographic clusters that are easier for readers to navigate. Scores and recordings, for example, might each be clustered in this way.

Formatting of References

In both the Chicago and APA referencing styles, the first line of each bibliographic citation is left-justified; all run-on lines are indented (referred to as hanging indents). The first line of each footnote or endnote citation is also left-justified; the indentation of run-on lines is optional. The indentation can be accomplished either by using the tab key, or by creating an indent on the ruler bar in the top menu,

Dealing with Irregular Sources

Irregular sources (those for which there is no exact referencing model) are not uncommon in music research. They can be a cause of considerable angst. The best approach in such cases is to begin with an existing model that comes closest to the irregular source, and to apply the same logic in the ordering and formatting of information. If the elements are separated by commas in the model, for example, they should be separated by commas in the irregular source. All identifying information must be included in a clear and logical way, with consistent formatting applied to similar sources.

Footnotes and Endnotes

Footnotes and endnotes (also referred to as notes) are used for two purposes: to provide citations for the sources that appear in the text (in the notes and bibliography referencing style, not in author-date referencing); and to present additional information that is relevant, although not central, to the main text. Such information might, for example, provide biographical or historical elaboration, or cite a related writing, or suggest additional sources the reader may wish to consult. Both referencing methods (notes and bibliography and author-date) use notes for this second purpose.

The only difference between a footnote and an endnote is where the information is located—respectively at the bottom (or foot) of each page, or at the end of each chapter, or clustered chapter-by-chapter at the end of a research proposal or thesis (before the bibliography in the Chicago style, and after it in the APA style).

Whether to use footnotes or endnotes is a matter of personal choice. The information in footnotes is easier for readers to access because everything is on the same page—text and footnote. On the other hand, a large number of footnotes, or footnotes that are particularly long, can take up a disproportionate amount of space on a page, leaving little room for the main text. In such cases, endnotes may be a better option. Endnotes, however, are less accessible as readers have to toggle between the main text and the notes.

Each chapter is usually given its own set of note numbers, with the notes in every chapter beginning at one (1). As a general rule, a sentence includes only one note. As noted earlier, the note number is usually placed at the end of the sentence, although there are times when a note number needs to be located mid-sentence, directly after the information to which it refers. If more than one note is needed in a sentence, it may be better to split the sentence into two, each with its own note. Alternatively, some of the footnote content might be relocated to the main body of the text. If neither of these alternatives works, more than one note number may be included in a sentence, but never as two consecutive note numbers at the end of a sentence.

The spacing of notes varies from one referencing system to the other. Chicago and APA both use single spacing for footnotes. Chicago also uses single spacing for endnotes; APA uses double.

Notes should be used with discrimination. They should only be used to convey significant information and should not include extraneous material that clutters the flow of thought. Notes that are overly long can also be problematic, drawing the reader's attention away from the main text. Some content belongs in a note, some belongs in the body of the text, some belongs in an appendix, and some does not belong at all. Don't try to say everything! Some elaboration can be interesting, and helpful. Too much can be counterproductive.

Appendices

The final item in a research proposal is an appendix (or appendices) of material that is subsidiary, but not central, to the main text. Appendices comprise such things as questionnaires, lists of compositions, lengthy musical examples, and figures and tables. They are only included when elaboration is needed, or when a lengthy segment of information would hinder the flow of thought in the main text.

There are no hard and fast rules for formatting appendices. In general, the following practices should be observed.

- Provide a parenthetical signpost to each appendix in the text, for example (see appendix A for a list of compositions).
- Begin each appendix on a separate page.
- Label the appendices alphabetically (A, B, C, etc.) or numerically (1, 2, 3, etc.); if there is only one appendix, it is simply labeled "appendix."
- Provide a brief descriptive title for each appendix, for example, "list of compositions." The title appears below the appendix heading. Both the heading and the descriptive title are centered on the page.
- The formatting of appendices is consistent with the formatting in the body of the text. The word "appendix" and the descriptive title, for example, are set in the style of the chapter titles.
- The spacing of the text is consistent with the spacing used in the body of the proposal or thesis—that is, either 1.5 or double spacing. If an appendix is derived from another source, it follows the spacing of the original source.[15]
- The appendices are sequenced in the order in which they appear in the text.

Coda

The research proposal provides a blueprint for the next few months of the research process. Once the proposal has been evaluated and approved by the university administration, the gathering of data can commence, following, step-by-step, the methodology and timeline set out in the proposal. The narrative of this book will resume with chapters 6, 7, 8, and 9, each of which deals with a different aspect of writing a thesis.

Exercises

Exercise 1: Seminar Debate

Exercise 1 is designed to draw attention to the ideological and methodological issues inherent in practice-based research. The exercise also offers an opportunity to develop the skills of critical thinking and argumentation.

Conduct a debate on the topic, "Practice-based research in music is a fraud." Three speakers in each team—the affirmative and the negative—will be decided through successive tosses of a coin or some other random selection process. The three affirmative speakers will comprise group 1; the three negative speakers will comprise group 2. The remainder of the class will be divided into groups 3 and 4.

As preparation for the debate, groups 1 and 2 will locate and read key writings on practice-based research in music. The writings will be discussed within each group and will be used to inform the case that is argued. Each group will decide on the order of the three speakers, and the information to be presented by each speaker.

Group 3 will conduct research into the rules of debating, draw up a set of guidelines, and distribute the guidelines to all class members.

Group 4 will comprise the adjudicating panel. Preparation will involve drawing up criteria for the evaluation of each speaker. The panel will appoint a chair, who—following a 10–15-minute period of deliberation at the conclusion of the debate—will present a report on the performance of each speaker and declare either the affirmative or negative team to be the winner of the debate.

NOTE: This exercise assumes a class size of 12–14 students. The exercise may need to be adapted for different class sizes.

Exercise 2: Research Proposal for Critical Evaluation

The following fictitious research proposal is littered with shortcomings in content, style, narrative continuity, syntax, spelling, punctuation, formatting, and typographical matters. Whilst the topic and its treatment may lead readers to question the seriousness with which the proposal is offered, the errors that have been built into it are in serious need of correction. Critically evaluate the proposal, using, as a guide, the information provided in this chapter together with the questions that follow the proposal. Then creatively rewrite the proposal, transforming it into a more appropriate document in both content and style.

134 Postgraduate Research in Music

Well may you chuckle at the shortcomings of this proposal . . . but beware lest you make the same mistakes!

A transcontinental investigation into the study of frog song looking at songs sung by frogs across different continents and using this information to forge a new postmodern style of composition

MARY JONES

Student number: 987654321

SUPERVISORS

Professor JB Croaker and Dr Terry Toad

RESEARCH PROPOSITION

2045

Faculty of Music

Introduction and Background

In 2025 I discovered frog song while I was on holiday with my parents in Asia. Before this I'd learned the tuba and sung in school choirs and I'd been on a few school excursions to the countryside where there were a lot of frogs but it didn't occur to me then that the frogs were singing I thought they were just croaking. Now I'd give anything to hear those frogs again but they're extinct now, global warming has wiped them out. Back to 2015. I don't know what changed in 2025 but I found myself hearing frog songs not frog croaking. From that moment I knew I wanted to study frog song. Other students in the class were choosing careers like engineering or teaching. I just wanted to study frog song. I most definately made the right choice. I also loved music and the tuba and composition. So when I reached university I had a bright idea. I could combine my passions for frog song, music and composition. My first thought was that I would also study biology so I could dissect frog's vocal chords to help me understand how frogs put their songs together but I realised you don't have to dissect human vocal chords to study opera so I enroled in a music degree majoring in composition and now all this has come together in a proposal to study frog song and how it can forge a new style of postmodern composition.

· More background. Once I got to uni I learned that Messiaen was fascinated by birds and he used bird song into his music, that was a real ah-ha moment for me. If Messiaen could write music based on bird song why couldn't I write music based on frog song. I just couldn't believe no-one else had done it. It wasn't just bird melodies that Messiaen used, he also used bird rhythm and he did it in big compositions and in small ones as well. He wasn't the first to do this. **One of the earliest known pieces of polyphonic music is a 13th-century song called Sumer is i'cumen in, where singers imitate the calls of a cuckoo. Vivaldi, Handel, Mozart and Beethoven, too, all wrote pieces of music that feature birdsong.** I also found out that John Cage was fascinated by mushrooms though from what I could see he didn't include mushrooms in his compositions. I also became interested in whale song and as I listened to spectrographic recordings of whale song I realised there might be parallels between whale song and frog song. This was my second ah ha moment. They are both mammals! What if there was an existing methodology that I could use as the starting point for my own ground breaking research that would save time and effort. But I soon realised, however, that my research goes further. Where whale song is used *with* music as an add-on, a sort of obbligato, I'll be using frog song to *generate* music. In other words, frog songs will be the *basis* of the composition. They will form the melodic motives, the rhythmic cells, the basis of the ensemble, they will shape the overall structure, the texture, the timbre and so on—there's nothing that won't be frog based.

Rational and aims

What Messiaen did for birds and Cage did for mushrooms I want to do for frogs. Before all the frog species become extinct. This is a rich source of un-tapped potential for postmodern composition.

There are three parts to this project. First, I want to study frog song in detail. This includes studying fog song across all eight continents and then analysing the data: My research aims are;

- identification of specific frog songs and transcontinental differences. How many different song types can be recognised? Do different frog speciies perform different songs?

136   Postgraduate Research in Music

- frequency range/s
- Pitch and rhythmic patterns within and across continents; are particular songs always sung at the same pitch or are they sometimes transposed? If so when? Higher or lower? How much higher or lower? What about rhythmic patterns, do they change? If so how? When? What is the musical effect of this?
- key operating principles such as call and response patterns (which frog sings what when and why, who imitates who and so on)
- Differences in tessitura between individual frogs and possible transcontinental differences as generated by habitat or other factors.
- frog ensembles—how many frogs per ensemble, gendered distribution, number of high and low voices etc. Are their different ensembles for different occasions?
- Differences in texture and transcontinental differences. Is the texture horizontal or vertical in regards to it's organisation? Layered? Chordal? Does it change within songs? Between songs? Between continents? If so when how and why. Ostinato patterns
- overall structure in frog song and transcontinental differences (e.g. ritornello-type pattern with solo frog alternating with a recurrent frog ensemble). Patterns of articulation (eg through changes in pitch or dynamic, cadential resolution, juxtaposed blocks of musical material, etc). Song climaxes—how and when reached, e.g. by higher pitch and/or increased textural density etc
- Do individual frog songs change and/or develop over time? We know that whale songs do—but what about frog snog?
- Are some frog snogs more popular than others? If so, what are the defining features of these songs?
- Seasonal differences, are particular songs sung according to the season, time of day and so on (like an Indian raga)
- What can frog snog tell us about frog social and cultural organisation? Why do they sing? Are these mating calls or is there more to it?
- Duration of snogs

Second and building on first, I iwll use the knowledge gained from my study of frog song and apply it to my own western art music composition, forging a new postmodern musical style that has implications for future directions in composition. To do this I will compose a symphony with nine short movements, each one corresponding to one of the continents. This is the creative component of the research project and as such it will be submitted as a separate piece of assessable work that is nonetheless closely linked with the exegesis and derives directly from the research that underpins the exegesis as the realisation of frog song in a symphonic context.

Research questions
The main research questions underlying this dissertation are as follows:

1. How musical are frogs?
1. How is frog snog structured and organised?
2. What are the embedded meanings in frog song?
5. How can frog song be translocated from animal to human culture and applied to symphonies in a a postmodern context?
3. What can frog snog tell us about frog social and cultural organisation? Why do they sing? Are these mating calls or is there more to it?

Methodology
This is a mixed method research project that mixes a number of different methods. These are.

1. **Ethnography:** this is field-based research in which I will spend an extended period of time in each of the seven continents recording and observing frog song.
3. autoethnography: the fieldwork will also be concerned with my own subjective experienc3 in the field. I will therefore diarise my own subjective responses to deepen my understanding of frog song. I will also be on the alert for the sort of emotional responses that are common in researchers listening to whale song/
2. Case-study approach: it is beyond the scope of this study to study all frogs in all locations on all continents. Through examining biological research on frogs I will identify one significant frog population on each continent which I will study as a series of case studies.
4. Spectrographic analysis of recorded frog song using the spectographic analysis of whale song as a methodology to identify recurrent pitch and rhythm and other patterns, providing a strong evidence base to support my own subjective impressions;
5. recording frog snog using underwater microphones and above water microphones. The aim hear is to here frog song communication in all the ways frogs hear it—in the water and out of the water;
2. reflective practice: I will be learning frog songs and singing along with the frogs in order to better understand aspects of ensemble, voice production, social and cultural organisation and so on. I will

138   Postgraduate Research in Music

document these experiences with a view to learning and improving the interactions. This direct communication will give me a unique insight into frog snog

6. Below–water submersion using scuba equipment to enable me to hear submersed frog song from a different perspective and to observe frog behaviour and social interaction in the water;

7. comparative Formal analysis of the musical structure of frog snogs from all six continents using the analytic rubrics set out above in rational.

8. Frog Blog: I will set up a Frog Blog so I can connect with other frog enthusiasts across the world and share information that will feed into my research

Significance

This research will forge a whole new musical language. This is particularly relevant in a postmodern world where the development of Western art music has pretty much ground to a halt. There are also potential environmental benefits with heightened audience awareness of how beautiful are the frogs. There is also broader application. Frog song Frog song could be used as an obbligato in meditation music in the way whale song is used currently. I can also see the potential for using frog song in lullabies, music to relax by, spa music, wedding music, body pump music, and so on. This is a highly versatile medium.

Limitations

For the purposes of this research frogs will be distinguished from toads, which are a species of frog but different to frogs in a number of ways including having a dry bumpy skin and spending less time in water.

Literature review

Whale song started to be recorded in the 1960s using underwater microphones. What started out as an exercise in detecting enemy submarines grew into something different. People started to here patterns in whale song and a hole new area of research started. Research in whale song is quite advanced and it might provide useful ideas for frog research. The same questions arise. Why do whales sing? Wikipedia has a good article about this.[1] This article details how marine mammals depend on sound to communicate because sight and smell don't work too well in water. This will provide deeper perspectives on why frogs sing. The limitation of this article however is that

---

[1] Whale vocalise https://en.wikipedia.org/wiki/Whale_vocalization, Wikipedia,

it does not deal with land based communication. Ultimately the question of why whales sing is unanswered in this article: 'The question of whether whales sometimes sing purely for aesthetic enjoyment, personal satisfaction, or 'for art's sake', is considered by some to be "an untestable question".

Other sources offer more concrete information. In *Whale Songs in the Pacific* this YouTube clip is based on research done by an academic at St Andrews's University.[2] She identifies 34–36 different sounds in the 'humpback repertoire" and songs that last anywhere from 5 minutes to a half hour. She says that like human music, 'whale song consists of repeated phrases and themes made up of individual units". This article is useful for my research because it uses spectrographic graphs, a method that will be useful for my own research. There are limitations however. I would have liked to see more connection made between whale song and human music in particular in regards to it's structural organisation. And the research did not touch upon frog song and it's links to whale song. All in all though a useful source.

Jack Brown and John White. Birds and bees in the antipodes. Vol.42/42, Kookaburra communal laughing as intervention in the treatment of clinical depression pp.42–60

Just as the iconic image of Australia is the kangaroo, so is the iconic sound the laughing of the kookaburra. In a landmark study, Brown and White (coincidentally the colours of the kookaburra) trained clinically depressed patients in the skills of kookaburra laughing then linked them with communities of kookaburras in the Australian bush with the instruction that the groups were to emulate the laughing of the kookaburras over a two-week period. With their concern that training in Western art music might colour the interactions, Brown and White divided the group into two, the first (control group) with choral or other musical training and the second without it. The aim of the study was to ascertain whether emulation of the laughing patterns of the kookaburras in extended sessions over a period of time would have a beneficial effect on the mental health of clinically depressed patients. The study also aimed to test the hypothesis that kookaburra interactions might be less effective in participants trained in Western art music. The findings of the study showed no improvement in the mental health of any participants. The limitation of this study—once again—is that frogs are not mentioned. Brown and White, however, establish a methodology that might be applied in future research in the context of frog song.

---

[2] *Whale Songs in the Pacific, https://www.youtube.com/watch?v=P99CR4y-TYw*, accessed on 17 July 2029

Appleby, Buzz, Journal of the natural world, 2007. 3/2. 'Bee Sting, Bee Sound and Bee hives, 22–23
An in depth look at the correlation between bee sting, bee sound and bee hives through looking at the case of a bee keeper who developed an allergy to bee sting and used recorded bee sound (humming) as a healing modality to neutralise the allergic reaction to the bee sting. Does not mention frogs or explore the findings in the context of homeopathy. Is nonetheless a valuable source as it builds on research that explores the synthesis of whale song and human music in meditation and calming music. Sets the scene for diverse applications of frog song as mentioned earlier in this proposal

Albert Jones, Whale song and cultural transmission (2010, London, Tantamount Press:)
Albert Jones is professor of music at the University of southern Springs, ethnomusicologist and performer in both western and south east Asian musical instruments. The book discusses many topics of relevance: differences in whale song in different geographical areas, gendered distribution in whale song performances, tessitura and high and low whale voices, melodic and rhythmic patterns in whale song, structural patterns, and patterns of cultural transmission both within and across whale populations. Does not mention frogs but provides a model for many of the questions I'll be asking in my own research.

An valuable source in the context of my research is a book written by professor JB Croaker (2014) that documents frog populations on all six continents including Antarctica. Providing a wealth of detail including frog numbers, frog locations, frog extinctions, frog mating patterns, frog teeth and so on. Also includes the difference between frogs and toads but there is no discussion of frog song. A useful source for identifying frog populations I will include in my research including extinct ones.

Frogs of the World (2003) is a chronological history of frogs from prehistoric times to the present with mention of the impact of the ice age, the agrarian revolution, the industrial revolution and global warming. The limitation is that it does not discuss frog song. Will be used to supplement Croaker's study and help me identify which frog populations to study

Another key researcher is David Rothenberg who has done groundbreaking research on the connection between humans and nature and bird song. He plays clarinet while birds sing and in this way establishes communication with them. His book *Why Birds Sing: A Journey Into the Mystery of Bird Song* (*Basic Books*) provides useful background information for my research as it looks at why birds sing and the mysteries of bird song. This book raises questions that I will be raising in my own research so although it has nothing to do with frogs, it actually has everything to do with them. The limitations of this source once again is that frogs are not mentioned.

Timeline

Task	Dates
Complete literature search	July 2030 inclusive (1 month)
Fieldwork/data gathering	August 2030 – June 2031 inclusive (11 months)
Data analysis	July 2031 – May 2032 inclusive (11 months)
Write chapters	June 2032 – April 2033 inclusive (11 months)
Final editing	May – June 2033 inclusive (2 months)
Submit exegesis	30 June 2033 inclusive

Budget

ITEM	COST
Round the world airfare	$3,000
Fieldwork accommodation	$6,692 (estimate) (includes cost of tent and camping equipment)
Food	$5,010 (estimate)
Travel to and from fieldwork sites	TBA
Scuba diving gear and air tanks	TBA
Stationary and incidentals	$300 (estimate)
TOTAL	$15,291

Bibliography

Albert Jones, Whale song and cultural transmission (Tantamount Press: London: 2010)

Jack Brown and John White. Birds and bees in the antipodes. Vol.42/42, Kookaburra communal laughing as intervention in the treatment of clinical depression pp.42–42

Whale vocalise https://en.wikipedia.org/wiki/Whale_vocalization, Wikipedia,

Whale Songs in the Pacific, https://www.youtube.com/watch?v=P99CR4y-TYw,

Smith, John, Journal of the natural world, 2007. 3/2. 'Bee Sting, Bee Sound and Bee hives, p.22–23

JB Croaker, JB, (2014) Frog Populations on the Continents of Planet Earth. (Nature and Nurture Press, 2014);

Green. Eric. *Frogs of the World*. 2006. Amphibian Press.

David Rothenburg, *Why Birds Sing: A Journey Into the Mystery of Bird Song* (*Basic Books*, 2005)

Frogs and perfect pitch; a study in time and motion

Terry Toad, 2015, Cane Toads: Towards a New Understanding of Habits and habitats. (Once Only Publishing, Galapagos)

142 Postgraduate Research in Music

Questions

1. Consider the sections that have been included in the proposal and address the following questions:
    (i) Of the key and optional sections described earlier in this chapter, which ones have *not* been included in the proposal? Should further sections be added? If so, which ones?
    (ii) Are the sections logically sequenced?
2. Title page
    (i) What is wrong with the title?
    (ii) There are further errors in the content of the title page. What are they?
    (iii) How should the content be ordered and formatted?
3. Introduction and Background
    (i) What is wrong with the heading?
    (ii) The second sentence of the first paragraph is in particular need of rectification. (Clue: Cumbersome sentences sometimes need to be split into two.)
    (iii) There is a plagiarized sentence in this section. Identify the sentence and the source from which it is taken. That source must be acknowledged in a citation. (Clue: Inconsistent fonts . . . Copying and pasting . . .)
    (iv) Observe the style in which the "Introduction and Background" is written. Is it appropriate in an academic context?
    (v) Using a highlighter, identify any narrative disjunctions in the text. Before doing this, you may wish to refer to the section in chapter 7 entitled "Unity and Cohesion."
    (vi) Are frogs and whales both mammals? What is the point of this question?
    (vii) Critically consider the syntax generally in the introduction, for example the following sentence: "But I soon realized however that my research goes further."
4. "Rational" and aims
    (i) There are two errors in the heading. What are they?
    (ii) How many continents are there? How many are mentioned in the proposal?
    (iii) The second paragraph indicates that there are three parts to the project. How many are actually mentioned?
    (iv) Comment on the scope of the project, as indicated in the aims. Is the project feasible? Redraft the aims, reducing, reordering, and correcting errors in spelling, punctuation, and formatting. The aims may also be reconceptualized.

Writing a Research Proposal   143

5. Research questions
   - (i) What is wrong with the research questions?
   - (ii) Reconceptualize the study as either a hypothesis or a research question. In doing this, consider the scope of the project and what it is seeking to do.
6. Methodology
   - (i) Are all of these methodologies needed? Redraft the methodology section, reducing, reordering, and rewriting as appropriate. Ensure that it is consistent with the redrafted aims.
   - (ii) What is wrong with the first sentence?
   - (iii) The methodology is littered with spelling, typographical and syntactical errors. Highlight each of them, and be sure not to include them in your reconstituted proposal.
7. Is the anticipated significance of the study, as stated in the proposal, credible? If not, why not?
8. Literature review
   - (i) Observe the way in which the review of literature is presented. Is it written as a literature review or as an annotated bibliography?
   - (ii) Are the sources cited appropriately?
   - (iii) Critically evaluate the sources that have been included in the proposal. Are they all relevant? You may wish to delete some sources, and to add others.
   - (iv) Have enough sources been included? If there are few sources to draw upon in a given area of research, how can this be dealt with in a literature review?
   - (v) Using a highlighter, identify any incomplete sentences in the literature review. Are incomplete sentences acceptable in this context?
   - (vi) What is wrong with the use of the first person in a literature review? Use a highlighter to identify where this occurs. Which person should be used?
   - (vii) How should a literature review begin and how should it end?
9. How feasible is the timeline? Does it include enough detail?
10. How credible is the budget? Does it include enough detail?
11. The bibliography is a mess in every respect! In your creative rewriting, consider the following questions:
    - (i) Which referencing style is appropriate for this project—the Chicago style, or the APA style? Apply this style accurately and consistently.
    - (ii) Should the listing of sources be referred to as a bibliography or a reference list?

Exercise 3: Abstract writing

Write an abstract for the reconstructed research proposal that is the subject of exercise 2, using, as a guide, the information on abstract writing set out in this chapter. The abstract should be no more than 300 words in length.

Reading List

Some of the sources in this reading list span more than one sub-disciplinary area. In such cases, the source will be cited in each of the areas in which it is relevant. This duplication ensures that key sources will not be overlooked in any particular area of enquiry.

Writing a Research Proposal

Booth, Wayne C., Gregory C. Colomb, Joseph M. Williams, Joseph Bizup, and William T. Fitzgerald. *The Craft of Research.* 4th ed. Chicago: University of Chicago Press, 2016.

Kumar, Ranjit. *Research Methodology: A Step-By-Step Guide for Beginners.* 5th ed. Los Angeles: Sage, 2019.

Orna, Elizabeth, and Graham Stevens. *Managing Information for Research: Practical Help in Researching, Writing and Designing Dissertations.* 2nd ed. Maidenhead: Open University Press, 2009.

Punch, Keith F. *Developing Effective Research Proposals.* 3rd ed. London: Sage, 2016.

Turabian, Kate. *A Manual for Writers of Research Papers, Theses and Dissertations: Chicago Style for Students and Researchers.* 9th ed. Chicago: University of Chicago Press, 2018.

Walliman, Nicholas. *Research Methods: The Basics.* London: Routledge, 2011.

Walliman, Nicholas. *Research Methods: The Basics.* 3rd ed. Abingdon, Oxon: Routledge, 2022.

Walliman, Nicholas. *Your Research Project: Designing and Planning Your Work.* 3rd ed. London: Sage, 2011.

Wentz, Elizabeth A. *How to Design, Write, and Present a Successful Dissertation Proposal.* Los Angeles: Sage, 2014.

Music as Artifact

Digital Musicology

"A Software Application for the Optical Recognition, the Superimposition and the Collation of Early Music Prints." Aruspix. Accessed June 2, 2020. http://www.aruspix.net/index.html.

"Digital Humanities Models." Accessed June 2, 2020. https://musicalgeography.org/digital-humanities-models-2-0.

"Digital Musicology." IMS Study Group. Accessed June 2, 2020. https:// musicology.org/ networks/sg/digital-musicology.

"Digital Musicology: Getting Started." Duke University Libraries. Accessed June 2, 2020. https://guides.library.duke.edu/c.php?g=857511.

"Digital Resources for Musicology." Adam | Eve. Accessed June 2, 2020. https://drm.ccarh.org.

"Music Encoding Initiative." MEI. Accessed June 2, 2020. https://music-encoding.org.

"Mapping Place and Movement Through Music History." The Musical Geography Project. Accessed June 2, 2020. https://musicalgeography.org.

"MUS381—Reference and Research Materials in Music: Digital Musicology." University of Texas Libraries. Accessed September 2, 2021. https://guides.lib.utexas.edu/mus381/digitalmusicology.

"Schenker Documents Online." Accessed February 5, 2022. https://schenkerdocumentsonline.org/index.html.

"Search, Browse and Analyse Complete Scores of Polyphonic Music, ca. 1420–ca. 1520." The Josquin Research Project. Accessed June 2, 2020. https://josquin.stanford.edu.

"SIMSSA: Single Interface for Music Score Searching and Analysis Project." Accessed June 2, 2020. https://simssa.ca.

"The ARC Research Centre for the History and Analysis of Recorded Music." CHARM. Accessed June 2, 2020. https://charm.rhul.ac.uk/index.html.

Historical Musicology

Brundage, Anthony. *Going to the Sources: A Guide to Historical Research and Writing*. 6th ed. Hoboken, New Jersey: Wiley Blackwell, 2018.

Crawford, Tim, and Lorna Gibson, eds. *Modern Methods for Musicology: Prospects, Proposals, and Realities*. London: Routledge, 2016.

Crist, Stephen A., and Roberta Montemorra Marvin, eds. *Historical Musicology: Sources, Methods, Interpretations*. Rochester, NY: University of Rochester Press, 2008.

Duckles, Vincent, et al. "Musicology." In *Grove Music Online*. Oxford University Press, 2001. https://doi-org.ezproxy.ecu.edu.au/10.1093/gmo/9781561592630.article.46710. See in particular the section by Glenn Stanley entitled "Historical Method."

Herbert, Trevor. "Social History and Music History." In *The Cultural Study of Music: A Critical Introduction*. 2nd ed., edited by Martin Clayton, Trevor Herbert, and Richard Middleton, 49–58. New York: Routledge, 2012.

Pruett, James W., and Thomas P. Slavens. *Research Guide to Musicology*. Chicago: American Library Association, 1985.

Wegman, Rob. C. "Historical Musicology: Is it Still Possible?" In *The Cultural Study of Music: A Critical Introduction*. 2nd ed., edited by Martin Clayton, Trevor Herbert, and Richard Middleton, 40–48. New York: Routledge, 2012.

Metric Theory

London, Justin. "Rhythm." In *Grove Music Online*. Oxford University Press, 2001. https://doi-org.ezproxy.ecu.edu.au/10.1093/gmo/9781561592630.article.45963.

Music Analysis

Bent, Ian D. "Analysis." Revised by Anthony Pople. In *Grove Music Online*. Oxford University Press, 2001. https://doi-org.ezproxy.ecu.edu.au/10.1093/gmo/9781561592630.article.41862.

Bent, Ian. *Analysis*. London: Macmillan, 1987.

Cadwallader, Allen Clayton, David Gagné, and Frank Samarotto. *Analysis of Tonal Music: A Schenkerian Approach*. 4th ed. New York: Oxford University Press, 2020.

Cook, Nicholas. *A Guide to Musical Analysis*. Oxford: Oxford University Press, 1996.

Kostka, Stefan, and Matthew Santa. *Materials and Techniques of Post-Tonal Music*. 5th ed. New York: Routledge, 2018.

Kostka, Stefan, Dorothy Payne, and Byron Almén. *Tonal Harmony*. 8th ed. New York: McGraw Hill, 2017.

146 Postgraduate Research in Music

La Rue, Jan. *Guidelines for Style Analysis*. Edited by Marian Green La Rue. Expanded 2nd ed. Sterling Heights, MI: Harmonie Park Press 2011.

Neumeyer, David, and Susan Tepping. *A Guide to Schenkerian Analysis*. Englewood Cliffs, NJ: Prentice Hall, 1992.

Pearsall, Edward. *Twentieth-Century Music Theory and Practice*. New York: Routledge, 2012.

Reti, Rudolph. *The Thematic Process in Music*. Westport, Conn.: Greenwood Press, 1978.

Roig-Francoli, Miguel A. *Harmony in Context*. 3rd ed. New York: McGraw Hill, 2020.

Roig-Francoli, Miguel A. *Understanding Post-Tonal Music*. 2nd ed. New York: Routledge, 2021.

Straus, Joseph. *Introduction to Post-Tonal Theory*. 4th ed. New York: W.W. Norton, 2016.

Sketch Studies

Marston, Nicholas. "Sketch." In *Grove Music Online*. Oxford University Press, 2001. https://doi-org.ezproxy.ecu.edu.au/10.1093/gmo/9781561592630.article.42828.

Music as Activity

Bernard, Harvey Russell. *Social Research Methods: Qualitative and Quantitative Approaches*. 2nd ed. Los Angeles: Sage, 2013.

Bresler, Liora. "Music in Qualitative Research." In *The Sage Encyclopedia of Qualitative Research Methods*, edited by Lisa M. Given, 534–537. Los Angeles: Sage, 2008.

Bryman, Alan. *Social Research Methods*. 5th ed. Oxford: Oxford University Press, 2016.

Creswell, John W., and Cheryl N. Poth. *Qualitative Inquiry & Research Design: Choosing Among Five Approaches*. 4th ed. Los Angeles: Sage, 2018.

George, Theodore. "Hermeneutics." In *Stanford Encyclopedia of Philosophy*, edited by Edward N. Zalta. Winter 2021 edition. https://plato.stanford.edu/archives/win2021/entries/hermeneutics.

Given, Lisa M., ed. *The Sage Encyclopedia of Qualitative Research Methods*. Los Angeles: Sage, 2008.

Kalaian, Sema A. "Research Design—Phenomenological Research." In *Encyclopedia of Survey Research Methods*, edited by Paul J. Lavrakas, 725–731. Thousand Oaks, CA: Sage, 2008. https://www-doi-org.ezproxy.ecu.edu.au/10.4135/9781412963947.n471.

Kumar, Ranjit. *Research Methodology: A Step-By-Step Guide for Beginners*. 5th ed. Los Angeles: Sage, 2019.

Punch, Keith F. *Introduction to Social Research: Quantitative and Qualitative Approaches*. 3rd ed. Los Angeles: Sage, 2014.

Thompson, William Forde, Alexandra Lamont, Richard Parncutt, and Frank A. Russo, eds. *Music in the Social and Behavioral Sciences: An Encyclopedia*. Los Angeles: Sage, 2014.

Walliman, Nicholas. *Research Methods: The Basics*. 3rd ed. Abingdon, Oxon: Routledge, 2022.

Wolf, James. "Self-Administered Questionnaire." In *Encyclopedia of Survey Research Methods*, edited by Paul J. Lavrakas, 804. Thousand Oaks, California: Sage, 2008. https://www-doi-org.ezproxy.ecu.edu.au/10.4135/9781412963947.n522.

Practice-based Research and Reflective Practice

Bassot, Barbara. *The Reflective Practice Guide: An Interdisciplinary Approach to Critical Reflection*. London: Taylor & Francis, 2016.

Bolton, Gillie, with Russell Delderfield. *Reflective Practice: Writing and Professional Development*. 5th ed. Los Angeles: Sage, 2018.

Borgdorff, Henk. *The Conflict of the Faculties: Perspectives on Artistic Research and Academia*. Leiden: Leiden University Press, 2012.

Burke, Robert, and Andrys Onsman, eds. *Perspectives on Artistic Research in Music*. Lanham, Maryland: Lexington Books, 2017.

Crispin, Darla, and Bob Gilmore, eds. *Artistic Experimentation in Music: An Anthology*. Leuven: Leuven University Press, 2014.

Doğantan-Dack, Mine. *Artistic Practice as Research in Music: Theory, Criticism, Practice*. London: Taylor & Francis, 2016.

Given, Lisa M., ed. *The Sage Encyclopedia of Qualitative Research Methods*. Los Angeles: Sage, 2008.

Huber, Annegret, Doris Ingrisch, Therese Kaufmann, Johannes Kretz, Gesine Schröder, and Tasos Zembylas, eds. *Knowing in Performing: Artistic Research in Music and the Performing Arts*. Bielefeld: transcript-Verlag, 2021.

Impett, Jonathan, ed. *Artistic Research in Music: Discipline and Resistance*. Leuven: Leuven University Press, 2017.

Knowles, J. G., and Ardra L. Cole, eds. *Handbook of the Arts in Qualitative Research: Perspectives, Methodologies, Examples, and Issues*. Los Angeles: Sage, 2008.

McNiff, Jean. *Action Research: Principles and Practice*. 3rd ed. Abingdon, Oxfordshire: Routledge, 2013.

Nelson, Robin, ed. *Performance as Research in the Arts: Principles, Protocols, Pedagogies, Resistances*. Basingstoke: Palgrave Macmillan, 2013.

Smith, Hazel, and Roger Dean. *Practice-Led Research, Research-Led Practice in the Creative Arts*. Edinburgh: Edinburgh University Press, 2014.

Thompson, Sue, and Neil Thompson. *The Critically Reflective Practitioner*. 2nd ed. Basingstoke: Palgrave Macmillan, 2018.

Referencing

Chicago Manual of Style: The Essential Guide for Writers, Editors, and Publishers. 17th ed. Chicago: University of Chicago Press, 2017.

Publication Manual of the American Psychological Association. 7th ed. Washington, DC: American Psychological Association, 2020.

Sampsel, Laurie J. *Music Research: A Handbook*. 3rd ed. New York: Oxford University Press, 2019.

Turabian, Kate. *A Manual for Writers of Research Papers, Theses and Dissertations: Chicago Style for Students and Researchers*. 9th ed. Chicago: University of Chicago Press, 2018.

Ethics Clearance

"Policy on the Ethical Conduct of Research Involving Human Participants and Personal Data." University of Oxford. Accessed August 26, 2021. https://researchsupport.admin.ox.ac.uk/governance/ethics/committees/policy.

"Research Integrity." University of Cambridge. Accessed August 26, 2021. https://www.research-integrity.admin.cam.ac.uk/research-ethics.

Other Sources Consulted

Rogers, Victoria. "John Blacking, Composer." *Ethnomusicology* 57, no.2 (Spring/Summer 2013): 311–329.

Rogers, Victoria. "The Musical Language of Peggy Glanville-Hicks." PhD. diss., University of Western Australia, 2000.

6

Writing a Thesis Part 1

Content, Organization, and Presentation

The stage is now set for writing a thesis. The research proposal has been subjected to rigorous scrutiny and the project has emerged as original, meaningful, viable, and achievable within the specified word count and timeframe. Key elements of the thesis have already begun to take shape in the research proposal with the drafting of an introduction, hypothesis or research question, literature review, and aims and methodology. Data have been assembled and further ideas have emerged as the research process has unfolded. All that remains now is to write a thesis!

Of course, writing a thesis isn't as easy as that. Like all of the steps in the research process, it requires particular skills and knowledge, as well as a sustained focus over a substantial period of time. Chapter 6 is the first of four chapters that discuss what is involved in writing a thesis. It considers what a thesis includes together with how the content is organized, presented, and formatted. Chapter 7 examines style in academic writing; chapter 8 documents the musical lexicon; chapter 9 focuses on efficiency and effectiveness.

Content, Organization, and Presentation

All these contain a number of core elements, as well as several optional elements whose inclusion is determined by the nature of the research, or by personal or institutional preference. Some of these elements are also included in research proposals and have already been discussed in chapter 5; others appear only in a thesis.

In the following list, the core elements are set in bold to distinguish them from the optional inclusions. The list is divided into three segments (front matter, chapters, and back matter) and provides a suggested ordering of sections, although this is just one of many possibilities. The sequencing of the front matter can vary. The ordering of the hypothesis or research question, literature review, and aims is also variable. And the back matter can also

Postgraduate Research in Music. Victoria Rogers, Oxford University Press. © Oxford University Press 2024.
DOI: 10.1093/oso/9780197616031.003.0007

be organized in different ways; endnotes, for example, are located before the bibliography in the Chicago style, and after it in the APA style.[1] The ensuing list is therefore not a rigid prescription, but rather a useful starting point for considering what to include in a thesis, and in which order. The guidelines that follow this list set out the what, the why and the how of each of these elements.

Front Matter
- **Title page**
- **Declaration of originality**
- Copyright page
- Dedication
- **Abstract**
- **Table of contents**
- List of musical examples
- List of tables
- List of figures
- List of definitions
- List of abbreviations
- List of symbols
- Preface
- **Acknowledgements**

Chapters (Main Text)
- **Introduction:** Contextual background; hypothesis or research question; literature review; aims, rationale, and significance; methodology.
- **Middle section:** Presentation and analysis of the research findings.
- **Concluding section:** Summary, discussion, and conclusion.

Back Matter
- **Endnotes**
- **Bibliography/reference list**
- Appendices

Front Matter

Title Page
There is no universal format for a title page. The content, however, is by and large standard. It is set out in the following points, then presented in the title

150   Postgraduate Research in Music

> ## The Musical Language of Diego Ferrera:
> ## A Sign of Things to Come?
>
> MARY SMITH
> BA MPhil (Oxon)
>
> This thesis is presented for the degree of Doctor of Philosophy
>
> Faculty of Music
> University of the Antipodes
>
> 2022

Figure 6.1. Title page for the fictitious doctoral thesis on the musical language of Diego Ferrera

page for the fictitious doctoral thesis referred to in chapter 5: a study of the musical language of the imaginary composer, Diego Ferrera (see figure 6.1).

- Title of thesis: The title is generally written in headline-style capitalization (the first letter of all major words is capitalized; also referred to as "title case"), although some institutions prefer sentence-style capitalization (only the first word of the title, the first word after a colon, and proper nouns are capitalized). The title should *not* be written in italics, or set within quotation marks, or followed by a period.
- Student name, in the order of first name then last name.
- Qualifications (if appropriate), listed from lowest to highest if there is more than one. If the awarding institution is different from the institution of enrolment, the abbreviated name of the awarding institution is included after the degree name(s). Qualifications are listed without periods, for example BA MPhil
- The degree for which the thesis is presented, for example: "This thesis is presented for the degree of Doctor of Philosophy." If the degree includes

both written and practical components, the wording is changed to reflect this, for example: "This thesis is presented in partial fulfilment of the requirements for the degree of Doctor of Musical Arts." There is no period at the end of the statement.

- School or Department and/or Faculty, and University, in this order.
- Month and year of submission.

The following points should also be noted:

- The title page does not include a page number, although it is sometimes counted as one (see the discussion below on pagination in the section entitled "table of contents").
- Attention needs to be paid to formatting (font type and size, and the spacing of information).
- All information on the title page should be centered on the page, not justified left or right.

Declaration of Originality

The declaration of originality affirms that the thesis is the work of the author, and that its content has not been submitted for a degree at any university. The declaration should be signed and include the date. The following wording is one of many possibilities.

I declare that this thesis is my own account of my research and that it contains as its main content work that has not been submitted for a degree at any university.

Signed: _____   Date: _____

Copyright Statement

A copyright statement is optional because a thesis, like any piece of writing, is automatically copyrighted once it has been committed to a fixed format (print or electronic). Nonetheless, a copyright statement provides very visible protection, placing ownership of the intellectual property completely beyond doubt. If a copyright statement is included, it should contain either, or both, the copyright symbol and the word "copyright," the name of the author, and the year from which copyright begins. It may also include the words "All Rights Reserved." In terms of formatting, it can be justified left or centered on the page, and set either on the same page as the declaration of originality or on a separate page:

© Mary Smith 2022

Dedication

A dedication is a tribute that is sometimes included to acknowledge one or more people for the role they have played in the author's life, or in the preparation of the thesis. People who might be named include parents, partners, mentors, or pioneers in a field of research. A dedication need not be long. It can be as succinct as: "For my parents." If a dedication is included, it should be set on a separate page and centered on the page.

Abstract

An extensive discussion of abstract writing has already been provided in chapter 5 ("Writing a Research Proposal"). The earlier account should be reviewed before writing the abstract for a thesis, for its content is replicated only in part in the ensuing discussion.

An abstract is a synopsis, or summary, of a larger document. It is an optional inclusion in a research proposal but obligatory in a thesis. An abstract for a thesis is more extensive than one written for a research proposal. It includes, in addition, the findings and conclusions of the research—information that usually occupies 30–40% of the word count. The abstract might therefore need to extend to 500 words, beyond the more typical length of 300–400 words. Precision and concision are of the essence, for there is space only for the key points. An abstract for a thesis contains the following information:

- Contextual background to the study.
- Overview of research already undertaken in the area and identification of the gap in the existing research.
- Hypothesis or research question, aims, rationale, significance, and methodology.
- Findings.
- Conclusions.

In style of presentation, there are, as noted in chapter 5, two approaches to abstract writing: the traditional one, and the one sometimes used in more recent scholarship. These approaches differ in two respects: whether the abstract is set in a single paragraph or multiple paragraphs; and whether the first person singular (I) is used. In other respects, the same stylistic conventions are followed. The two approaches are summarized in table 6.1.

When writing an abstract, be efficient. Begin by considering the main sections, then jot down, in bullet points, the content that will be incorporated into each of these sections, and in which order. Try to include some key terms from the thesis to ensure that the abstract and the thesis are well aligned.

Table 6.1. Two approaches to abstract writing

The more traditional approach	The approach in some contemporary practice
One paragraph	More than one paragraph
First sentence not indented	First sentence of opening paragraph not indented
Complete sentences only	Complete sentences only
Present and past tenses predominate	Present and past tenses predominate
Use of third person	Use of first person and third person
Active voice preferred	Active voice preferred

Decide which style of abstract writing to follow—the traditional approach, or the one sometimes used in more recent scholarship. Once this planning has been completed, a first draft can be written. It will in all likelihood be too long and need to be pruned back. Gradually, over successive drafts, chisel away at the content and reduce the word count. Every idea must be critically evaluated to see whether it is essential, or whether it might be deleted. Every phrase needs to be scrutinized to see if there is a more succinct way of saying the same thing. A word here, a phrase there; gradually an abstract can be whittled down to fit within the specified word count.

One final point to consider is when to write the abstract. Although it is the first thing a reader encounters, it should be written last, once the thesis has taken its final form. Only then is an abstract certain to be a complete and accurate synopsis of the thesis.

Figure 6.2 sets out an abstract for the fictitious doctoral thesis on the music of Diego Ferrera. This abstract has been adapted from the one set out in figure 5.4 of chapter 5. It would be fruitful to compare the two abstracts to see how the content varies from one context to the other, and the extent to which an abstract from a research proposal can form the basis of one written for a thesis—provided, of course, that it is done well in the first place.[2]

Table of Contents

Where a table of contents is optional in a research proposal, it is essential in a thesis. The table of contents is one of the first things a reader looks at to get an idea of the content, scope, and overall shape of a thesis. It is an important reference point.

Guidelines for compiling a table of contents have already been set out in chapter 5. The earlier account should be reviewed before writing the table of contents for a thesis, for it is recapitulated only in part in the ensuing discussion.

154   Postgraduate Research in Music

> **ABSTRACT**
>
> The Peruvian composer Diego Ferrera (1910–85) studied in Paris with Lucia Boucher and in Vienna with Gustav Waschenwasser before moving to the USA, where he spent fifteen years as a high-profile figure in the musical life of New York. In the early 1960s he moved to Greece, where he wrote many of his major works. He returned to Peru in 1975 and spent his final years in Lima in relative obscurity. Ferrera left a legacy of 157 works, including twelve operas, fourteen ballets, and many vocal and instrumental works. After his return to Peru, several brief, largely biographical newspaper articles were written about him and a number of film and radio programmes were made. There has been some study of his music—mostly student dissertations—but there has been no comprehensive investigation of his musical language, its development over five decades, or its significance in twentieth-century composition. This thesis addresses this gap by examining Ferrera's musical language from the early works of the 1930s through to the late works of the 1970s. The study concludes that the musical influences from Ferrera's formative years in Peru permeate his entire compositional output, and that the privileging of melody and rhythm in the late works together with the use of Peruvian folk song, a consonant musical idiom, and a pared-down musical texture, added a unique musical voice to twentieth-century composition. The study further concludes that whilst there is stylistically little to connect Ferrera's music with the wide and divergent range of sounds and approaches that are grouped under the umbrella of Postmodernism, the conceptual foundation of his music nonetheless has a clear resonance with aspects of Postmodern thought, anticipating the emergence, later in the century, of the Postmodern aesthetic of consonance, simplification, accessibility, and a renewed interest in non-Western musics.

Figure 6.2. Abstract for the doctoral thesis on the music of Diego Ferrera

A table of contents is referred to simply as "contents." It lists all of the sections in the ensuing pages (not including the preceding ones), together with the starting page number of each section. Where a contents page in a research proposal may simply list the major sections, it is more detailed in a thesis and includes both the major sections and the sub-sections within them.

A contents page is easier to read when the sub-sections are demarcated by indentation. The further an indentation sits to the right, the lower the section sits within the structural hierarchy of the thesis. This hierarchy can be reinforced through capitalization/non-capitalization, different fonts, and numerical and/or alphabetical labeling.

A further consideration is the matter of pagination. Two systems of pagination are used in a thesis: lower case Roman numerals (i, ii, iii, iv, etc.) for the front matter; and Arabic numerals (1, 2, 3, 4, etc.) for the remainder (the body of the thesis and the back matter). As noted earlier in this chapter, the title page is not always counted as a page. If it *is* counted, it does not include a page number and the page following the title page (the declaration of originality) is numbered ii. The page numbering therefore begins before the table of contents—and of course the contents page itself is given a page number. For neatness, the page numbers are justified right.

Accuracy is crucial in the documentation of page numbers. It is so easy to make last-minute changes in the body of a thesis and forget to amend the page numbers in the contents page. One of the last tasks prior to submitting a thesis should be to check the accuracy of the pagination. How irritating it is for readers to refer to a table of contents, only to find that the pagination is incorrect.

Figure 6.3 sets out a contents page for the doctoral thesis on the music of Diego Ferrera. It illustrates the key principles discussed in this section: differentiated headings; indentation of sections; and appropriate pagination.

CONTENTS

LIST OF MUSICAL EXAMPLES	v
LIST OF TABLES	vii
ABSTRACT	viii
PREFACE	ix
ACKNOWLEDGEMENTS	x
CHAPTER 1: INTRODUCTION	
Contextual background	1
Biographical overview	6
Literature review and research question	10
Aims, rationale, and methodology	20
CHAPTER 2: FORMATIVE MUSICAL INFLUENCES	
Peruvian folk music	22
European art music	26
CHAPTER 3: THE EARLY WORKS	
Background	33
Four Folk Songs for Voice and Piano	36
Choral Suite	48
Sonatina for Panpipe and Piano	60
Summary and discussion	62
CHAPTER 4: THE NEOCLASSICAL WORKS	
Background	64
Pre-Columbian Prelude and Presto	65
Inca Concerto	75
Musica Antiqua	87
Summary and discussion	100

Figure 6.3. Table of contents for the doctoral thesis on the music of Diego Ferrera

List of Musical Examples

Musical examples provide evidence for the analysis that is presented in a thesis. They are listed in the front matter in the order in which they appear in the text. Each example is identified by a caption (numerical identifier and descriptive title) and set on a new line, together with the page number on which it appears in the thesis. The page numbers are justified right. If a descriptive title runs onto a second line, the page number is aligned with the second line of the title. The list of examples is set in 1.5 or double spacing, and set on a separate page.

Guidelines for the presentation, content, and formatting of musical examples are set out in appendix C.

List of Tables

A table is a summary, or aggregation, of research data that have been grouped into meaningful clusters and presented in a grid of vertical columns (top to bottom) and horizontal rows (left to right). Conventions for the listing of musical examples (as described above) apply equally to tables.

Guidelines for the presentation, content and formatting of tables are set out in appendix D.

List of Figures

A figure is a diagram or pictorial illustration that helps to explain information in the text. A figure may take the form of a graph, a map, a photograph, or some other image. Conventions for the listing of musical examples and tables (as described above) apply equally to figures.

Guidelines for the presentation, content and formatting of graphs are set out in appendix E.

List of Definitions

Definitions are often listed alphabetically in the front matter of a thesis, grouped together on a separate page. Alternatively, terms may be defined at first mention in the text, or in the methodology section.

List of Abbreviations

Abbreviations that need clarification are listed alphabetically in the front matter, grouped together on a separate page.

List of Symbols

Symbols requiring explanation are listed by order of appearance in the text, grouped together on a separate page.

Preface

A preface is a brief statement that precedes the body of a thesis. It is an optional, though usual, inclusion. A preface adds a personal dimension to the research, describing, for example, how the topic of the thesis came about. It is generally written in the first person and often concludes by acknowledging the people who have contributed to the thesis. Alternatively, the acknowledgements may be set out in a separate section.

Acknowledgements

Acknowledgements are typically extended to supervisors for their guidance and support; to family and other people who have provided encouragement; to library and archive staff who have helped to locate sources of information; and to departments or universities that have provided financial or other assistance. At the very least, supervisory and institutional support should be acknowledged as a matter of courtesy.

Chapters (Main Text)

Just as a novel is divided into chapters, so too is a thesis. Chapters are a way of organizing the content into clearly defined segments, each of which deals with a particular aspect of a topic. In this way a case can be built up progressively over the course of a thesis, leading to the conclusions that are set out in the final chapter. Chapter divisions also allow a thesis to "breathe," giving readers a chance to assimilate the content of each chapter before moving onto the next one.

There is no set rule as to how many chapters should be included. As few as four may suffice for a short thesis; more are needed for a longer one. It is the subject matter that determines the division of content and the number of chapters.

There is also no set rule as to the length of individual chapters. For a doctoral thesis of 80,000–100,000 words, a chapter length of 6,000–10,000 words is typical. If a chapter extends beyond ca. 15,000 words, it is generally split into two. For shorter theses, a shorter word count per chapter is appropriate. Ultimately, the length of each chapter is determined by its content. Chapters do not need to be uniform in length, and shorter chapters may be interspersed with longer ones.

The chapters within a thesis can be grouped into three segments: an introduction to the research; a middle section in which the research findings are presented and analyzed; and a conclusion that draws the threads together and discusses the findings.

Introduction

The introduction presents particular challenges for a writer; indeed, some say that this is the most difficult section to write. One of the greatest challenges lies in finding the *right* opening idea and the *right* opening sentence; readers need to be ushered—even enticed—into a thesis. Through this metaphorical opening of the door, readers can then be acquainted with what the thesis is about, the scholarly context from which it has emerged, what it aims to do, how it will do this, why it is significant, and how it will proceed. Without this foundation in place, the remainder of a thesis makes little sense.

The idea of introducing the research has already been discussed in the context of writing a research proposal (see chapter 5). These two introductions are not quite the same thing, however. In a research proposal, the introduction is limited to the contextual background, the main issues (and possibly key researchers) in the area of research, and a statement of what the study is about and why it is being undertaken. In a thesis, almost the entirety of the research proposal is incorporated into the introductory chapter, expanded and amended to incorporate new information and further ideas that have emerged since the proposal was written. The earlier document therefore functions as an important starting point for the opening chapter of a thesis.

The following content is included in the introduction to a thesis, typically in the following order:

- Contextual background to the study.
- Hypothesis or research question (arising from the contextual background).
- Literature review (arising from the contextual background, and from the hypothesis or research question).
- Aims and rationale (emerging from the gap identified in the literature review).
- Scope of the study, including any limitations (may also be incorporated into the aims).
- Methodology (the "how" of the aims).
- Definitions of key terminology (alternatively, may be set out in the front matter of the thesis).
- Structure of the thesis (emerging from the aims and methodology).

This content and its ordering are appropriate for most theses, but not for all. If, for example, a literature review were to be particularly extensive, it might be set as a separate chapter following the introduction. Occasionally, too, as noted in chapter 4 ("Writing a Literature Review"), there is little or no existing research on or around a topic. In such cases, the aims and methodology might immediately follow the contextual background. The key point to be noted is that the exact content and its ordering vary from project to project; every thesis is unique and has its own logic. Even the heading can vary, as noted in chapter 5. "Setting of the Study," "Background," or some other heading might be used instead.

The sections within an introduction, as outlined in the preceding dot points, have already been discussed in chapters 4 and 5. These chapters should be reviewed before writing the introductory chapter of a thesis.

When Should an Introduction Be Written?

There is no hard and fast rule as to when to write an introduction. Some scholars write it first, not only to clarify their thinking but also to keep them on track as they write the remaining chapters. If the introduction is written first, it is important to be flexible and to adjust it later on; the very nature of research ensures that things will change as the writing proceeds. Other scholars write the introduction last—a strange reversal, perhaps, and a rather contrived way of going about things. This approach makes sense, however, because a thesis is a retrospective report, the documentation of a process that has already been completed. Writing the introduction last ensures that it is consistent with the other chapters in the thesis. The optimal approach may be to draft an introduction first, and to return to it after the body of the thesis has been written. This offers the best of both worlds.

What is the Difference Between an Abstract and an Introduction?

An abstract and an introduction are not the same thing. They are similar, but they are also different. Both provide a contextual background to the study; both indicate what the research is concerned with and the methods it will use; and both refer to the literature in the area of research. They may even share some phrases and sentences. An abstract, however, is a very condensed document; an introduction, by comparison, is more expansive (although more limited in subject matter). As a summary of an entire thesis, an abstract includes findings and conclusions; an introduction does not—indeed, it cannot because the findings have not yet been presented. An abstract does not outline the structure of a thesis. This, however, is set out at the end of the introduction so that readers have a clear idea as to how the thesis will proceed. These two parts of a thesis—an abstract and an introduction—have different

160 Postgraduate Research in Music

functions and should not be confused. One summarizes an entire thesis; the other introduces it. The similarities and differences between the two are set out in table 6.2.

Table 6.2. Abstract and introduction compared

Abstract	Introduction
Includes a brief contextual background to the study	Includes a broad contextual background to the study
Signals the research question or hypothesis	Defines the research question or hypothesis
Makes brief reference to the relevant literature	Makes detailed reference to the relevant literature
Gives a brief indication of the aims and methodology	Sets out detailed aims and methodology
Might make brief reference to the scope of the study	Defines the scope of the study
Includes a brief synopsis of the findings and conclusions	Does not include the findings and conclusions
Does not indicate how the thesis will be structured	Indicates how the thesis will be structured

Organization and Presentation of the Research Findings

The presentation of the research findings is the most extensive part of a thesis. Three factors need to be considered when writing this section: how the findings will be organized; how they will be presented; and how they will be analyzed. Organization and presentation are examined in this section. The analysis of findings will be discussed in chapter 7 in the section entitled "Evidence and the Analytical Process."

Organization of the Findings

Two levels of planning need to be taken into account when organizing the research findings: the macro, and the micro. The macro level, or outer framework, outlines the chapter divisions and the allocation of content between the chapters. The micro level, or inner scaffolding, maps the sections within each chapter, and the content within each section. The ordering of content must be logical both between and within the chapters to ensure that an argument can be built up progressively over the course of the thesis.

It is far more effective—and far easier—to follow a good plan than to lurch from one idea to the next with little idea of how the thesis will unfold. A useful approach is to consider the following questions, working progressively from the macro to the micro:

- What is the hypothesis or research question, and what are the aims of the thesis?

- Which clusters, or categories, of information have emerged from the research data?
- What is the best way of dividing this information into chapters?
- What is the optimal ordering of chapters?
- Which specific content will be included in each chapter?
- How will the content be sequenced within each chapter?

The plan that emerges from these considerations can be documented as a series of headings, sub-headings, and bullet points. It is not a rigid blueprint from which no deviation is possible; even with the best planning, flexibility will always be needed because writing is a creative and evolving process. Content that may seem to belong in one place may later need to migrate to another—or even to toggle to and fro until the optimal destination is found.

Presentation of the Findings

Further reflection is needed to work out how the research findings will be presented. A beginning-to-end account is generally not the best approach; an interminable, bar-by-bar analysis of a score, for example, can be impenetrable for readers and contribute little to addressing the aims of the research. In most projects, a better approach is to cluster the data into meaningful thematic groups that have a clear correlation with the aims of the research.

Imagine, for example, a study that explores the performative application of notions of taste in late eighteenth-century British keyboard music.[3] Imagine also that the secondary literature sheds little light on the subject. The next task would therefore be to undertake a survey of late eighteenth-century writings on the subject of taste. This could be presented as a writer-by-writer account, but it would be difficult for readers to distil the essential points. A thematic approach would be more effective, shifting the focus from the individual writers to the common themes that emerge from the writings—such as imagination, refinement, and judgement. This approach would also shift responsibility to the writer of the thesis, rather than the reader, to distil the key points and to make sense of the information.

Imagine, as a second example, a study of the musical language of an early twentieth-century composer. A beginning-to-end description of each work would embed the key information in a sea of unnecessary detail, making it difficult for the reader to glean the essential points. Once again, a thematic

162 Postgraduate Research in Music

approach would be more effective—in this case a series of analytic rubrics such as structure, melodic design, tonal organization, texture, and rhythmic usage. These rubrics could be used as a framework for the discussion of individual works, distilling the musical language to its essence and enabling meaningful comparisons to be made between the compositions.

Illustrations

Some of the research findings may also be presented in illustrations—in other words, in images that help to explain the information presented in the text. Illustrations distil a large amount of information into visual representations that can be easily comprehended by readers.

Illustrations must be presented well if they are to make their point effectively. This section sets out general conventions governing the use of illustrations.[4] Appendices C, D, and E provide detailed guidelines for three of the illustrative categories that need particular discussion: musical examples, tables, and graphical formats.

All illustrations are governed by conventions as to how they are identified, formatted, introduced, discussed, and located in the text. Musical examples are referred to as "examples"; tables are referred to as "tables"; other illustrations such as bar charts, line graphs, pie charts, photographs, and maps are referred to as "figures."

Each of these illustrative categories (musical examples, tables, and figures) is given its own set of identifying captions, each of which includes two elements: (1) the number of the illustration; and (2) a descriptive title, or a brief explanatory text. The caption is justified left and does not include a period at the end. The captions are generally placed above the illustrations; captions for figures in the Chicago style, however, are placed below.

The system that is used for the numbering of illustrations combines two Arabic numerals: first, the number of the chapter in which the illustration appears; and second, the number of the illustration as determined by its order of appearance in the chapter. The two numbers are separated by a period. Taking tables as an example, the first table in chapter 6 would be labeled table 6.1; the second would be labeled table 6.2, and so on. If only one table were to appear in chapter 6, it would be labeled table 6.1. When two or more tables are closely related, each is given a separate numerical identifier (6.1, 6.2, 6.3), rather than linked alphabetical identifiers (6.1A, 6.1B, 6.1C). Illustrations that are particularly long or less immediately relevant may be included as appendices, rather than in the chapter itself, and labeled as appendix 1, appendix 2, and so on.

The captions may be formatted in different ways; the key is to be consistent in applying a single approach to all captions. Two of the styles commonly used in music research—the Chicago style and the APA style—are summarized below and illustrated in table 6.3.

Chicago-style formatting:
- All information in the caption is located on the same line.
- The caption number is separated from the descriptive title either by a period and a space, or by an em space (three spaces). If an em space is used, the numerical identifier is highlighted in bold, and there is no period.
- Sentence-style capitalization is used.
- Italics are not used unless the caption includes an element that requires italics, such as the title of a musical work.

APA-style formatting:
- The illustration number is set in bold above the descriptive title.
- The descriptive title is set a double-spaced line below the number, in italics.
- Headline-style capitalization is used.

Table 6.3. Formatting of captions in Chicago and APA styles

Chicago style	APA style
Example 6.1. *Nausicaa*, prologue, bars 1–5 OR: **Example 6.1** *Nausicaa*, prologue, bars 1–5	Not applicable because the APA style is not used in humanities research
Table 6.1. Two approaches to abstract writing OR: **Table 6.1** Two approaches to abstract writing	**Table 6.1** *Two Approaches to Abstract Writing*
Figure 6.1. Distribution of frog song in Antarctica OR: **Figure 6.1** Distribution of frog song in Antarctica	**Figure 6.1** *Distribution of Frog Song in Antarctica*

There are further conventions that govern how illustrations are introduced. One of the golden rules of academic writing is to create a smooth flow of ideas, without any disjunctions in the text. An illustration must not suddenly pop up in the text, seemingly out of nowhere. Readers need to be led to it through one or two introductory sentences that foreshadow the information that is about to be presented. These sentences often include some of the wording in the caption itself, creating an easy transition from text to illustration.

164   Postgraduate Research in Music

How this works in practice is illustrated in the following example, which refers to a fictitious (and highly unlikely) study of frog song across the continent of Antarctica. The statistical findings of the study are documented in a table whose caption reads as follows:

Table 6.1. Frog song in Antarctica: Distribution by pitch collection and region

This table could be introduced in a number of ways, including the following:

Frog song based variously on pentatonic, diatonic, and chromatic pitch collections is common across the continent of Antarctica. Its distribution can be seen in table 6.1, which documents the numerical occurrences by pitch collection and region.

Or:

Frog song based variously on pentatonic, diatonic and chromatic pitch collections is common across the continent of Antarctica. Table 6.1 documents its distribution by pitch collection and region.

Or:

Frog song based variously on pentatonic, diatonic and chromatic pitch collections is common across the continent of Antarctica. These pitch collections vary in number from region to region (see table 6.1).

In each of these examples, the word "table" is not capitalized unless it appears at the beginning of a sentence. This is consistent with the Chicago style, in which the words "table," "example," and "figure" and are set in lower case when used in the text, but capitalized in captions. Other styles such as the APA capitalize "table," "figure," and "example" whenever they appear with a number, whether in the text or a caption.

Convention—and good scholarship—also decree that it is not enough simply to present an illustration. Equally important is the discussion that follows. Any significant elements, recurrences, differences, correlations, and implications need to be addressed. The "So what?" question is critical here. What does this information actually *mean*? As noted earlier in this chapter, it is the task of the writer, not the reader, to make sense of the data.

As a general rule, an illustration is placed immediately after the paragraph in which it is first mentioned. Another approach is to cluster the illustrations at the ends of chapters, or, if they are overly long or less immediately relevant, as appendices at the end of the thesis. For ease of reading, however, it is better to locate each illustration close to the text to which it refers—where possible *after* its first mention and not before, for it can be confusing for readers to see an illustration before it has been introduced.

Conclusion

The word "conclusion" has two related meanings. It can be defined as the final part of a document, often containing a summation of what has gone before. It can also be defined as a judgement, or deduction, that is reached through a process of argumentation and logic. Taken together, these two meanings encapsulate the content and purpose of the concluding section of a thesis.

The conclusion begins by summarizing the findings of the research and discussing their significance. It also returns to the hypothesis or research question set out earlier in the thesis, and addresses the all-important "So what?" question. What do the findings actually *mean*? What are their implications? Are they significant, and if so, why? What deductions or conclusions can be drawn from them?

Just as the introduction proceeded from the broad to the narrow, so should the conclusion proceed from the narrow to the broad, moving beyond summation, analysis, and discussion of the findings to a broader contextualization of the study. This contextualization might, for example, relate the findings to wider debates and ideas on the subject, as set out in the literature review. It might question earlier writings or theories on the subject, based on the evidence that has been presented. It might also point to areas for future research.

It is important to highlight any new knowledge that has emerged from the study, and the significance of that knowledge. To do this is not arrogance or conceit, but a necessary part of good scholarship. It should not be left to the reader to try to work out why a study is significant, and what it adds to the existing body of knowledge. An approach that fails to point this out is as flawed as one that exaggerates the findings.

Back Matter

The back matter follows the main text and includes the endnotes (if used instead of footnotes), the bibliography (referred to in APA referencing as the list of references), and the appendices (if included in the thesis). The endnotes might also be located at the end of each chapter, rather than clustered at the end of the thesis.

Endnotes

A discussion of endnotes (and footnotes) has already been provided in chapter 5, "Writing a Research Proposal." Readers are referred to the earlier discussion when assembling the endnotes for the thesis.

166 Postgraduate Research in Music

Bibliography/Reference List
Readers are referred to the extensive discussion of referencing in chapter 5, and to the referencing models provided in appendices A and B.

Appendices
Readers are referred to the guidelines for appendices which are set out in chapter 5.

Formatting

Matters of formatting have arisen in a number of places in this chapter. Such considerations also extend to the thesis as a whole, for the way in which a thesis is formatted and presented undoubtedly has a bearing upon how it is perceived.

In formatting, as in so many matters of scholarship, there is a plethora of different approaches. The following guidelines are based upon four principles: readability, comprehensibility, neatness, and consistency. These guidelines overlap in various ways with those set out in the *Chicago Manual of Style*, the *Publication Manual of the American Psychological Association*, Turabian's *A Manual for Writers of Research Papers, Theses and Dissertations*, the *MHRA Style Guide*, the *MLA* Handbook, and Irvine's *Writing About Music*.[5] It is important to apply a single approach consistently, whether that of a particular style guide, that of the institution of enrolment, or that set out in the following discussion.[6]

Margins

The top, bottom, and right margins should be one inch (2.54cm) wide. The left margin should be wider to allow for binding of the thesis (1.75 inches, or 4.5 cm).

Justification of Margins

The left margin is justified. The right margin is generally not justified ("ragged"), although some scholars find it neater to right-justify as well. Right justification, however, may distort some of the line spacings.

Font and Font Size

A clear font should be selected, such as Times New Roman 12-point. The same font should be used throughout a thesis, with the possible exception of headings, sub-headings, tables, and other illustrations, which may be set in different fonts to differentiate them from the main text.

Line Spacing

The following elements are either 1.5 or double spaced: abstract, lists in the front matter, preface, acknowledgements, main text, and appendices. There are differing approaches to the remaining elements. The guidelines set out in table 6.4 prioritize readability and economy. If these guidelines are inconsistent with the style guide that is being followed for other matters, the style guide should be followed to ensure consistency in all matters.

Table 6.4. Line spacing in a thesis

1.5 or double spacing	Single spacing
Abstract	Block quotations
Lists in the front matter (tables, illustrations, etc.)	Footnotes and endnotes (with a blank line between each note)
Preface	
Acknowledgements	Table and figure captions
Main text	Notes or sources cited below illustrations
Appendices (but an appendix from another source follows the spacing of the original source)	Bibliography/reference list (with blank lines between entries)
	Text within tables
	Lists in appendices

Begin Each Major Element on a New Page

Each chapter begins on a new page, as do other major elements such as the preface, introduction, bibliography, and each appendix.

Headings

Headings encapsulate the structure of a thesis and make it easier for readers to follow the flow of thought. A thesis gains in clarity through the addition of headings.

168   Postgraduate Research in Music

Differentiated headings reflect the position of a section or sub-section within the structural hierarchy of a thesis. Headings that sit higher in the structural hierarchy (for example, major sections within chapters) are indicated by such things as larger font size, capital letters, headline-style capitalization, and bold typeface; headings that sit lower in the structural hierarchy (sections within sections) are characterized variously by a smaller font size, lowercase letters, sentence-style capitalization, and italics. A sixteen-point, capitalized heading in bold therefore sits higher in the structural hierarchy than a twelve-point, sentence-style heading.

A maximum of four heading levels will generally suffice; more than four may confuse rather than clarify. Consistency is crucial in the formatting of headings, for the style of an individual heading signifies where the section fits within the overall structure of a chapter.

A hierarchy of headings can either be individually crafted or generated by computer software that provides a selection of differentiated heading styles (heading 1, heading 2, heading 3, etc.). Computer-generated headings offer two benefits: automatic formatting, and the insertion of appropriate spaces between the headings and the preceding and ensuing text.

Table 6.5 presents a typical hierarchy of headings. Four heading levels are included, each corresponding to a different structural level within the thesis.

Table 6.5. Hierarchy of headings

Level	Category	Example
Level 1 (centered on the page or left aligned)	Sections in the front matter (e.g. preface), chapter titles, and sections in the back matter (for example, bibliography)	**Cambria 16 Point, Bold**
Level 2 (left aligned)	Major sections within chapters	**Cambria 14 point, bold**
Level 3 (left aligned)	Sections within major sections	**Times New Roman, 12 point, bold**
Level 4 (left aligned)	Sub-sections within sections	*Times New Roman, 11 point, italics*

Indentation of Paragraphs

The first line of the opening paragraph of a chapter or section should be left-justified. The first line of each ensuing paragraph within the section is indented. The indentation can be accomplished either by using the tab key, or by creating an indent on the ruler bar in the top menu, with the indentation set at one centimeter or some other appropriate measure.

Exercises

Exercise 1: Critical Evaluation of an Existing Thesis

Using the "searching for sources" skills set out in chapters 2 and 3 of this book, locate a masters or doctoral thesis on a topic relevant to your area of research. The thesis should be at least 20,000 words in length. Alternatively, you may wish to return to the masters or doctoral thesis whose literature review you critically evaluated as exercise 2 of chapter 4. Critically evaluate the content of the thesis, using the following questions as the basis of your evaluation. Restrict the evaluation to no more than 1,500 words. Bullet points may be used.

Front Matter
- Observe the sections in the front matter. To what extent do they adhere to, or differ from, the guidelines set out in this chapter? Is the ordering of sections logical? Do you have any suggestions for improvement?
- Comment on the effectiveness of the abstract, comparing it with the guidelines set out in both this chapter and chapter 5. Observe how long it is; which information is included; whether it is set as a single paragraph or multiple paragraphs; which person, tense, and voice are used; and whether it gives a clear indication of what the thesis is about.
- How has the table of contents been formatted? Have capitalization and indentation been used to good effect? If numerical and/or alphabetical labeling have been used, is there a systematic hierarchy of numerals and/or letters? Are the page numbers justified right? Do they correspond accurately to the page numbers in the body of the thesis? Is the ordering of content logical?

170 Postgraduate Research in Music

- Observe the style and content of the preface and acknowledgments. Identify three things you might seek to emulate, or not emulate, in your own thesis.

Chapters
Introduction

- Critically evaluate the introductory chapter of the thesis, using the guidelines set out in this chapter to inform your evaluation. Observe which of the following sections it contains: contextual background; hypothesis or research question; literature review; aims and rationale; scope of the study; methodology; definitions of key terminology; structure of the thesis. Has anything been left out that should be there? Has anything been included that should not be there? Is there a smooth and logical flow of ideas from one section to the next?
- Compare the introduction and the abstract. Do they overlap, and if so, how? Do they differ, and if so, how?

Presentation of Research Findings

- Critically evaluate the chapters in which the findings are set out. How are the data organized and presented? Is it logical? Effective? Why or why not?
- Is an argument built up systematically over the course of the thesis? If so, how is it done? If not, how is it not done?
- If illustrations are included, are they effective? Why or why not?

Conclusion

- Critically evaluate the conclusion. Does it provide an effective summary of the findings? Why or why not? Does it explore the implications of the findings and address the all-important "So what?" question? Does it move beyond summation to a broader discussion and contextualization of the findings? Does it highlight the significance of the study, and/or any new knowledge that has emerged? Does it point to areas for future research?

Back Matter

- Critically evaluate the bibliography/reference list. How is it organized? Which referencing style is used? Is the referencing style appropriate for the sub-discipline of the research? Is the referencing accurate and consistent?
- Are appendices included? If so, is the information they contain appropriate? Why or why not?

Exercise 2: Planning the Thesis Structure

Prepare a table of contents for your thesis, using, as a conceptual starting point, the contents page set out in figure 6.3 of this chapter. Work systematically from the macro to the micro levels of organization and address the following questions:

- Which front matter will be included, and in which order?
- What will each chapter deal with?
- What is the optimal ordering of chapters?
- Which sections and sub-sections will be included within each chapter?
- What is the optimal sequencing of the sections and sub-sections?
- Which back matter will be included, and in which order?

Include brief, appropriate titles for the chapters and for the sections and sub-sections within them.

Reading List

Some of the sources in this reading list span more than one subject area. In such cases, the source will be cited in each of the areas in which it is relevant. This duplication ensures that key sources will not be overlooked in any particular area.

Writing a Thesis

Booth, Wayne C., Gregory C. Colomb, Joseph M. Williams, Joseph Bizup, and William T. Fitzgerald. *The Craft of Research*. 4th ed. Chicago: University of Chicago Press, 2016.

Dunleavy, Patrick. *Authoring a PhD: How to Plan, Draft, Write and Finish a Doctoral Thesis or Dissertation*. Basingstoke: Palgrave Macmillan, 2003.

"Graduate Research & Writing: Reporting and Discussing your Findings." Monash University. Accessed July 29, 2021. https://www.monash.edu/rlo/graduate-research-writing/write-the-thesis/writing-the-thesis-chapters/reporting-and-discussing-your-findings.

High, Chris, and Jane Montague. "Planning and Organizing Your Research." In *Doing Postgraduate Research*, 2nd ed., edited by Stephen Potter, 92–113. London: Sage, 2006.

Morley, John. "Academic Phrasebank." University of Manchester. Accessed May 26, 2021. https://www.phrasebank.manchester.ac.uk.

Phillips, Estelle M., Derek Salman Pugh, and Colin Johnson. *How To Get a PhD: A Handbook for Students and Their Supervisors*. 6th ed. Maidenhead, Berkshire: McGraw-Hill Education, 2015.

Turabian, Kate. *A Manual for Writers of Research Papers, Theses and Dissertations: Chicago Style for Students and Researchers*. 9th ed. Chicago: University of Chicago Press, 2018.

172 Postgraduate Research in Music

Editorial Matters

Chicago Manual of Style: The Essential Guide for Writers, Editors, and Publishers. 17th ed. Chicago: University of Chicago Press, 2017.

New Oxford Style Manual. Oxford: Oxford University Press, 2016.

Publication Manual of the American Psychological Association. 7th ed. Washington, DC: American Psychological Association, 2020.

Turabian, Kate. *A Manual for Writers of Research Papers, Theses and Dissertations: Chicago Style for Students and Researchers*. 9th ed. Chicago: University of Chicago Press, 2018.

Formatting

Chicago Manual of Style: The Essential Guide for Writers, Editors, and Publishers. 17th ed. Chicago: University of Chicago Press, 2017.

Irvine, Demar. *Irvine's Writing About Music*. Revised by Mark A. Radice. 3rd ed. Portland, Oregon: Amadeus Press, 1999.

MLA Handbook, 8th ed. New York: The Modern Language Association of America, 2016.

Publication Manual of the American Psychological Association. 7th ed. Washington, DC: American Psychological Association, 2020.

Richardson, Brian, Robin Aizlewood, Derek F. Connon, Malcolm Cook, Gerard Lowe, Graham Nelson, and Chloe E. M. Paver. *MHRA Style Guide: A Handbook for Authors and Editors*. 3rd ed. London: Modern Humanities Research Association, 2015. See also *MHRA Style Guide Online*. Accessed June 9, 2021. http://www.mhra.org.uk/style.

Turabian, Kate. *A Manual for Writers of Research Papers, Theses and Dissertations: Chicago Style for Students and Researchers*. 9th ed. Chicago: University of Chicago Press, 2018.

Illustrations

Cowdery, James R., Carl Skoggard, and Barbara Dobbs Mackenzie. *How to Write About Music: The RILM Manual of Style*. 2nd ed. New York: Répertoire International de Littérature Musicale, 2006.

Holoman, D. Kern. *Writing About Music: A Style Sheet*. 3rd ed. Oakland, California: University of California Press, 2014.

Irvine, Demar. *Irvine's Writing About Music*. Revised by Mark A. Radice. 3rd ed. Portland, Oregon: Amadeus Press, 1999.

"Keeping it simple: Four myths on data presentation." Accessed July 29, 2021. http://www.plain figures.com/downloads/four_myths_of_data_presentation.pdf.

Publication Manual of the American Psychological Association. 7th ed. Washington, DC: American Psychological Association, 2020.

"Reporting Results." University of Manchester. Accessed July 29, 2021. http://www.phraseb ank.manchester.ac.uk/reporting-results.

Tufte, Edward R. *The Visual Display of Quantitative Information*. 2nd ed. Cheshire, Connecticut: Graphics Press, 2001.

Turabian, Kate. *A Manual for Writers of Research Papers, Theses and Dissertations: Chicago Style for Students and Researchers*. 9th ed. Chicago: University of Chicago Press, 2018.

Wingell, Richard. *Writing about Music: An Introductory Guide*. 4th ed. Upper Saddle River, New Jersey: Pearson Prentice Hall, 2009.

Referencing

Chicago Manual of Style: The Essential Guide for Writers, Editors, and Publishers. 17th ed. Chicago: University of Chicago Press, 2017.

Publication Manual of the American Psychological Association. 7th ed. Washington, DC: American Psychological Association, 2020.

Sampsel, Laurie J. *Music Research: A Handbook*. 3rd ed. New York: Oxford University Press, 2019.

Turabian, Kate. *A Manual for Writers of Research Papers, Theses and Dissertations: Chicago Style for Students and Researchers*. 9th ed. Chicago: University of Chicago Press, 2018.

Other Sources Consulted

Huntingford, James. "Tasteful Piano Performance in Classic-Era Britain." Masters diss., Edith Cowan University, 2021.

Rogers, Victoria. "The Musical Language of Peggy Glanville-Hicks." PhD. diss., University of Western Australia, 2000.

Rogers, Victoria. "Avant-Garde or Postmodern? The Melody-Rhythm Concept in Peggy Glanville-Hicks's *Sinfonia da Pacifica*." In *Analytical Essays on Music by Women Composers: Concert Music, 1900–1960*, edited by Laurel Parsons and Brenda Ravenscroft, 229–54. New York: Oxford University Press, 2022.

7

Writing a Thesis Part 2

Style in Academic Writing

Chapter 6 explored the first aspect of writing a thesis: content, together with its organization and presentation. Chapter 7 examines the second: style in academic writing. The academic style is a particular way of writing. It is concerned with the exposition and analysis of facts, and with rhetoric—in other words, with argumentation and persuasion.[1] It uses logic to explain and discuss the evidence that is presented, and to argue a case that establishes new knowledge of some kind. As such it needs a special style, one that is formal, considered, and objective. This chapter discusses key elements of the academic style, and examines the stylistically appropriate use of language within an academic context.

Key Elements of the Academic Style

Regardless of the area in which the research is undertaken, there are several key elements that characterize the academic style. These elements can usefully be grouped into seven categories: (a) defining terms; (b) the notion of argument; (c) evidence and the analytical process; (d) objectivity; (e) unity and cohesion; (f) quoting sources; and (g) the avoidance of plagiarism. These categories will now be discussed in turn.

Defining Terms

In the academic style, terms are defined when they cannot be assumed to be common knowledge within a discipline, or when they are used in a particular way. Defining terms is important because writer and reader need to share the same understanding. Without the clarity that definitions provide, confusion can easily arise.

Definitions can be located in the text itself, or in footnotes or endnotes—always, of course, at first mention of a term. If a thesis includes a number of

Postgraduate Research in Music. Victoria Rogers, Oxford University Press. © Oxford University Press 2024.
DOI: 10.1093/oso/9780197616031.003.0008

terms that need to be defined, they might, as an alternative, be aggregated in a definitions page in the front matter of the thesis or set out in the methodology.

The Notion of Argument

The term "argument" is generally used to mean a disagreement between people. There is, however, a further meaning, and it is this that applies to academic writing. In an academic context, the term "argument" is used to refer to "a coherent series of reasons, statements, or facts intended to support or establish a point of view."[2] The argument is conducted through the presentation, analysis, and discussion of the research data (evidence) and runs as a thread through a thesis, bringing continuity and cohesion to the writing as a whole.

Playing the role of devil's advocate is important in assembling an argument. Any possible weaknesses in an argument need to be anticipated and nullified through such expressions as: Whilst it might be suggested that . . . , the facts indicate . . .

Evidence and the Analytical Process

Evidence is information that is presented to support an argument. In music research evidence takes many different forms, including statistical data sets, data from interviews, musical examples, different editions of scores, historical treatises, newspaper articles, correspondence, recordings, and personal observations through reflective practice.

The presentation of evidence (as discussed in chapter 6 in the section entitled "Presentation and Analysis of the Research Findings") is followed by analysis and discussion. Significant findings need to be explored, and the implications of the data need to be explained. There might, for example, be notable continuities, or contradictions, in the evidence. Any inconsistencies need to be accounted for; results that do not fit a pattern must not be ignored, for they are important and often yield a rich discussion. Comparison and analogy are also important. They locate the findings in a wider context and help to make sense of them. The neoclassical works of a mid–twentieth-century composer, for example, may usefully be discussed within the context of Stravinskian neoclassicism; and a study of choral participation by sufferers from Parkinson's disease might be compared with similar studies of choral participation by people with Alzheimer's disease.

176   Postgraduate Research in Music

The "So what?" question is implicit in this. How do the research findings relate to the hypothesis or research question set out at the beginning of the thesis? Is there a broader context in which they need to be understood? How do they relate to other research? What conclusions can be drawn? Are the findings significant? What does the information actually *mean*? These questions, which incorporate aspects of the critical thinking guidelines set out in chapter 4, provide a framework for analyzing the research findings. The analytical scalpel should be applied systematically to each segment of the research findings, and, of course, in the concluding chapter of the thesis.

The following checklist can be used as a guide for the analytical process:

- Which significant points emerge from the data?
- Are there continuities, contradictions, and/or inconsistencies in the data?
- What are the implications of the data?
- How do the findings and conclusions relate to the research question or hypothesis set out at the beginning of the thesis?
- Is there a broader context within which the findings can be located, and within which they can be better understood? How do they relate to other research?
- So what? Why are the findings significant? What conclusions can be drawn? What do the findings actually *mean*?

Objectivity

Academic research has traditionally been grounded in the idea of objectivity—the notion of maintaining distance between the observer and the phenomenon being observed, free from preconceived notions and unaffected by personal beliefs or opinions. This idea has less currency in contemporary scholarship, particularly in the social sciences and humanities where subjectivity is often seen as an implicit part of the research process. This, however, does not offer a carte blanche for researchers to indulge in excessive subjectivity. Even when the findings of a study are overtly subjective, as in reflective practice, objectivity—or distancing—is necessary in the analysis of the findings, and evidence is needed to support any conclusions that are drawn.

Although the notion of objectivity is less credible than it once was, it is important to remember why it emerged in the first place. It was seen as a mechanism for arriving at fact, or truth. Its modus operandi was, and remains, rigorous enquiry.

Unity and Cohesion

Like any piece of writing, a thesis must hold together—in other words, it needs unity and cohesion. This happens at two levels: the macro, and the micro.

At a macro level, a thesis must form a unified whole. This is achieved through the logical ordering of chapters, and by ensuring that the thread of the argument is ever present. The thread of the argument is the flow of ideas that leads from the hypothesis or research question, through the research findings and discussion, to the conclusion of the thesis. The thread may be invisible but it must always be present, underpinning the case that is built up over the course of a thesis. The "So what?" question must be a constant companion, questioning why every piece of information is included and what it adds to the case that is being assembled. This ensures that the argument does not veer off track, and that the thesis is unified at a macro level.

A thesis must also be cohesive at a micro level. This is achieved through the logical sequencing of content within each chapter, and through the use of connecting words and phrases to maintain continuity from sentence to sentence, from paragraph to paragraph, and from section to section. This "connective tissue" can be used to indicate continuation, or elaboration, or a new direction (see table 4.3 in chapter 4 for a list of connecting words and phrases). A related technique is to use a repeated word or phrase as a bridge from one sentence, or segment, to the next; paraphrased expressions can also be used in this way. Above all, cohesion is created through the flow of ideas; one thing must follow on logically from another, without disjunctions in the text.

Signposts are a further aspect of unity and cohesion. In an academic context, a signpost is a sentence or phrase that links a paragraph, section, or chapter to the flow of the argument, or to the broader enquiry of the thesis. The opening sentence of this paragraph is a signpost, reminding readers that this section of the chapter is about unity and cohesion. These conceptual landmarks can look forward or back, referring either to content that is yet to come, or to something that has already been presented. Without them, readers (and writers) can easily become lost.

Closely related to signposts are summative statements—sentences or paragraphs that draw the threads together at the ends of sections and chapters, going beyond the detail to ask the "So what?" question. In doing so, the hypothesis or research question is kept constantly in mind and the thread of the argument is maintained. There is a difference between drawing the threads together at the ends of sections and chapters and the overall summation in the concluding chapter of a thesis. The section-by-section and chapter-by-chapter summaries should be largely restricted to the content that immediately

178 Postgraduate Research in Music

precedes them. In the final chapter, the findings are discussed in a broader context.

Logic of chronology also plays a role in ensuring that a thesis is unified and cohesive. Chronologies typically run from earliest to latest. A discussion of the stylistic periods of a particular composer, for example, usually flows from the early to the late works to reflect a stylistic development over time. Chronological disjunctions steer an argument off course and should be avoided.

The techniques through which unity and cohesion can be achieved are summarized in the following guidelines:

1. Maintaining the thread of the argument:
   - Construct a logical ordering of content that enables a case to be built up progressively from the hypothesis or research question through to the concluding chapter of the thesis. Every idea and every piece of evidence must follow on logically from the preceding one to maintain the thread of the argument.
   - Keep the hypothesis or research question constantly in mind, referring to it in a direct or oblique way from time to time throughout the thesis.
   - Keep the "So what?" question constantly in mind. Ask constantly: "What does this *mean*? What does it contribute to the argument?"
   - Include summative paragraphs at the ends of sections and chapters before moving onto a new section or chapter. These summations include critical analysis, critical evaluation, and critical synthesis.
2. Creating continuity from sentence to sentence, from paragraph to paragraph, from section to section, and from chapter to chapter. This can be done by:
   - Using connecting words and phrases to link one sentence to the next, signaling either the continuation or elaboration of an idea, or a departure in a new direction.
   - Repeating a word or phrase as a bridge from one sentence, paragraph, or section to the next. Paraphrased expressions can also be used.
3. Using signposts to link segments of information to the flow of the argument, or to the broader enquiry of the thesis.
4. Ensuring that the chronology is sequential.

Quoting Sources

Sources are quoted for four reasons in academic writing: to locate the research within the existing body of writings; to provide evidence that supports the argument being presented; to precipitate discussion; and to avoid plagiarism (see the ensuing section for a discussion of plagiarism). Quoting sources is an important aspect of the academic style, yet its deployment is often a source of confusion. The following guidelines seek to dispel this confusion, dealing in turn with the two ways in which sources can be quoted: as direct quotations, and through paraphrasing.

Direct Quotations

A direct quotation is a literal replication of content from another source. Such content may derive from written sources; from interview or survey data; from websites, social media, and blogs; from radio programs, film, or videos; or from communication such as email.

There are two types of direct quotation: those that run on in the text (referred to as run-on, or run-in, quotations); and block quotations (also referred to as indented quotations). The difference between them is essentially one of length. A run-on quotation is shorter and is subsumed within a sentence, with the quoted material enclosed by quotation marks. Block quotations are longer and comprise around thirty-five words or more. They are indented, set in a smaller font, and not enclosed by quotation marks. In the Chicago style, block quotations are single spaced and separated from the surrounding text by an extra space above and below. In the APA style, they are double spaced and not separated from the surrounding text by an extra space above and below.

Direct quotations range in length from a single word to one or more paragraphs. If a quotation involves the literal citing of paragraph after paragraph of an original source to "let it speak for itself," however, it is replication, not research. Only in special circumstances, and for very good reason, should this be done. It is the task of the writer, not the reader, to extract the salient information from a source.

Single or Double Quotation Marks

Whether to enclose run-on quotations by double or single quotation marks is a matter of style. American scholarship generally uses double, and single within double. The so-called British style reverses this practice and use single to enclose a quotation, and double within single. Block quotations do not need quotation marks because the indentation in itself indicates that the material is quoted from another source. Quotations within block quotations are enclosed by double quotation marks in American scholarship, and by single quotation marks in the British style.

180 Postgraduate Research in Music

Introducing and Quitting Quotations

All quotations, regardless of their length, must be woven seamlessly into the text. They must be foreshadowed in the text that precedes them and followed by text that emerges smoothly from them. There are techniques that can be used for this, as illustrated in the following examples.[3]

> *Technique 1: Using the first part of a sentence to introduce an idea that is completed in the quotation in the second part*
> She condemned serialism as "a camouflage for the ungifted: its expressive limitations and technical cerebrality have become an art medium only in the hands of the very few who, by breaking its tenets, have transcended its grip."

> *Technique 2: Splitting a quotation into two parts by interspersing an attributing phrase between them*
> "Nothing," she wrote, "is guaranteed to alienate the affections of an audience so fast as the acid and despairing sounds of a twelve-toner."

> *Technique 3: Anticipating what is to come in a block quotation by using some of the same words or ideas in the text that introduces it. In this example, "a viable way forward" in the introductory sentence corresponds to "a more fruitful evolution," and the "horizontal concept" corresponds to "the contrapuntal"*
> Yet despite her condemnation of the method, and although referring to Schoenberg as "the one I hate most," she nonetheless credited him with creating a viable way forward through re-introducing the horizontal concept:
>> The serial led in the end to a more fruitful evolution in that it turned us from the vertical concept and the harmonic structure to the contrapuntal. But of course the row was wrong. You cannot have all twelve sounds. It's like building a solid concrete building with no windows.

> *Technique 4: Creating a seamless transition from a quotation to the text that follows. In the following example, words from the quotations are repeated in the content that follows: "seven months" from the block quotation, and "record" from the run-on quotation*
> Glanville-Hicks expressed her misgivings in a letter to Diana Menuhin (wife of Yehudi):
>> Had I been a man I'd have told San Francisco that a seven-month deadline for a full length opera was impossible, absolutely impossible. Being a woman I did not have

that privilege, as it would have been ascribed to my sex that I had not been able to make a deadline that no man would accept. Thus, the deadline will be made.

Seven months and eleven days after starting work on the opera, Glanville-Hicks penned the final notes. "Dear Larry," she wrote to Durrell, "Sappho has sung her last aria—the curtain is down and the house lights are up! Seven months and eleven days—a record!" It was a record that Glanville-Hicks was to rue. *Sappho* was rejected for performance by the commissioning body and the opera remained unperformed until 2012, when a recording of the work was made.

Punctuation Preceding a Quotation

There are four possibilities when punctuating the end of a phrase or sentence that precedes a quotation: a comma, a colon, a period, or no punctuation at all.[4]

A comma is typically used after verbs such as observed, responded, and asked. A colon is sometimes used as an alternative to set the quotation off in sharper relief.

> Smith observed, "This young artist is set for a glittering career."
> Smith observed: "This young artist is set for a glittering career."

If a quotation is preceded by a complete sentence, a colon is generally used. A period is sometimes used as an alternative; a colon is preferable, however, because the two punctuation marks mean different things. A period signifies the conclusion of an idea; a colon signifies the opening out of thought, as in the following example:

> The critic's response was laudatory: "This young artist is set for a glittering career."

If a quotation is introduced by the word "that," or by a word or phrase with a similar function, no punctuation is needed.

> The critic observed that "this young artist is set for a glittering career."

Punctuation Following a Quotation

A key question when punctuating the end of a quotation is which comes first: the closing quotation mark, or the punctuation mark. The answer is that it depends. It depends upon which punctuation mark is used, and whether the American or British style is followed. In the context of this discussion, it

182   Postgraduate Research in Music

is useful to group the punctuation marks into three categories: commas and periods; semicolons and colons; and exclamation marks and question marks.

Both the Chicago and APA styles locate commas and periods before the closing quotation mark, regardless of whether they form part of the quoted material. This is sometimes referred to as the American style. The so-called British style, on the other hand, locates commas and periods after the closing quotation mark unless the punctuation is part of the quotation itself, in which case it is located before the closing quotation mark. Whether to follow the American or British approach is a stylistic choice which, once made, must be followed consistently.

Semicolons and colons always follow a closing quotation mark because they signal an opening out of thought that happens not within but beyond the quotation.

Exclamation marks and question marks are included before the closing quotation mark if they are part of the quotation. If they are extraneous to the quotation, they are placed outside the closing quotation mark, as in the following example:

> To whom is "we" referring in such expressions as: "We can see, here, an unexpected resolution of the augmented sixth chord"?

Changing a Punctuation Mark at the End of a Quotation

A punctuation mark at the end of a quotation may need to be changed to conform to correct syntactical usage. It is acceptable to do this, provided there is no change to the meaning of the quoted material. If, for example, a semicolon or colon were to conclude the quoted segment in the original source, it would be replaced by a comma, a period, or nothing at all, as appropriate.

Capitalization and Lowercase

It is acceptable in both the Chicago and APA styles to change capital letters to lowercase and vice versa at the beginning of a quotation (run-on or block), provided the change complies with correct grammatical usage. If a quotation is integrated into a sentence, for example through the word "that," the first letter of the quotation is set in lowercase regardless of how it appears in the original source.

> *Original*
> "The art of music above all the other arts is the expression of the soul of a nation."[5]

> *Quotation integrated into a sentence*
> Vaughan Williams observed that "the art of music above all the other arts is the expression of the soul of a nation."

Writing a Thesis Part 2 **183**

Omissions, Insertions, and Emphases

Sometimes it is better to omit part of a quotation so that readers can focus on the relevant points. These omissions are indicated by an ellipsis (three successive dots). An extensive discussion of the ellipsis is provided in appendix F.

There are also times when material needs to be inserted into a quotation, either to clarify the meaning or to reduce the length of the quotation. In such cases, the added or amended content is enclosed by square brackets.

> "It [music] may be defined as the displacement of air."

An error is acknowledged by the word [sic], or [*sic*], in square brackets, immediately after the errant text.

> "The players will be performing Haydn's 'Quark' [sic] Quartet in the first half of the program."

When a writer wishes to emphasize part of a quotation, the words are italicized and followed immediately by [emphasis added], in square brackets before the closing punctuation.

> "Music may be understood as a combination of sounds, but it is perhaps better defined as *the displacement of air* [emphasis added]."

Citations for Quotations

The sources of quotations must be provided, using an appropriate referencing style (see chapter 5 for a discussion of referencing). In notes and bibliography referencing, the superscript number is located at the end of a sentence if the quoted material relates to the entire sentence, or directly following the quotation within a sentence if the remainder of the sentence is not attributable to that source. The superscript number for a block quotation is located at the end of the quotation.

Of the following three quotations, the first two are run-on with the superscript number located appropriately in each case (respectively in the middle and at the end of the sentence). The third is a block quotation, with the superscript number located at the end of the quotation. The superscript numbers in these examples are illustrative only and do not point to actual footnotes or endnotes.[6]

> *Example 1*
> Varèse's rejection of harmony as a "dated decorative device" and his advocacy of rhythm as "the starting point for new organic design"[1] resonated strongly with her.

184 Postgraduate Research in Music

Example 2

It was "not a musical form but a mechanical gadget," in her analysis.[2]

Example 3

The serial led in the end to a more fruitful evolution in that it turned us from the vertical concept and the harmonic structure to the contrapuntal. But of course the row was wrong. You cannot have all twelve sounds. It's like building a solid concrete building with no windows.[3]

In APA author-date referencing, the parenthetical (in-text) citation includes the author, year, and page number. The first two of the following examples are run-on quotations; the second is an alternative way of citing the same source. The third example is a block quotation, double spaced as is the convention in the APA style.[7]

Example 1

She condemned atonality as "a camouflage for the ungifted: its expressive limitations and technical cerebrality have become an art medium only in the hands of the very few who, by breaking its tenets, have transcended its grip" (Glanville-Hicks, 1966, p. 201).

Example 2

Glanville-Hicks (1966) condemned atonality as "a camouflage for the un-gifted: its expressive limitations and technical cerebrality have become an art medium only in the hands of the very few who, by breaking its tenets, have transcended its grip" (p. 201).

Example 3

America has a tiny minority of composers, often referred to as exotic, who are

not content to make a new arrangement of the old sounds or a fresh version

of the old forms. They want to change the whole sound and substance of

the musical language and find new structural principles to govern their new

materials (Glanville-Hicks, 1950, p. 112).

Referencing a Quotation Within a Quotation

When citing a source that includes a quotation from another source (a "source within a source"), the question that arises is whether to acknowledge both sources in the citation. The best approach in such cases is to consult the source within the source and to cite it directly. If the source within the source cannot be located and thus cited directly, it is acknowledged within the citation for the "secondary source," using the words "quoted in," or "as cited in." In the Chicago style, full bibliographic details are given for both the "primary" and "secondary" sources. In the APA style, full bibliographic details are given only for the "secondary" source.[8]

The following examples illustrate the referencing of sources within sources in the Chicago and APA styles. The abbreviation N indicates footnote; B indicates a bibliographic reference.

Chicago style[9]
N: Peggy Glanville-Hicks, "Tapesichord: The Music of Whistle and Bang," *Vogue* 122 (July 1953), 108, quoted in Victoria Rogers, *The Music of Peggy Glanville-Hicks* (Farnham: Ashgate, 2009), 90.

B: Glanville-Hicks, Peggy. "Tapesichord: The Music of Whistle and Bang." *Vogue* 122 (July 1953): 80–81, 108. Quoted in Victoria Rogers, *The Music of Peggy Glanville-Hicks* (Farnham: Ashgate, 2009).[10]

APA style
In-text citation: (Glanville-Hicks, 1953, p. 108, as cited in Rogers, 2009, p. 90)
B: Rogers, Victoria. (2009). *The Music of Peggy Glanville-Hicks*. Ashgate.

Quotations from Interview or Survey Data
Citations are not needed for quotations from interview or survey data that have been generated by the research. Interviewees are simply referred to in the text (for example, Participant 1 reported . . .). This practice ensures that the participants remain anonymous.

Paraphrasing
Paraphrasing is the second way in which sources can be cited. It involves the rewording of a passage in a more succinct form, capturing the key content and leaving out information that is less relevant to the context of the para-phrase. If the original source is succinct, compelling, and entirely relevant, a direct quotation should be used. If the original is long and/or contains infor-mation that is not relevant to the thesis, paraphrasing may be a better option. Paraphrasing can also be helpful when the meaning of an original source is difficult to unravel.

The skillful deployment of paraphrasing can be facilitated by the following process:

186 Postgraduate Research in Music

- Extract the essential ideas from the source. Jot them down. Be careful not to leave out key content, thereby distorting the meaning of the original.
- Make a list of synonyms for the key ideas. A good thesaurus can be helpful, such as the WordHippo website (https://www.wordhippo.com).
- Consider how the ideas will be shaped in the paraphrased content. Will the ordering of content change? Will ideas from different paragraphs, or even different sections of the original, be conflated into one or more sentences?
- Talk the paraphrased content out loud and jot the ideas down in everyday language. Also consider whether the paraphrased content will be interspersed with direct quotations.
- Rewrite the paraphrased content in an academically appropriate style (see the discussion below on language usage in the academic style).
- Ensure that the wording of the paraphrase is substantially different from the original source, otherwise it is plagiarized—even if the source is acknowledged.[11]
- Be sure to connect the paraphrased segments with words, phrases or sentences that create continuity.
- Acknowledge the source of each paraphrased segment.

The following passage from Charles Rosen's book, *The Classical Style*, illustrates the principles—and the challenges—of paraphrasing. Rosen's text is quite dense and the meaning is not easy to untangle. The first challenge is therefore to work out what Rosen is actually saying. The next challenge is to decide what to omit from the original, and how to organize the paraphrased and directly quoted content.

Original quotation
"It is often difficult to distinguish the defining characteristics from the acquired characteristics of a form, partly because as time goes on the latter tend to become the former. That is, we must distinguish between what an eighteenth-century composer would have called a sonata (how far he would have stretched the term and at what point he would have said, 'This is not a sonata, but a fantasia') and the way sonatas were generally written (the patterns they gradually fell into and which were later unhappily considered as rules). The line between the two is often blurred, and it is doubtful if even the composers of the period would have been able to draw it with any certainty."[12]

Paraphrase
In his book *The Classical Style*, Charles Rosen observes that musical forms change over time, and that what a form becomes is often what defines it.[13] In

Rosen's analysis, there is therefore a need to differentiate between "what an eighteenth-century composer would have called a sonata" and "the patterns [sonatas] gradually fell into."[14]

Avoidance of Plagiarism

The avoidance of plagiarism is one of the most fundamental principles of academic writing. Plagiarism can be defined as "presenting, intentionally or unintentionally, the ideas or work of another person as one's own ideas or work, without appropriate referencing or acknowledgement."[15] Whether the plagiarism is intentional or unintentional makes no difference. Whether the ideas arise from print, visual, online, electronic, or some other source, also makes no difference. Plagiarism is intellectual theft, for which there are severe penalties—including failure of a thesis. Paraphrased material (the restatement of a text using different words) is not exempt. Here, too, the source of the information must be acknowledged.

Plagiarized information can be distinguished from common knowledge. That J. S. Bach was born in 1685 and died in 1750, for example, is common knowledge. It is a widely known fact, the source of which does not need to be cited. If an idea or fact is uniquely attributable to a particular source, however, that source must be cited. Notwithstanding this apparent dichotomy, the line between plagiarized content and common knowledge is not always clear in practice. If there is any doubt, caution should be exercised and sources cited.

Plagiarism can be avoided by observing a few simple rules:

- During the note taking phase of a research project, record the full bibliographic details of each source. Meticulously document the page numbers of both direct quotes and paraphrased material, and be sure to enclose direct quotes within quotation marks. Any of your own ideas that are generated by a source should be distinguished clearly from the summarized material. This fastidious attention to detail minimizes the chance of inadvertent plagiarism.
- Ensure that the wording of a paraphrase is markedly different from the original, and that the source is cited appropriately. If the wording is not markedly different, the paraphrase is considered to be plagiarized, even if the source is acknowledged.[16]
- Even if only a few words are taken directly from a source, those words must be enclosed by quotation marks (and of course cited appropriately). Failure to enclose the words in quotation marks is considered to be plagiarism, even if the source is cited.[17]

- Be careful when your text includes two consecutive sentences that are attributable to the same source. If a citation were only provided for the second sentence, the first one would be considered to be plagiarized, albeit unintentionally. Such plagiarism can be avoided by providing consecutive citations, or by combining the two sentences into one, with a single citation.
- Meticulously document every source to which reference has been made (see chapter 5 for a discussion of referencing).

There is no need to plagiarize. A thesis is enhanced by citing the work of other scholars. It adds authority and credibility. Moreover, by the time the research is at the advanced stage of writing a thesis, the student scholar is a genuine authority on the topic. Ideas do not need to be pilfered from elsewhere. The greatest danger comes from inadvertent plagiarism, which can be avoided by the fastidious handling of sources and information.

Language Usage in the Academic Style

Just as there are a number of key elements that are intrinsic to the academic style, so too are there stylistically appropriate practices in the use of language. This section discusses nine of these practices: (1) precision and concision; (2) which person to use; (3) which tense to use; (4) which voice to use; (5) avoidance of contractions, colloquialisms, and clichés; (6) use of acronyms; (7) gender-neutral language; (8) italics for emphasis; and (9) matters of punctuation. The matter of grammar is a notable omission from this list. It is a subject so vast as to be beyond the scope of this book—yet it lies at the very heart of proficient language usage. Readers who have not received instruction in the mechanics of grammar would do well to seek such instruction.

Precision and Concision

Words, like musical notes, have the capacity to convey subtle nuances of meaning. Just as the flavor of an authentic cadence shifts slightly when either the root, third, or fifth of the triad is the uppermost note of the final chord, so too is meaning inflected slightly by the use of a word that is similar but subtly different in meaning from another one. The delight—and the dilemma—of words is that different words can convey more or less the same meaning;

"surprised," for example, is similar to astonished, but at the same time slightly different. Words must be used to convey the *precise* meaning that is intended; there is no place for approximation. Words need to be polished and finessed until they sparkle with clarity.

The ordering of words is equally important, for an incorrect ordering can confuse, or even distort, the intended meaning. This can be seen in the following example, the incorrect version of which is correct grammatically. The problem is that it does not convey the intended meaning with precision because the adverb "almost" is in the wrong place..

Incorrect version:
Jane almost arrived in time for the concert.

Correct version:
Jane arrived almost in time for the concert.

Sentences must be finessed with the same attention to detail. Overly long or complex sentences should be avoided unless, through the skillful ordering of words and use of punctuation, the sentence "breathes" in the right places. If a sentence is unduly long, consider splitting it into two shorter ones. Include a mix of sentence lengths, and remember that short, punchy sentences can make their point very effectively. Above all, don't try to sound academic! Yes, there is a particular style of writing that is used in an academic context— but being academic is not about writing long-winded sentences or filling the text with jargon. The best academic writing expresses complex ideas clearly, directly, and economically—in other words, with precision and concision. Complexity of thought is necessary; complexity of expression is not.

Consider the second of the following sentences. It may seem to be "academic" at first sight, but it is too long and contains too many qualifications and ideas. In short, it reads as gobbledygook.

The effectiveness of a chord progression consists of a mutual interplay between the sequence of chords and the apprehension of the listener. The mechanism through which this process takes place is that faculty or faculties of the mind, or certain powers of the mind, which affect, or are affected by, or which form a judgment of, the sensory impulses created by the displacement of air; and the historically contingent mode of subjectivity and the disposition of those subjective perceptions renegotiated by the endless forms of imagination through which apprehension is effected.[18]

190 Postgraduate Research in Music

Now consider, as a further example, the title of the flawed research proposal presented as exercise 2 in chapter 5:

A transcontinental investigation into the study of frog song looking at songs sung by frogs across different continents and using this information to forge a new postmodern style of composition

This title contains three repetitions: investigation/study of; transcontinental/different continents; and study of frog song/looking at songs sung by frogs. The first of these repetitions is also glaringly imprecise: an "investigation into the study of."

Precision and concision require constant vigilance and attention to a number of questions:

- Do the words convey the *precise* meaning that is intended?
- Are the sentences unwieldy in length or content?
- Which words, phrases, and sentences are unnecessary and can be excised?
- Which phrases and sentences can be conflated?

Reducing the number of words does not in itself lead to better writing, however. It can be taken too far. Connecting words and phrases, signposts, and words of explanation, for example, create a flow of ideas that is integral to polished, cohesive writing. They should not be excised. There is also the matter of personal style. Good writing has personality; it engages the reader. Consider, for example, the following sentence, which has been taken from the introduction to this book: "Every note is important; every word is important." This sentence could be reduced to: "Every note and word are important." The repetition in the first version, however, creates a greater impact. Writing that is devoid of personality, imagination, and engagement is not good writing. If these elements are omitted, the principle of concision has been taken too far. Working out what can be removed and what can remain is part of the challenge of good academic writing.

Which Person to Use?

As noted in chapter 4 ("Writing a Literature Review"), the term "person" refers to the pronoun that is used: I/we (first person); you (second person); or he/she/it/they (third person). Of these, the third person is employed through the entirety of a thesis. The second person is avoided because its role is to address people directly. The use of the first person is less clear-cut. Whilst it is inappropriate in the context of a literature review, there are differing schools of thought as to whether it should be used in other parts of a thesis.

Traditionally in music research, as in other areas of scholarship, the first-person singular was avoided because the subjectivity it encapsulated ran counter to the objectivity that was sought. More recently, however, the influence of the social sciences and the emergence of reflective practice have led to a loosening of the traditional approach. The first-person singular is now employed in some areas of music research to acknowledge what is seen as the implicit element of subjectivity in all research.

The best approach to the first person is to use it with discrimination. There are times when it needs to be used (for example, in reflective practice research), times when it might be used (for example, in a preface), and times when it is better avoided (for example, in reporting research findings). Some scholars use the term "the present writer" as a way of circumventing the issue. This, however, is a somewhat stilted expression, implying that there is also a past writer—which of course is nonsensical. This expression is not used often and is better avoided.

Related to the use of "I" is the deployment of "we," which is the plural of "I." The identity of "we," however, is never explained. To whom is "we" referring in such expressions as: "We can see, here, an unexpected resolution of the augmented sixth chord"? Not only is the identity of "we" never established; "we" also assumes that the readers' perceptions mirror those of the writer, and that the reader will join the writer in whatever is being proposed ("We move on now to consider . . . "). There is an implication of coziness, of familiarity, between writer and reader that is inappropriate in the context of a thesis—not least because some of the readers are the examiners. Indeed, "we" is inappropriate more broadly in academic writing, which—as noted at the beginning of this chapter—requires a style that is formal and objective. "We" is a mannerism that should be avoided.

The following examples illustrate three different ways of presenting the same information. The first example (in the first person) clothes the information in opinion. The second example ("the present writer") is somewhat clumsy; it is also grounded in opinion. The third example uses the passive voice to distance the writer from the phenomenon being observed ("appear to have been enhanced"; see the discussion below on the active and passive voices). This is an appropriate academic style.

192   Postgraduate Research in Music

First person
I believe that this approach to training has enhanced students' aural skills.

"The present writer"
It is the view of the present writer that this approach to training has enhanced students' aural skills.

Use of the passive voice
Students' aural skills appear to have been enhanced through this approach to training.

Which Tense to Use?

As noted in chapter 4 ("Writing a Literature Review"), tenses are concerned with the temporal (or time) aspect of an action—that is, whether the action takes place in the past, the present, or the future. The earlier discussion is now expanded to explore the tenses that are used when documenting the aims and methodology, and when reporting, discussing, and evaluating the research findings.

Documenting the Aims: Present Tense
The aims of a study are stated in the present tense. This provides a sense of immediacy, presenting the aims as both a present-moment event and an ongoing process. If the aims are set out numerically, each aim begins with an infinitive (the base form of a verb), for example "to ascertain," "to investigate" (see chapter 5, "Writing a Research Proposal," for a discussion of the numerical listing of aims).

> The aim of this study is to explore possible links between Blacking's musical compositions and his work as an ethnomusicologist and social anthropologist.

Documenting the Methodology: Present, and Present Perfect Tenses
Two tenses are typically used in the methodology section: the present, and the present perfect (present past). Of these, the present tense predominates.

> This study draws upon three analytic methods: formal analysis, basic shape analysis, and harmonic analysis.

The present perfect tense is used when discussing the methods that have been employed by other researchers. This tense describes an action that has happened once or many times in the past, and which may continue. It combines the present form of the verb "to have" (has/have) with a past participle (for example, "used").

> Other researchers have used a similar approach.

Reporting the Research Findings: Past Tense

The past tense is used to report and describe the research findings. This tense is appropriate because the actions that are being reported took place before the time of writing and have been completed.

> Fifty participants completed the questionnaire; of these, thirty took part in semi-structured, face-to-face interviews.

Discussing the Research Findings: Present Tense

The present tense is used when the research findings are discussed. This tense projects the discussion as a present-moment event, sometimes with ongoing implications.

> The analysis shows that . . .
> The study concludes that . . .
> Table 7.1 indicates that . . .
> The implications of these findings are profound, suggesting that . . .

The present tense is also used when research findings are accepted as being universally true, for example:

> Studies from around the world show perfect pitch to be a universal phenomenon, and this is no less the case in the present study.

Evaluating the Research Findings: Present, Future, and Conditional Tenses

The present tense predominates when the research findings are being evaluated. The future tense also plays an occasional role.

> The findings of this study are significant and will inform future research into Baroque ornamentation.

194   Postgraduate Research in Music

The conditional tense can also be useful, signaling what would, could, should, or might happen. The conditional clause is often introduced by the word "if."

> If the study were to be replicated with a larger sample, the results would be unlikely to differ.

Which Voice to Use?

As noted in chapter 4 ("Writing a Literature Review"), there are two voices that can be used in academic writing: the active voice, and the passive voice. The active voice is employed when the subject of a sentence is the one performing the action. When the passive voice is used, the sentence is reordered so that the subject is the recipient of the action. The verb is also different in the passive voice, which combines some form of the verb "to be" (for example, "is") with a past participle (for example, "discussed"). The following example serves as a reminder of the earlier discussion.

> *Active voice*:
> Broadwood manufactured English square pianos in the late eighteenth century.

> *Passive voice*:
> English square pianos were manufactured by Broadwood in the late eighteenth century.

Both voices have a role to play in writing a thesis, although the active voice is generally preferred because it is clear and direct. Notwithstanding this, the passive voice should not be disregarded. It changes the emphasis within a sentence and provides syntactical variation.

Avoidance of Contractions, Colloquialisms, and Clichés

Contractions, colloquialisms, and clichés are part of the lexicon of everyday speech. A contraction combines two words into one, using an apostrophe to indicate the missing letter(s)—for example, it's, there's, and we'll. Colloquialisms are words or expressions that are conversational in nature; "bloke," "dodgy," and "grog" are examples of colloquialisms. A cliché is an expression that has become trite through overuse. "You can't judge a book by its cover," and "he is as strong as an ox," are commonly encountered clichés. These are casual, informal ways of communicating and run counter to the formal, serious tone of academic writing. They should be avoided, and only incorporated into the text if they appear in a quotation from another source.

Use of Acronyms

An acronym is a word formed from the initial letters of a group of words, for example, historically informed performance (HIP). Acronyms are an economical way of referring repeatedly to multi-word titles and concepts and can be fashioned individually for particular contexts. They are commonly used in academic writing. An acronym should be written out at first mention, with the acronym following immediately in parentheses. In subsequent mentions, only the acronym is needed. An acronym is set in capital letters; there are no periods or spaces between the letters because the acronym is seen as a complete word in itself.

Gender-Neutral Language

Gendered language uses words in a way that is implicitly biased towards the male gender. It employs male pronouns (he/him/his) to refer to people in general; it also includes gender-specific nouns that implicitly exclude the female gender (for example, chairman). Taken literally, such language excludes around fifty per cent of the population. Terms such as "man's search for meaning," for example, imply that women do not search for meaning— which is self-evidently an absurd proposition. Gendered language should be avoided.

The use of male pronouns in a generic way is particularly problematic. They are sometimes replaced with clumsy paired pronouns (she and he, or he and she); pronoun amalgams are also used (he/she, s/he; his/her). Style guides generally avoid pronoun amalgams and suggest that they should only be used if there is no better alternative. Another possible solution is to replace a singular (male) pronoun with a plural, un-gendered pronoun ("they" or "their"). It is grammatically incorrect, however, to use a plural pronoun to refer to a singular subject.[19] Notwithstanding this, the practice is gradually gaining traction in academic writing and is now endorsed by the *Publication Manual* of the *American Psychological Association*. The *Chicago Manual of Style*, on the other hand, does not endorse the practice. The best solution is to rephrase the sentence, thereby avoiding the problem altogether.

Consider the following statement:

A student who mindlessly copies his teacher risks losing his own creative voice.

The term "student" is used here in a generic sense to refer to students in general—male and female. The problem lies with the male pronoun "his," for female students also risk losing their creative voices. There are a few ways in which this statement could be rephrased to be gender neutral.

Rephrasing 1
A student who mindlessly copies his/her teacher risks losing his/her own creative voice.

This rephrasing is gender-neutral. It is somewhat clumsy, however, and is better avoided.

Rephrasing 2
A student who mindlessly copies their teacher risks losing their own creative voice.

This rephrasing mixes a singular subject (student) with a plural pronoun (their). It is now gender-neutral, but grammatically incorrect. It is better avoided.

Rephrasing 3
Students who mindlessly copy their teachers risk losing their own creative voices.

The statement is now gender-neutral and grammatically correct. The subject and the pronoun agree; both are plural. This is an appropriate solution.

There is always a gender-neutral alternative to gendered language. The *Chicago Manual of Style* sets out nine techniques that can be used; the *Publication Manual of the American Psychological Association* also includes a number of strategies, as well as an extended chapter on bias-free language more generally.[20]

Italics for Emphasis

Italics can be used to emphasize a particular word or point, as illustrated in the following example. They lose their impact if they are overused, however, and should be employed sparingly.

> Centuries should be spelled out rather than written as numerals—hence the twentieth century, *not* the 20th century; twentieth-century music, *not* 20th-century music.

Matters of Punctuation

Codes of meaning and shared understandings are embedded in punctuation, just as codes of meaning are embedded in words. Both are symbols that convey something beyond themselves. The right punctuation mark is therefore as important as the right word, or the right tense. A comma, for example, conveys a very different meaning from a question mark. Punctuation also clarifies meaning by grouping words and ideas that belong together, and by separating those that do not. It articulates thought and allows the text to breathe.

There are eight punctuation marks that are often poorly understood and wrongly deployed in academic writing: commas, semicolons, and colons; the apostrophe; the ellipsis; and the hyphen, en dash, and em dash. They are discussed in appendix F.

Exercise

This exercise builds upon exercise 1 in chapter 6, which involved the critical evaluation of the content of an existing masters or doctoral thesis. Provide a stylistic evaluation of the same thesis, using the following questions as the basis of your evaluation. Restrict the evaluation to no more than 1,500 words. Bullet points may be used.

Key Elements of the Academic Style

1. Is the style of writing appropriate for an academic context? Why or why not?

198   Postgraduate Research in Music

2. Comment on the quality of the rhetoric in terms of:
   - The evidence that is provided.
   - The argument that is presented, and the thread of the argument through the thesis.
   - The analysis and discussion of the research findings, and the extent to which the author has addressed the "So what?" question.
3. Which techniques, if any, are employed to create unity and cohesion? Does the author use connecting words and phrases, signposts, and summative statements? If so, give two examples of each. If not, give three examples of disjunctions in the text.
4. Observe the way in which quotations are used in the thesis and address the following questions: (a) Are the quotations foreshadowed in the text that precedes them, and followed by text that emerges smoothly from them? Or are there disjunctions between the text and the quotations? Provide two examples to support your observations. (b) Which referencing style is used? Is it applied accurately and consistently? Provide two examples to support your observations. (c) Are the quotations preceded and followed by appropriate punctuation? Provide two examples to support your observations.
5. Observe the way in which paraphrasing is used in the literature review. Is it used skillfully and effectively? Provide two examples to support your observations.
6. Provide two definitions of plagiarism, other than the definition given in this chapter, and cite the sources of the definitions. Why is plagiarism reprehensible?

Stylistically Appropriate Use of Language within an Academic Context

1. Observe the syntax in the thesis. Is language used with precision and concision? Illustrate your response with two examples.
2. Is the first-person singular employed in the thesis? If so, where? Is it appropriate? Is the first-person plural used? If so, where? Is it appropriate? In which person is the greater part of the thesis written? Is it appropriate? Why or why not?
3. Read the section about tables in appendix D of this book. Create a table, following the guidelines set out in appendix D, and document the tenses that are used in: (a) the literature review; (b) the aims; (c) the

methodology; (d) reporting the research findings; (e) discussing the research findings; and (f) evaluating the research findings. In a brief paragraph following the table, or in three or four bullet points, evaluate the appropriateness and effectiveness of the tenses that are employed in these sections of the thesis.

4. Is the thesis written in the active or passive voice, or a mixture of the two? Is this aspect of style handled appropriately? Why or why not? Provide two examples to support your observations.

5. Observe whether gender-neutral language is used. Provide two examples of either gender-neutral or gender-biased language, or one of each.

6. Select two of the punctuation marks that are discussed in appendix F. Track the way in which they are used in one chapter of the thesis. Provide three examples that illustrate either the correct or incorrect use of each of the two punctuation marks. Comment briefly on whether they are used effectively.

Overall Evaluation

In no more than four sentences, provide an overall evaluation of the thesis. What mark out of one hundred would you award it?

Reading List

Key elements of the academic style

Andrews, Richard. *A Theory of Contemporary Rhetoric*. New York: Routledge, 2014.

"Avoiding Academic Misconduct: Plagiarism." Edith Cowan University, Student Intranet—My Studies. Accessed October 14, 2021. https://intranet.ecu.edu.au/student/my-studies/academic-integrity/avoiding-academic-misconduct.

Booth, Wayne C., Gregory C. Colomb, Joseph M. Williams, Joseph Bizup, and William T. Fitzgerald. *The Craft of Research*. 4th ed. Chicago: University of Chicago Press, 2016.

Bowman, Vibiana, ed. *The Plagiarism Plague: A Resource Guide and CD-ROM Tutorial for Educators and Librarians*. New York: Neal-Schuman Publishers, 2004.

Brooks, Cleanth, and Robert Penn Warren. *Modern Rhetoric*. 4th ed. New York: Harcourt Brace Jovanovich, 1979.

Dunleavy, Patrick. *Authoring a PhD: How to Plan, Draft, Write and Finish a Doctoral Thesis or Dissertation*. Basingstoke, Hampshire: Palgrave Macmillan, 2003.

Herrick, James A. *Argumentation: Understanding and Shaping Arguments*. 6th ed. State College, PA: Strata Publishing, 2019.

Lillis, Theresa, and Sarah North. "Academic Writing." In *Doing Postgraduate Research*. 2nd ed., edited by Stephen Potter, 114–51. London: Sage, 2006.

200 Postgraduate Research in Music

Toye, Richard. *Rhetoric: A Very Short Introduction*. Oxford: Oxford University Press, 2013.
Turabian, Kate. *A Manual for Writers of Research Papers, Theses, and Dissertations: Chicago Style for Students and Researchers*. 9th ed. Chicago: University of Chicago Press, 2018.

Stylistically appropriate use of language within an academic context

"Academic Phrasebank." University of Manchester. Accessed May 26, 2021. https://www.phrasebank.manchester.ac.uk.

Chicago Manual of Style: The Essential Guide for Writers, Editors, and Publishers. 17th ed. Chicago: University of Chicago Press, 2017.

Cowdery, James R., Carl Skoggard, and Barbara Dobbs Mackenzie. *How to Write About Music: The RILM Manual of Style*. 2nd ed. New York: *Répertoire International de Littérature Musicale*, 2006.

Fish, Stanley Eugene. *How to Write a Sentence and How to Read One*. New York: Harper, 2011.

Garner, Bryan A. *The Chicago Guide to Grammar, Usage, and Punctuation*. Chicago: University of Chicago Press, 2016.

"Graduate Research & Writing: Reporting and Discussing your Findings." Monash University. Accessed July 29, 2021. https://www.monash.edu/rlo/graduate-research-writing/write-the-thesis/writing-the-thesis-chapters/reporting-and-discussing-your-findings.

Holoman, D. Kern. *Writing About Music: A Style Sheet*. 3rd ed. Oakland, California: University of California Press, 2014.

Irvine, Demar. *Irvine's Writing About Music*. Revised by Mark A. Radice. 3rd ed. Portland, Oregon: Amadeus Press, 1999.

New Oxford Style Manual. Oxford: Oxford University Press, 2016.

Publication Manual of the American Psychological Association. 7th ed. Washington, DC: American Psychological Association, 2020.

Richardson, Brian, Robin Aizlewood, Derek F. Connon, Malcolm Cook, Gerard Lowe, Graham Nelson, and Chloe E. M. Paver. *MHRA Style Guide: A Handbook for Authors and Editors*. 3rd ed. London: Modern Humanities Research Association, 2015. See also *MHRA Style Guide Online*. Accessed June 9, 2021. http://www.mhra.org.uk/style/.

Seely, John. *The Oxford Guide to Effective Writing and Speaking: How to Communicate Clearly*. 3rd ed. Oxford: Oxford University Press, 2013.

Strunk, William Jr. *The Elements of Style*. Revised by E. B. White. 4th ed. Boston: Allyn and Bacon, 2000.

Sword, Helen. *Stylish Academic Writing*. Cambridge, Massachusetts: Harvard University Press, 2012.

Turabian, Kate. *A Manual for Writers of Research Papers, Theses, and Dissertations: Chicago Style for Students and Researchers*. 9th ed. Chicago: University of Chicago Press, 2018.

Other sources referred to

Burke, Edmund. *A Philosophical Enquiry into the Origin of Our Ideas of the Sublime and Beautiful, with an Introductory Discourse Concerning Taste, and Several Other Additions*. 9th ed. London: J. Dodsley, 1782.

Glanville-Hicks, Peggy. "Musical Explorers: Six Americans Who Are Changing the Musical Vocabulary." *Vogue* 116 (November 1950): 112–13, 134, 137, 139.

Glanville-Hicks, Peggy. "Tapesichord: The Music of Whistle and Bang." *Vogue* 122 (July 1953): 80, 81, 108.

Glanville-Hicks, Peggy. "Music: How it's Built." *Vogue* 147 (March 1966): 200–1, 207–8, 210.

Rogers, Victoria. *The Music of Peggy Glanville-Hicks*. Farnham: Ashgate, 2009.

Rosen, Charles. *The Classical Style: Haydn, Mozart, Beethoven*. Rev. ed. New York: Norton, 1998.

Vaughan Williams, Ralph. *National Music*. London: Oxford University Press, 1934.

8

Writing a Thesis Part 3

The Musical Lexicon

Musical terminology is a frequent source of discombobulation for music scholars. Not only is it unique in the concepts and structures it describes; it is also documented in different ways. Whether to capitalize major and minor, the church modes, and scale degrees; how to document artists' names and the titles of musical works; how to refer to notes and note names . . . these are just some of the many confusions that arise when writing about music. Chapter 8 brings clarity to the issue by discussing nine key elements within the musical lexicon: (1) capitalization; (2) artists' names; (3) the titles of musical works; (4) notes and note names; (5) time signatures; (6) chords; (7) non-English terms; (8) numbers; and (9) abbreviations.[1]

Capitalization

Confusion about capitalization can generally be avoided by applying a basic rule of grammar. Proper nouns—those referring to specific people, places, or things—are capitalized. Common nouns—those referring generically to categories of people, places, or things—are not capitalized.[2] Terms that are frequently used in music research will now be considered in this context.

Historical Periods, Musical Styles, and Artistic Movements

Historical periods are proper nouns. They are therefore capitalized, regardless of whether they are used as nouns or adjectives. The only exception to this is the adjective "medieval," which, for no apparent reason, is often written in lowercase. When historical terms are used in a general, ahistorical way, however, they are not capitalized. These conventions are illustrated in table 8.1.

The capitalization of musical styles and artistic movements is less straightforward. Impressionism, Expressionism, Symbolism, Futurism, Neoclassicism,

Postgraduate Research in Music. Victoria Rogers, Oxford University Press. © Oxford University Press 2024.
DOI: 10.1093/oso/9780197616031.003.0009

Table 8.1. Capitalization of historical periods

Capitalized	Not capitalized
the Middle Ages; the medieval/Medieval period	a medieval attitude
the Renaissance; Renaissance music	a renaissance of moral behavior
the Baroque; Baroque music; the Baroque era	The architecture could only be described as baroque in its excess.
the Classical period; Classical balance	They prefer classical music; they do not like popular music.
Romanticism; the Romantic period	a theme that is romantic in character; a romantic dinner for two

Primitivism, and Minimalism, for example, are not capitalized in style guides such as the *Chicago Manual*, but this is not a universal practice.[3] Whether to capitalize these terms is ultimately a matter of interpretation. If they are seen as proper nouns—in other words, as referring to specific things—they are capitalized. If they are seen as common nouns—as referring generically to categories of things—they are not capitalized.

Artistic styles and movements that are spelled in German, however, are capitalized as a matter of course because all nouns in German are capitalized. *Stürm und Drang* and *Empfindsamkeit*, for example, are capitalized—although the adjectival form of *Empfindsamkeit* is not capitalized because adjectives in German are generally not capitalized (the *emfindsamer Stil*, or the *empfindsamer* style).[4] The French term *galant*, too, is not capitalized because adjectives in French are generally not capitalized (the *galant* style).

Centuries

Centuries are set in lower case because they are common nouns. They should be spelled out rather than written as numerals—hence twentieth century, *not* 20th century; twentieth-century music, *not* 20th-century music.

Genres and Forms

Musical genres and forms are not capitalized when they are referred to generically. When a musical genre or form is part of a specific title, however, it is capitalized because it becomes a proper noun in that context.

Beethoven wrote nine symphonies.
Beethoven, Symphony No. 6
Bruckner's Ninth Symphony
Mozart's Fifth Violin Concerto
C. P. E. Bach's Rondo in C Minor, Wq. 59, no. 4, H. 283
The movement is set in rondo form.
The opera begins with a prologue.
The opening movement is in sonata form.

Movements and Sections within a Composition

The names of movements and sections within a composition are not capitalized when they are used as generic terms.

A detailed analysis of the second movement is provided in chapter 3.
An aria is stylistically different from a recitative.
Nineteenth-century composers preferred the more capricious scherzo to the stately minuet.
The ritornello is woven through the entire movement.
The thematic material is set out in the exposition.
The second theme is set in the dominant key.
In rondo form, the refrain alternates with a number of episodes.

Capitalization *is* necessary, however, when the titles of specific movements are used as proper nouns—that is, when they are referred to in the context of specific compositions.

The Prelude sets out the thematic material on which the opera is based.
The Scherzo is set in triple meter.
In Act 2, Scene 1 of *Rigoletto* . . .

Church (Ecclesiastical) Modes

The church (ecclesiastical) modes are capitalized in both their authentic and plagal forms because their names are derived from specific regions of ancient Greece.

Dorian   Hypodorian
Phrygian   Hypophrygian

Lydian	Hypolydian
Mixolydian	Hypomixolydian
Aeolian	Hypoaeolian
Ionian	Hypoionian

The movement begins in the Dorian mode. In measure sixteen there is an abrupt shift to the Aeolian mode, then two bars later to G Lydian.

Major and Minor

The words "major" and "minor" are not capitalized when they are used generically. They *are* capitalized, however, when they appear in the title of a work because they become proper nouns in that context.

The first cello sonata by Brahms is in the key of E minor; the second is in F major. Brahms's Sonata in F Major for Cello and Piano was composed in 1886.

Scale Types

Scale types are generic categories; they are therefore not capitalized.

chromatic
diatonic
major
minor
melodic minor
pentatonic
octatonic
whole tone

Scale Degrees

Scale degrees are also generic categories and not capitalized.

tonic
supertonic
mediant
subdominant

206 Postgraduate Research in Music

dominant
submediant
leading tone

Dynamics, Tempo, and Other Performance Instructions

Dynamics, tempo, and other performance instructions are generally not capitalized and are set in italics. Some non-English terms that have become universal are sometimes set in roman font rather than italics (for example, "pizzicato").

piano, pianissimo
forte
adagio
allegro ma non troppo
crescendo, diminuendo
a tempo
allargando
poco allargando
a cappella
torna frettolosa
esitando
alle Pausen gut gehalten ("Pausen" is capitalized because nouns in German are capitalized)
mit dem Bogen geschlagen
mit Dämpfer
nicht zu schnell
très espressif (un peu en dehors)
sans sourdines
sur la touche
un peu animé
The dynamic marking changed abruptly from *pianissimo* to *forte*.
In Strauss's *Pizzicato Polka*, the strings play pizzicato throughout.

Musical Instruments

Musical instruments are not capitalized when they are referred to generically. When an instrument forms part of a title, however, it is capitalized because it is a proper noun in that context.

Schumann wrote one concerto for the cello.
Schumann, Cello Concerto in A Minor, op. 129

Artists' Names

A number of factors need to be taken into account to ensure that artists' names are documented accurately and appropriately. Names of non-English origin require particular attention, not only in their spelling but also in the observance of diacritics and particles.

First and Subsequent Mentions

The full name of an artist is given at first mention, together with the dates of birth and death. Only the last name is given in subsequent mentions. Both dates include four digits, even if they fall within the same century. The dates are set in parenthesis and are separated by an en dash (see appendix F for a discussion of the en dash). If the artist is still alive, the date of birth is either followed by an en dash, or preceded by the letter *b*. If the flow of the text renders it clumsy to include the dates immediately after a name, the text should either be rearranged or the dates provided in a footnote or endnote.

Johannes Brahms (1833–1897)
John Smith (1995–) *or* (b. 1995)

Multiple Spellings, and Identification of Family Members

Some composers' names have multiple spellings. The name of the Renaissance composer Josquin des Prez, for example, is also spelled as Desprez, Després, and des Prés. In such cases, the best approach is to follow the spelling in *Grove Music Online* or some other authoritative source, unless there is a particular reason not to do so.

Related to this is the specification of a particular family member when the family contains several known musicians. The music of Bach, for example, might be attributed to Johann Sebastian or to one of his sons, Carl Philipp Emanuel, Johann Christian, Wilhelm Friedemann, or Johann Christoph Friedrich. The particular family member should be clarified at first mention, either by writing the name out in full or by using the appropriate initials.

208 Postgraduate Research in Music

When initials are used, each letter is followed by a period and a space—for example, C. P. E. Bach.

Diacritics

A diacritic is a sign that is attached to a letter to indicate its pronunciation, for example Béla Bartók, György Kurtág, Antonín Dvořák, and Gabriel Fauré. It is intrinsic to the spelling of a name and should be included unless the name has become anglicized through repeated use. In the anglicized spelling of Händel, for example, the umlaut is omitted from the letter *a* (Handel); in the case of Schönberg, the umlaut is omitted from the letter *o* and an *e* is added (Schoenberg).

Particles in Last Names

A particle in a last name (d', de, la, le, van, von, etc.) is always included at first mention of the name. Whether it is included in subsequent mentions is generally optional; the practice that is often followed is to omit the particle in subsequent mentions, unless it is connected to the name by an apostrophe. If there is any doubt, it is best to be guided by the spelling in *Grove Music Online* or some other authoritative source.

A particle is always capitalized at the beginning of a sentence or footnote, regardless of whether it is capitalized in the name itself. It is generally set in lower case mid-sentence. In Dutch names, particles are usually lowercased when the name is given in full (for example, Vincent van Gogh) and capitalized when only the last name is given, both at the beginning of a sentence and mid-sentence (for example, Van Gogh). The conventions governing the documentation of particles are set out in table 8.2.

Possessives

Writing the possessive form of a name is generally straightforward: add an apostrophe and an *s* (for example, Bach's sons, Beethoven's quartets). Less straightforward is how to write the possessive form of a name that ends in *s*, *x*, or *z*. There are two ways of doing this. The first is simply to add an apostrophe after the *s* (although not an *x* or *z*), for example Strauss' waltz (but *not* Josquin des Prez' music). The second way is to add an apostrophe and an *s*, for

Writing a Thesis Part 3   209

Table 8.2. Particles in last names

First mention	Beginning of sentence	Mid-sentence
Bart van Oort	Van Oort, or Oort	Van Oort, or Oort
Carl Maria von Weber	Von Weber, or Weber	von Weber, or Weber
Elizabeth Jacquet de La Guerre	De La Guerre, or La Guerre	de La Guerre, or La Guerre
Jean Henri D'Anglebert (or d'Anglebert)	D'Anglebert	d'Anglebert
Vincent d'Indy[a]	D'Indy	d'Indy

[a] Where the particle in d'Anglebert is often capitalized at first mention, the particle in d'Indy's name is generally set in lower case at first mention.

example Strauss's waltz, Josquin des Prez's music (although the latter, notably, is generally referred to as Josquin's music, Josquin's life, etc). Both approaches are acceptable, although style guides and grammar books generally favor the use of an apostrophe and an *s*.

Titles of Musical Works

The titles of musical works include some or all of the following information (as appropriate for each work), and in the following order:

Composer
Title of work
Number (position in a series of works within a particular genre)
Key
Opus (and, if appropriate, number within an opus)
Thematic catalogue number
Common usage (descriptive) title

Titles can be grouped into six categories, each of which has its own conventions of presentation: generic titles, individual titles, common usage titles, titles within a work, liturgical titles, and titles referred to in two languages.

Generic Titles

A generic title is one that groups a composition with other works that share a number of classificatory features. Generic titles include symphonies, sonatas, piano trios, string quartets, concertos, masses, and requiems.

Content and Formatting

Generic titles include the generic classification (for example, symphony), the number within a series (for example, no. 2), and the key. To this are added, variously and as appropriate, the opus number, thematic catalogue number, and common usage title. The series number and the opus number are generally abbreviated, respectively to no. and op. All elements are separated by commas, with the exception of parenthetical common usage titles.

Some of the elements within generic titles are capitalized: the name of the work (using headline-style capitalization), the key, and the thematic catalogue number. The opus number is not capitalized. There are differing approaches to the capitalization of series numbers. The *Chicago Manual of Style*, for example, does not capitalize them, nor does Donahue in his *Style and Usage Guide to Writing About Music*.[5] Holoman, on the other hand, distinguishes between a series number (which he capitalizes) and a number within an opus (which he does not capitalize)—a style he describes as "strongly preferred in the profession"[6] (for example, Schubert, String Quartet No. 14 in D Minor, op. 7, no. 3). Ultimately there is no right and wrong in this; it is a matter of stylistic preference.

Key

If a key includes a flat or a sharp, the accidental can be written either with the appropriate symbol or spelled out. The use of a superscript *b* (^{b}) to denote a flat and a superscript hash sign ($^\#$) to indicate a sharp are generally avoided, for these signs denote different things. The similarity, moreover, is only approximate, as can be seen in the following example:

To be used:	G♭ and G♯ (accidentals)
To be avoided:	G^b and G$^\#$ (superscript *b* and the hash sign)

If a key containing an accidental is spelled out, it is generally hyphenated (for example, E-flat major). This indicates that the two elements belong together because the key is a compound term. Not all compound terms are hyphenated, however, and for this reason a key containing an accidental is sometimes written without a hyphen (for example, E flat major; see appendix F for a discussion of the hyphen). Both spellings are correct. One approach should be chosen and applied consistently.

Thematic Catalogue Number

A thematic catalogue is an index of a composer's works, organized by chronology or by some other principle (for example, by type of composition).

A thematic catalogue includes such information as the title of a work; an incipit of the opening notes; the instrumentation, genre and opus number; the location of the autograph score and first edition; and the date and place of composition. Thematic catalogues have been compiled for the works of many, but not all, composers. If there is a thematic catalogue number for a work, it is included when the title is cited in full.

A thematic catalogue assigns an Arabic number to each work within the catalogue. The number is preceded by one or more letters that usually denote the name of the person who compiled the catalogue, for example, *K.* for Köchel (for the works of Mozart), and *Hob.* for Hoboken (for the works of Haydn). In some cases, the letters *WV* (*Werkverzeichnis*, or works catalogue) are used; examples include thematic catalogues for the music of J. S. Bach (BWV), Buxtehude (BuxWV), Handel (HWV), and Mendelssohn (MWV).

Some thematic catalogue numbers can be formatted in different ways. The thematic catalogue number for Mozart's Symphony No. 40, for example, could be written as K. 550, K.550, K550, or K 550. In such cases, the formatting is a stylistic choice which, once made, needs to be applied consistently. The formatting of *WV* catalogue numbers, on the other hand, is invariable: there are no periods or spaces between the letters, and there is a space between the group of letters and the number.[7] The thematic catalogue number for Bach's *St Matthew Passion*, for example, is BWV 244.

New thematic catalogues are in some cases superseding the old ones. The compositions of Wagner, Mendelssohn, Tchaikovsky, and Berlioz are three of a number of composers whose works have been re-indexed in new catalogues. The compositions of Bartók have been catalogued in four ways: Bartók's own (incomplete) opus numbers; the DD numbers; the Sz numbers; and the (most recent) BB numbers. The most recent thematic catalogue number should generally be used; in some cases an explanatory note may be necessary.

Examples of Generic Titles

Bach, Prelude and Fugue in A Minor, BWV 543
Beethoven, String Quartet No. 8 in E Minor, op. 59, no. 2
Brahms, Symphony No. 4 in E Minor, op. 98
Corelli, Concerto Grosso in G Minor, op. 6, no. 8
Fauré, Requiem in D Minor, op. 48
Haydn, String Quartet in E-flat Major, op. 33, no. 2, Hob. III:38
Mozart, Symphony No. 40 in G Minor, K. 550
Schubert, String Quartet No. 14 in D Minor, op. 7, no. 3, D. 531

Postgraduate Research in Music

Schumann, Cello Concerto in A Minor, op. 129
Beethoven's String Quartet No. 8; Beethoven's Eighth String Quartet (*but*: By the time Beethoven had written his eighth string quartet . . .)
Brahms's Symphony No. 4 was composed over the two-year period, 1884–1885. (*But*: When Brahms began work on his fourth symphony in 1884, . . .)

Individual Titles

An individual title is one that has been given to a work by the composer. Individual titles are assigned to such compositions as operas, musicals, oratorios, songs, song cycles, and tone poems. From time to time, individual titles are given to other genres, for example symphonies and masses.

Content and Formatting

Where generic titles are set in roman font, individual titles are italicized. There is one exception to this: the titles of single song settings, which are set either in italics or quotation marks (for example, Schubert's *Erlkönig*, or Schubert's "Erlkönig"). Although both formats are acceptable, italics are preferable because they identify single song settings as individual works and distinguish them from songs within a song cycle (the latter are discussed in the section below entitled "titles within a work").

Individual titles in English generally follow headline-style capitalization. In a language other than English, capitalization follows the conventions of the language in which the title is written. In German, as noted earlier in this chapter, nouns are capitalized but adjectives are not (for example, *Das wohltemperierte Clavier*). In French, nouns are not capitalized other than the first noun of a sentence (for example, *Pavane pour une enfante défunte*). If a French title begins with a definite article (*le, la, l', les*), the first noun following the article is sometimes capitalized, for example, *Le Diable dans le beffroi* (or: *Le diable dans le beffroi*); and *La Mer* (or: *La mer*). It is also acceptable to use English headline-style capitalization for non-English titles that have become anglicized through repeated use (for example, *Le Sacre du Printemps*).

If an individual title contains an opus number and/or thematic catalogue number, the numbers are included after the title. The key is not included.

Examples of Individual Titles

Bach, *Die Kunst der Fuge*, BWV 1080
Bax, *Tintagel*

Elgar, *The Dream of Gerontius*
Haydn, *Die Schöpfung*, Hob. XXI:2
Messiaen, *Messe de la Pentecôte* (Pentecôte is a proper noun, hence capitalized)
Ravel, *Pavane pour une enfante défunte*
Schubert, *Erlkönig*, D. 328
Schumann, *Dichterliebe*, op. 48
Strauss, *Pizzicato Polka* (or *Pizzicato-Polka*)
Vaughan Williams, *A Sea Symphony*
Vaughan Williams, *The Lark Ascending*
Verdi, *La forza del destino*

Common Usage Titles

A common usage (or descriptive) title is one that has been attributed to a work, usually by someone other than the composer. It is the title by which the work is commonly known.

Common usage titles are capitalized, written in roman font, set in quotation marks, and enclosed by parentheses. They are sometimes written in italics rather than quotation marks. Quotation marks are preferable, however, because they distinguish common usage titles from (italicized) individual titles.

Examples of Common Usage Titles

Corelli, Concerto Grosso in G Minor, op. 6, no. 8 ("Christmas Concerto")
Haydn, String Quartet in E-flat Major, op. 33, no. 2, Hob. III:38 ("The Joke")
Schubert, String Quartet No. 14 in D minor, op. 7, no. 3, D. 531 ("Death and the Maiden")

Titles within a Work

Titles within a work include individual songs within song cycles, arias from operas, choruses from oratorios, and individual pieces from larger instrumental works. They are set in quotation marks and are generally followed by a comma. English titles within a work usually follow headline-style capitalization. In languages other than English, capitalization follows the conventions of the language in which the title is written.

Examples of Titles within a Work

"La muse victorieuse," from Couperin's *Vingt-cinquième ordre*
"Vanitas vanitatum," from Schumann's *Fünf Stücke im Volkston*
"Bewundert, o Menschen," from Bach's *Nun Komm der Heiden Heiland*
"When the Foeman Bares his Steel," from Gilbert and Sullivan's *The Pirates of Penzance*
"Kyrie," from Bach's Mass in B Minor
"Im wonderschönen Monat Mai," from Schumann's *Dichterliebe*
"La vita è inferno all'infelice," from Verdi's *La forza del destino*

Liturgical Titles

The titles of liturgical works and the movements within them are capitalized and set in roman font. An individual title for a liturgical work, however, is set in italics.

Berlioz's Requiem is a work of grand proportions.

Kyrie	Gloria	Credo
Sanctus	Benedictus	Agnus Dei

Stravinsky's late works include the *Requiem Canticles* (1966).
Britten's *Festival Te Deum* was written in 1944.

Titles Referred to in Two Languages

If a work from another language is generally known by its English title, the English title should be used (with a parenthetical translation to the original language at first mention). If a work from another language is generally known by its non-English title, that title should be used (with a parenthetical translation into English at first mention).

The Art of Fugue (*Die Kunst der Fuge*)
Winterreise (*Winter Journey*)

Notes and Note Names

Note names are written in roman font and in uppercase letters. This is not to be confused with the use of a lowercase letter to signify a minor key at the beginning of a harmonic analysis.

Middle C on the piano
Trumpet in D
The A string on a cello

Note Names as Compound Adjectives

When a note name is used as a compound adjective, it is hyphenated. When a note name is used as the sole adjective, it is not hyphenated.

The B-flat clarinet *but:* The clarinet in B flat
The D-minor chord *but:* The key of D minor
The key of C-sharp minor
The note name of G-double-sharp
The A-flat-major triad *but:* The key of A-flat major
The G-major scale *but:* The key of G major
The E-minor chord *but:* The key of E minor

Accidentals

Accidentals can be written either as symbols or words. If symbols are used, they must be used consistently; if accidentals are spelled out, they must be spelled out consistently. When double flats and double sharps are spelled out, hyphens should be added to link the elements together (E-double-flat, rather than E double flat).

As noted in the earlier discussion of keys, it is important to avoid the use of a superscript b (^{b}) to denote a flat and the superscript hash sign ($^\#$) to indicate a sharp, because these signs denote different things.

G♭   G flat
G♭♭   G-double-flat
G♯   G sharp
G×   G-double-sharp
G♮   G natural

The G♯ in bar 3 is soon contradicted by a G♮ in bar 4.
Or: The G sharp in bar 3 is contradicted by a G natural in the ensuing bar.
Not: The G♯ in bar 3 is contradicted by a G natural in the ensuing bar.
Not: The G sharp in bar 3 is contradicted by a G♮ in the ensuing bar.

Plurals

The plural of a note name simply adds an *s*. An apostrophe should *not* be inserted between the note name and the *s* because an apostrophe denotes possession.

> Cs, C sharps; *not* C's, *not* C sharp's
> The second theme is chromatically inflected with B flats and E flats.

Succession of Notes or Keys

In a succession of notes or keys, the individual note names are written in uppercase and connected by en dashes.

> A circle of fifths progression that moves from D–G–C–F
> The four-note pattern A–B–C–D
> *But*
> Successive key areas of C major, G major, and D major

Time Signatures

Time signatures should not be written as fractions (with a slash separating the numbers) because fractions denote something quite different.

> $\frac{3}{4}$ *not* 3/4
> $\frac{12}{8}$ *not* 12/8

Chords

Chord inversions should not be written as fractions. If a second inversion chord, for example, is referred to in Arabic numerals, it is written as $\frac{6}{4}$, *not* as 6/4. A second inversion chord on the dominant would be written as V$\frac{6}{4}$. Chords can also be described in words, for example, a six-four chord on the dominant (or a second inversion chord on the dominant).

Non-English Terms

Non-English terms are set in italics unless they have become part of everyday English. If a non-English term is set in italics and used repeatedly, the italics may be omitted after the first (italicized) mention of the term.

The *fin de siècle* aesthetic was one of radical departure from previous artistic practices.

The *Affektenlehre*, known as the Doctrine of the Affections, was central to the Baroque musical aesthetic.

Frédéric Chopin wrote many études for the piano.

The ostinato is an important structural device in Stravinsky's music.

The Leitmotiv is closely associated with the operas of Richard Wagner.

Numbers

The question of whether to write numbers as numerals or words is a frequent source of confusion. Amidst the multiplicity of approaches, the easiest solution is to follow either the Chicago style or the APA style.

In the Chicago style, there are two ways of documenting numbers. In research that does *not* include a large amount of numerical data, numbers from one through to (and including) one hundred are spelled out; numbers above one hundred are written in Arabic numerals. When the research includes a substantial amount of numerical data, numbers from one to nine are spelled out in words; numbers ten and above are presented as Arabic numerals.[8] In all cases, a number that begins a sentence must be spelled out.

Research that does not include a substantial amount of numerical data
Of the 120 participants in the study, ninety-five attended at least two concerts.
Sixty-five of the participants

Research that includes a substantial amount of numerical data
Of the 120 participants in the study, 95 attended at least two concerts.
Sixty-five of the participants

218 Postgraduate Research in Music

The same rules apply for ordinal numbers—that is, those showing the position of something, rather than how many (first, fifth etc.).

> The fourth quartet
> The twelfth symphony (*or* the 12th symphony if there is a large amount of numerical data)
> One fifth of the respondents
> On the ninety-second day after the première (*or* the 92nd day if there is a large amount of numerical data)
> The third movement of Beethoven's Fifth Symphony

Related numbers in a sentence are written as numerals, regardless of the thresholds above and below that would otherwise apply.

> Of the 120 participants in the study, 95 attended one concert, 20 attended two or more concerts, and 5 attended no concerts at all.

The APA style is more straightforward. In this approach, numbers ten and above are expressed in Arabic numerals; those below ten are written in words.[9] In all cases, a number that begins a sentence must be spelled out.

> Of the 95 participants in the study, 11 attended two concerts and five attended none at all.
> Ninety-five of the participants

The same rule applies for ordinal numbers—in other words, numbers 1–9 are expressed in words and those ten and above are written as numbers.

> The fourth quartet
> The 12th symphony
> One fifth of the respondents
> On the 92nd day after the première
> The third movement of Beethoven's Fifth Symphony

Abbreviations

Abbreviations are generally avoided in the running text (for example, chapter, *not* chap.; that is, *not* i.e.; introduction, *not* introd.), although some terms are routinely abbreviated (for example, b. 1910; ca. 1920). The most frequently used abbreviations in music research are captured in the following list; most but not all are followed by a period.

anon.	anonymous
arr.	arranged
b.	born (used with birth dates); b. 1930
c. *or* ca.	approximately (generally used with dates); c. 1930
CD	compact disc
chap., chaps.	chapter(s)
comp.	compiled by
diss.	dissertation
ed., eds.	editor(s)
ex.	example
e.g.	for example
ff.	indicates the ensuing content without stipulating a final page number
fig., figs.	figure(s)
LP	vinyl (long playing) record
m., mm.	measure(s)
n., nn.	footnote(s) (used in a footnote that makes reference to another footnote)
n.d.	no date (used in bibliographical citations which do not have a date)
no.	number
n.p.	no place (used in bibliographical citations which do not have a place of publication)
op., opp.	opus (opp. is the plural)
op. posth.	opus posthumous (work published after the death of the composer)
p., pp.	page(s)
trans.	translation, or translated by (used in bibliographical citations)
vol., vols.	volume(s) (used in bibliographical citations; is sometimes capitalized)

Coda

Many elements in the musical lexicon are unambiguous in their documentation. Others are variable. The guiding principle must always be consistency. If Impressionism is capitalized, for example, Expressionism must also be

220   Postgraduate Research in Music

capitalized. If the first of Mozart's thematic catalogue numbers is written as K. 123, subsequent Köchel numbers must follow the same pattern. If a symbol is used at first reference to an accidental, subsequent accidentals must also be documented as symbols, and not as words. Consistency is the key in all stylistic matters. Whether to use American or British spelling; how to document numbers; whether to use single or double quotation marks; how to document references . . . the detail *is* important. Readers can be confident that a stylistically consistent thesis is likely to be accurate in other respects as well.

Exercise

The following text is in serious need of editing. It presents a highly abbreviated, simplistic history of Western Art Music and is offered *not* as a complete historical account, but rather as a vehicle for the sort of stylistic errors and inconsistencies that are not uncommon in student theses. Particular historical elements are included not because they are necessarily more significant than others, but because they serve the purpose of this exercise. Provide an edited version of the text, using the information in this chapter to inform your editorial choices.

The history of western art music in less than one thousand words

The history of western art music is generally divided into a number of historical periods: the medieval period; the renaissance; the baroque; the classical Period; the romantic period; and the 20th century. Within each of these periods, there were different styles, genres, and Aesthetic Foundations. In the baroque period, for example, the Concerto emerged as an important genre, and along with it the Ritornello as a key organizing principle. Antonio Vivaldi (1678–41) wrote around five hundred Concerti, of which "*the four seasons*" Op.8 is the best known. Bach also wrote many concertos (1685—1750), including the 6 Brandenburgs and the concerto in d-minor for 2 violins B.W.V.1043.

A key aesthetic principle in baroque music was the doctrine of the affections (affektenlehre), which ascribed specific emotions to particular musical gestures and keys. The transition from Modality to Tonality was a further key element in the baroque. In the Medieval and renaissance periods, music had been based on the 6 church modes, each of which had its own unique flavor: dorian, phrygian, lydian, mixolydian, aeolian, and ionian. During the baroque, these Modes were replaced by the Major and Minor Scales, the genesis of which can be seen in the Late Renaissance. Equal temperament emerged as the main tuning system, and with it the circle-of-fifths as a pillar of the harmonic syntax—successive chords a fifth apart, for example B,E,A,D.

In the mid eighteenth century, the baroque aesthetic was overtaken by the empfindsamer-style – an approach to composition that was associated with CPE Bach and other composers from North Germany. Elsewhere in Europe, the style was known as Galant. Empfindsamkeit was concerned with the expression of subjective emotions and with sudden changes of mood; it marked a clear aesthetic departure from the baroque. This new way of writing music favored light, elegant, periodic melodies set in a Homophonic Texture. The melodic ornamentation was more extensive in galant music than in the empfindsamer stil.

The classical period grew out of the empfindsamer style and the galant; Haydn and Mozart were its most notable composers. Haydn produced a large body of compositions, many of which form part of today's Canonic Repertoire. They include one hundred and four symphonies, the best known of which is, perhaps, the symphony no. 101 in D major hob 1: 101 (*clock symphony*). Mozart wrote 41 symphonies, the final one of which was the so-called jupiter symphony k551 in c major.

Empfindsamkeit prepared the way for the emergence of the sturm und drang movement in the mid-late 18th century. Sturm und drang began in the literary arts and spread to the other arts, including music. The sturm und drang aesthetic rejected the rationalism of the enlightenment and cultivated strong emotion, individualism, and subjective expression. In music it can be seen, for example, in Mozarts' opera Idomeneo K366, which was written between 1780-81.[1] This opera begins with a dramatic, Fortissimo D Major Chord. The sturm und drang lay the aesthetic foundation for the emergence of romanticism in the early decades of the 19th century. By the 1820's, the Romantic sensibility had superseded the classical style.

Romanticism in music was an artistic response to the profound social, cultural, and political changes triggered by the French Revolution, the industrial revolution, and the rise of the middle class. New genres emerged, such as the lied, the symphonic poem, and the one-movement piano piece. Chopin's Nocturne no. 1 in B flat minor Op. 9 No. 1, and his Nocturne no. 5 in F♯ major, op. 15 no. 2. exemplify the One-Movement-Piano Piece. The classical symphony underwent a profound transformation, as evidenced in Beethoven's Symphony no. 5 in c Minor Op. 67, and in Berlioz's "Symphonie Fantastique" op.14. The quest for expressive means was reflected in an expanded tonal

---

[1] Clue: See table F.2 in appendix F for information about the documentation of date ranges.

language, with composers writing increasingly Chromatic music and venturing into increasingly remote key areas. A modulation from F-major to the remote key of G Sharp Minor, for example, would not be surprising in the 19th century, but almost inconceivable in the baroque era.

The turn of the 20th century heralded the collapse of Tonality—the tonal system that had sustained Western Art music through the common practice period. New scales replaced the Major and Minor scales, including the Pentatonic, Octatonic and Whole Tone Scales. Such radical changes to the tonal dimension were inevitably accompanied by radically different structural principles: Schoenberg's egalitarian, chromatic, serial method, in which no single tone was more important than another; and Stravinsky's neoclassicism, in which the Ostinato was a key structural element. The fin de siecle turmoil was perhaps most potently expressed in the riot that accompanied the premiere of Stravinsky's Le Sacre du printemps ("The Rite of Spring"), at the Theatre des Champs Elysees in Paris on the twenty ninth of May nineteen thirteen. Around mid-century there were even more radical developments, including Total Serialism, Cage's Indeterminacy, and electronic music.

The advent of recording around the turn of the twentieth century was, in its own way, no less radical. Recording changed the way in which music is consumed – first wax cylinder's then 78's, LP's, CD's, and more recently the streaming of MP3's.

Reading List

Chicago Manual of Style: The Essential Guide for Writers, Editors, and Publishers. 17th ed. Chicago: University of Chicago Press, 2017.

Cowdery, James R., Carl Skoggard, and Barbara Dobbs Mackenzie. *How to Write About Music: The RILM Manual of Style.* 2nd ed. New York: *Répertoire International de Littérature Musicale,* 2006.

Donahue, Thomas. *A Style and Usage Guide to Writing About Music.* Lanham, Maryland: Scarecrow Press, 2010.

Holoman, D. Kern. *Writing About Music: A Style Sheet.* 3rd ed. Oakland, California: University of California Press, 2014.

Irvine, Demar. *Irvine's Writing About Music.* Revised by Mark A. Radice. 3rd ed. Portland, Oregon: Amadeus Press, 1999.

Lester, Mark, and Larry Beason. *The McGraw-Hill Handbook of English Grammar and Usage.* 3rd ed. New York: McGraw-Hill, 2018.

MLA Handbook. 8th ed. New York: The Modern Language Association of America, 2016.

New Oxford Style Manual. Oxford: Oxford University Press, 2016.

Publication Manual of the American Psychological Association. 7th ed. Washington, DC: American Psychological Association, 2020.

Richardson, Brian, Robin Aizlewood, Derek F. Connon, Malcolm Cook, Gerard Lowe, Graham Nelson, and Chloe E. M. Paver. *MHRA Style Guide: A Handbook for Authors and Editors*. 3rd ed. London: Modern Humanities Research Association, 2015. See also *MHRA Style Guide Online*. Accessed June 9, 2021. http://www.mhra.org.uk/style/.

Turabian, Kate. *A Manual for Writers of Research Papers, Theses and Dissertations: Chicago Style for Students and Researchers*. 9th ed. Chicago: University of Chicago Press, 2018.

9
Writing a Thesis Part 4
Efficiency and Effectiveness

Chapter 9 is the last of the four chapters that explore various aspects of writing a thesis. Content, style, and the musical lexicon have occupied the preceding three chapters. This chapter focuses on strategies and understandings that lead to greater efficiency and effectiveness in the writing process. These strategies and understandings can usefully be grouped into seven categories: (1) finding a way into each chapter; (2) getting the ideas down on paper; (3) building in breaks; (4) good scholarship is slow scholarship; (5) making the most of supervision; (6) editing; (7) saving and backing up.

Finding a Way into Each Chapter

Finding a way into each chapter can be one of the most challenging tasks in writing a thesis. For this, a systematic approach is needed. The first step is to review the chapter outline that was included in the research proposal, then to read through the entirety of the data that have been assembled for the chapter—research findings, notes, interview transcripts, and so on. Once this has been done, the data can be organized into clusters that correspond to the headings and sub-headings in the chapter outline; if necessary, the outline can be adjusted. It is important to work from printouts because it is easier to see the whole picture in hard copy, rather than scrolling up and down a screen to try to piece things together.

After the data have been reviewed and organized, a way needs to be found into the chapter. What will the chapter focus on? Is some contextual background needed? Is there an idea, an angle, that may captivate the reader's interest? Should reference be made to a previous chapter to show how the new chapter fits into an evolving narrative (for example: This is the second of two chapters that explore . . .)? Is a forward-pointing signpost needed to the chapter that follows (for example: This is the first of two chapters that examine . . .)? This introduction to the chapter is followed by an outline of what the chapter will be dealing with, and in which order.

Postgraduate Research in Music. Victoria Rogers, Oxford University Press. © Oxford University Press 2024.
DOI: 10.1093/oso/9780197616031.003.0010

If it proves to be impossible to find a way into a chapter, stop! Don't waste time when the flow of ideas has completely dried up; good ideas cannot be forced. If an effective introduction does not come to mind after a reasonable amount of effort (whether for a chapter or a section), leave it until later. The subconscious mind will weave its magic; in time, the ideas will come. Just get on with writing the chapter and return later to the matter of how to begin it.

Getting the Ideas Down on Paper

Regardless of whether the words flow easily or whether they are reluctant to come forward, bullet-point planning is a useful strategy for getting the ideas down on paper. Without a plan, muddled thinking is likely to prevail. The following approach is often helpful and can be applied not only to sections but also to the sub-sections within them.

- Talk the ideas out aloud to yourself in everyday speech. A "discussion" of this kind might begin with: "Now, what am I actually trying to say here?" Have a conversation with yourself.
- Jot down what you have just said in dot points, using everyday language.
- Sequence the bullet points into a logical flow of ideas by annotating the points with numbers. The annotated points then become the structure for the section or sub-section.
- Fill in the detail, still using everyday language.
- Convert the language into an appropriate academic style.
- Edit and finesse the text over time.

Every sentence does not need to be perfect in the first draft. The key is to get the ideas down on paper. Follow the steps outlined above, then let the draft sit and come back to it later—many times over. The perspective of time will bring refinement after refinement until the text expresses the *exact* meaning that is intended. A perfectionistic approach in the early stages of writing is generally not the most efficient use of time.

Building in Breaks

Breaks are a necessary part of writing a thesis. When the flow of thinking and writing stops, take a break. Creativity cannot be forced. More often than not, good ideas emerge when deliberate effort is *not* being made. When an idea emerges during a break, jot it down and only return to the writing when the desire to do so returns. Many significant understandings and insights emerge from this process—not when effort is being made, but when effort is *not* being made. Less can be more, although of course little effort at all will never produce much in the way of results. It takes time to develop an awareness of when effort is necessary, and when it is to no avail.

Good Scholarship Is Slow Scholarship

Successful research outcomes stem from both the conscious and subconscious minds. This book has been largely concerned with conscious thought processes, for they are the bedrock of good research. There is also a creative process that can be tapped into, for deep analyses and insights often emerge not from the conscious mind, but from the subconscious mind. This is the intuitive voice that musicians work with on a daily basis; it is present no less in research and writing than in making music. Taking breaks, as discussed in the previous section, is part of this process. The other part is time. Good scholarship cannot be rushed. It needs time, and large amounts of it. This understanding needs to be factored into the writing process. Good scholarship is slow scholarship.

Making the Most of Supervision

Supervisors' time and expertise are critical to the success of a research project. The roles and responsibilities of both student and supervisors should therefore be clarified at the outset. One of the roles of a student, for example, is to prepare an agenda for each supervision meeting to ensure that the meeting is conducted in an efficient and effective way. Table 9.1 sets out some roles and responsibilities that can be used as a starting point for discussion.

Editing

Editing involves the ruthless criticism of your own work. It happens at a number of levels, and at different stages of the writing. Cross checking, formatting, and tidying up the referencing are best done when the writing has been completed. Textual editing, on the other hand, is an ongoing process,

Writing a Thesis Part 4 **227**

Table 9.1. Supervisor and student roles and responsibilities

Role of supervisor/s	Role of student
To advise on the scope and shaping of the project	To formulate a detailed timetable/program of study
To advise on: (a) relevant literature and theoretical frameworks; (b) draft sections and chapters; (c) the complete draft of the thesis	To follow up on advice given by the supervisor(s)
To set deadlines for the submission and reading of drafts	To adhere to deadlines and to communicate with the supervisor(s) if things fall behind schedule
To provide regular supervision meetings	To ensure that regular appointments are made (and kept!) for supervision meetings, and to prepare an agenda and list of questions for each meeting.
To read drafts of student work and be well prepared for supervision meetings	To ensure that written work is prepared for each supervision meeting and submitted to the supervisor/s at least three days before each meeting, or at a time agreed to by both student and supervisor

with each draft subjected to rigorous review until the text is optimally precise and concise. It can be hard to abandon a cherished sentence or segment of writing that has been painstakingly assembled. If, however, it adds nothing to the argument, it must be discarded—no matter how much it hurts!

Textual editing often benefits from reading the text out aloud. This highlights the natural breathing points and exposes sentences that may be overly long or unwieldy. If a text speaks well, it will read well.

It can be helpful to work from a checklist of editorial tasks, undertaking the tasks methodically, one at a time, to ensure that nothing is missed. Table 9.2 captures the key editorial tasks that need to be undertaken.

Saving and Backing Up

A system for saving and backing up is essential. Years of work can be lost if proper processes have not been set in place; indeed, the history of scholarship is riddled with horror stories of lost data. Backups must be made at the end of each day's work—at least three e-copies of every file (for example, the computer copy, a copy on the university server, and a thumb drive copy). In

228 Postgraduate Research in Music

Table 9.2. Editorial checklist

Editorial element	Questions to be asked	When
Ideas and the flow of the argument	• Is the argument watertight? • Is it presented in a clear and logical way? • Is the ordering of content optimal? • Are there any disjunctions in the text? Are further linking words and signposts needed to create a more cohesive narrative?	Ongoing
Condensing and conflating	• Which words, phrases, sentences, and sections are unnecessary and can be excised? • Which phrases and sentences can be conflated?	Ongoing
Correcting	• Are the syntax, grammar, spelling, and punctuation accurate?	Ongoing
Permissions	• Have the requisite permissions been procured for replication of musical examples or other content?	Nine months prior to submission
Double checking and cross checking	• Are the data accurate? • Are the quotations accurate? • Are the page references in the table of contents accurate? • Do the headings in the table of contents correspond exactly to those in the text? • Is the numbering of illustrations in the text correct? • Do the captions in the lists of illustrations correspond exactly to those in the text? • Is the numbering of the appendices accurate? • Do the appendices referred to in the text match the ordering of the appendices at the end of the thesis?	Final stages of writing
Formatting	• Are the fonts and spacings consistent throughout the thesis? • Is the hierarchy of headings consistent throughout the thesis? • Is Roman pagination used in the front matter of the thesis, and Arabic pagination in the remainder? • Are the illustrations formatted correctly and consistently? • Are the appendices formatted correctly and consistently? • Is there consistency in all matters of style, such as quotation marks, American or British spelling, capitalization, musical nomenclature, and so on? • Check that there are no headings at the bottom of a page with the ensuing text beginning at the top of the next page.	Ongoing and final stages of writing
Referencing	• Is the referencing style applied consistently and accurately throughout the thesis? • Is each citation accurate and correctly formatted? • Has each footnote or in-text reference been recorded in the bibliography/reference list (with the exception of personal communication and reference works such as dictionaries)?	Final stages of writing

addition, it is sound practice to print off a copy of each segment of data, and each chapter, once they have been completed.

An efficient system is also needed for the labeling of files (see also the discussion of filing in chapter 5, "Writing a Literature Review"). The best method is to give each file a number, followed by the file name and the date. Each file should be "saved as" each day it is worked on, giving it a new number and date stamp. This ensures that all drafts are kept. *Never* delete a draft, for it may subsequently be preferred to a later one. The numerical sequencing of files also makes it easy to keep track of the individual files because they are stored sequentially. This is illustrated in the following example:

1. Ch. 9, Efficiency, 15 Nov. 2021
2. Ch. 9, Efficiency, 16 Nov. 2021
3. Ch. 9, Efficiency, 18 Nov. 2021
(and so on)

Coda

The journey of writing a thesis is now coming to an end. One question remains: What lies beyond the thesis? This question will be addressed in chapter 10.

10

Beyond the Thesis

This brief concluding chapter is a metaphorical dipping of the toes into the academic world that beckons following completion of the thesis. With the skills acquired through writing a thesis, students are now equipped to take on new challenges: those of presenting their research findings at conferences and in publications. This chapter provides an overview of the where, the what, and the how of presenting a conference paper, and of publishing the research in academic journals and books. The practical advice that is offered facilitates the transition from student to scholar and provides a pathway for continuing involvement in the world of scholarship.

Conference Papers

Presenting papers at conferences is one way of sharing the insights and knowledge that have been documented in the thesis. Conference attendance also provides an opportunity to build a profile in the research community, and to develop further skills: those of public speaking and networking.

Where to Present

In terms of where to present, aim high. Join the professional associations that are appropriate for the area of research (such as the American Musicological Society and the Society for Ethnomusicology) and check their conference schedules. This information is available online and includes details about the submission of abstracts and registration. Planning needs to be done months in advance. Travel and accommodation also need to be planned well ahead of time.

What to Present

Each conference paper should form a topic in itself and address a meaningful issue. Some chapters of a thesis will be appropriate for presentation at

Postgraduate Research in Music. Victoria Rogers, Oxford University Press. © Oxford University Press 2024.
DOI: 10.1093/oso/9780197616031.003.0011

conferences; others will not. The thesis as a whole might also raise broader questions that can be addressed in a conference paper.

Like a thesis, a conference paper contains three sections: an introduction that sets out the contextual background, aims (and methods if appropriate), and plan for how the paper will proceed; a middle section in which the research findings are presented; and a conclusion in which the findings are summarized, discussed, and contextualized. The key elements of the academic style should be kept in mind, for they apply as much to presenting a conference paper as to writing a thesis (see chapter 7 for a discussion of these elements).

Conference presentations are typically twenty minutes long, with a further ten minutes allocated for questions. Precision and concision are therefore of the essence. The major points need to be distilled from a large body of information and presented within a relatively short timeframe.

How to Prepare and Present a Conference Paper

The key to a successful conference presentation lies in the preparation. The following guidelines set out the main considerations for preparing and presenting a paper.

- Use PowerPoint. PowerPoint presentations are effective, and they look professional. PowerPoint makes it easier for the audience to follow the argument.
- Ensure that the PowerPoint presentation has a clear and logical flow of ideas. The points and headings on the slides should mirror the plan set out in the introductory segment of the presentation.
- Do not include too much information on any single PowerPoint slide— no more than five or six points.
- Audio and video files (as well as images) can be embedded in the slides. It is quicker and easier to click on an audio or video link than to open it in another program.
- In addition to the PowerPoint presentation, prepare a full, written text of the paper. The text should include cues for the PowerPoint slides. It should be printed in double spacing to make it easier to read.
- It is perfectly acceptable to read (not mumble!) a paper in its entirety. It is also common practice to ad-lib from the PowerPoint slides, although papers that are ad-libbed are particularly prone to running overtime.
- Be mindful of the difference between spoken and written language. Conversational language is more colloquial, and the sentences are

shorter and less complex. In written language, colloquialisms and clichés are generally avoided, and the sentences are often longer and more complex. Whilst the content of a conference paper must be grounded in the academic style, its manner of presentation can be more conversational and colloquial.

- Speak your paper as you write it—sentence after sentence, over and over again as you craft and re-craft the words. This will eliminate sentences that are long and unwieldy. If a sentence does not fall easily from the tongue, re-write it.
- Be meticulous with the punctuation. As noted in chapter 7 and in appendix F, punctuation articulates thought; the various punctuation marks do this in different ways. The skillful use of punctuation allows the text to breathe in the right places.
- It is also helpful to italicize words and phrases that need to be emphasized. This leaves nothing to chance in the presentation and ensures that the reading will be polished and engaging.
- It is essential to time the presentation beforehand, practicing it several times and pruning it back until the timing is exact or, better still, a couple of minutes under time to allow for contingencies. Operating the PowerPoint should be part of the test runs. Papers that run over time are generally cut off by the chair of the session when the allotted time is up, even if the presentation has not been completed.
- Remember: No matter how interesting the content may be, a paper makes little impact when a presenter races through the text, barely drawing breath, in order to get through too much material within the allotted time. The worst presentations are those in which the presenter has too much to get through, resulting in a garbled race against time in the final minutes of the presentation.
- Take a back-up of the PowerPoint to the conference session and be sure to have a printout just in case there is a catastrophic failure of equipment.
- Arrive well before the scheduled time of the presentation to ensure that the equipment is working.

Publications

Writing journal articles and books are further ways of disseminating the research findings and building a profile in the research community. Writing at this level also presents opportunities for the continuing development of writing skills, for the feedback from reviewers is invariably helpful.

Where to Publish

Aim for the top journals and the top academic publishers. The pre-eminent journals and publishers within a field of study will already have become apparent during the research process.

Seek to publish journal articles only in refereed journals. The status of a journal can be checked through the *Ulrichsweb* database (see chapter 2). *Ulrichsweb* also provides further information about the journal, such as the number of issues per year; this information can also be found on the journal's website.

To find an appropriate publisher for a book, visit the websites of key academic publishers to determine their areas of publication strength. Oxford University Press was a logical destination for this book, for example, because it had already published bibliographic texts in the area of music research.

As a matter of ethics, only approach one journal or publisher at a time. Journal editors and the commissioning editors of books send submissions to two or three reviewers. A huge amount of time is invested in the reviewing process. It is not fair to waste the time of either the editors or the reviewers by later rejecting an offer to publish.

Don't be discouraged if submissions for publication are rejected. It can take time before an article or book finds the right publication fit. Knockbacks are not setbacks, and criticism is not a personal attack. The feedback that accompanies an unsuccessful submission can be put to good use in improving the next one.

What to Publish

Conference papers are often reconstituted as journal articles, expanded appropriately in content and scope. Like a conference paper, an article should form a topic in itself and address a meaningful issue. Some chapters of a thesis will be appropriate for re-crafting as articles; others will not. The thesis as a whole might also raise broader questions that can be discussed in an article.

Like a thesis and a conference paper, a journal article contains three sections: an introduction that sets out the contextual background, aims (and methods if appropriate), and a plan for how the article will proceed; a middle section in which the findings are presented; and a conclusion in which the findings are summarized, discussed, and contextualized. The key elements of the academic style, together with the stylistically appropriate use of language, are as relevant here as they are in a thesis. They remain primary considerations.

234 Postgraduate Research in Music

A doctoral thesis may also lend itself to publication as a book, although some reshaping of the thesis will be necessary. The formal exposition of a hypothesis or research question, aims, rationale, and methodology, for example, is subsumed into a general introduction in a book, and documented in a less literal and more subtle way. The detailed reporting of research findings is condensed in a way that is no less rigorous in its scholarship, but is less detailed and more engaging in its presentation. A book is more narrative in its approach. It is more supple and readable and might, for example, include further contextualization and additional content. A considerable amount of thought and work are needed to transform a thesis into a book; this is not a literal transplantation from one context to the other.

How to Prepare and Present a Publication Submission

The convention in academic publishing is to submit a completed article to the editor of a journal, and a detailed publication proposal to the commissioning editor of a book publisher. The key to a successful publication submission, like a successful conference paper, lies in the preparation. The evaluations of reviewers are based on what is presented, not on what *might* have been presented if more time had been spent on the submission. There is only one chance to make a good impression.

When sending an article to a journal, be sure to check the journal's submission guidelines, which can be found on the journal's website. These guidelines include such things as the permitted word count, the journal's referencing style, and what to include in the covering letter. It would reflect very poorly on a submission if, for example, notes and bibliography referencing were used when in-text referencing is the house style of the journal. It is the quality of the article, however, that is of paramount importance—the topic, the argument, and the writing. An article should be submitted only when it has been reworked so many times that no further improvements can seemingly be made. Critical feedback from thesis supervisors and others is part of this process.

When making a submission to an academic book publisher, check the submission guidelines on the publisher's website and follow them strictly. These guidelines provide a framework through which a case can be argued for the proposed book. Each rubric, as set out in the guidelines, should be used as a heading in the proposal, and in the same order. A good publication proposal should be engaging and compelling, showing, beyond doubt, that the project is unique, valuable, and viable. The skills learned in presenting an argument in a thesis can now be put to good use, albeit in a slightly different context.

It takes time to prepare a detailed publication proposal. Weeks should be set aside for it—not two weeks, but four, five, or six weeks. The information on competing books, for example, must be meticulously researched and presented. As noted earlier, there is only one chance to make a good impression. A submission should only be lodged when no further improvements can be made, either conceptually or syntactically.

Coda

Conference presentations and publications mark the end of one journey—writing a thesis—and the beginning of another. Rudyard Kipling's "six honest serving men," as described in the introduction to this book, will continue to be loyal and indispensable companions on the new journey; so, too, the skills that have been learned through writing a thesis. Postgraduate research in music is inevitably a springboard to new worlds, not only through the enrichment of artistic practice but also through continuing involvement in the world of scholarship. Research and creating music are not separate activities, for, as noted in the introduction to the book, research *enhances* the creative capacity of musicians. The complete musician is, indeed, the scholar-musician.

Notes

Prelims

1. Ruth Watanabe, *Introduction to Music Research* (Englewood Cliffs, New Jersey: Prentice Hall, 1967).
2. Jonathan Bellman, *A Short Guide to Writing About Music*, 2nd ed. (New York: Pearson Longman, 2007); Trevor Herbert, *Music in Words: A Guide to Researching and Writing About Music* (London: Associated Board of the Royal Schools of Music, 2001); and Richard Wingell, *Writing About Music: An Introductory Guide*, 4th ed. (Upper Saddle River, New Jersey: Pearson Prentice Hall, 2007).
3. D. Kern Holoman, *Writing About Music: A Style Sheet from the Editors of 19th-Century Music* (Berkeley: University of California Press, 1988); Demar Irvine, *Irvine's Writing About Music*, rev. Mark A. Radice, 3rd ed. (Portland, Oregon: Amadeus Press, 1999); and James R. Cowdery et al., *How to Write About Music: The RILM Manual of Style*, 2nd ed. (New York: *Répertoire Internationale de Littérature Musicale*, 2006).
4. Phillip D. Crabtree and Donald H. Foster, *Sourcebook for Research in Music*, rev. Allen Scott, 2nd ed. (Bloomington: Indiana University Press, 2005).
5. The more recent editions of these books are: Pauline Shaw Bayne, and Edward M. Komara, *A Guide to Library Research in Music*, 2nd ed. (Lanham, Maryland: Rowman & Littlefield, 2020); Jane Gottlieb, *Music Library and Research Skills*, 2nd ed. (New York: Oxford University Press, 2017); Laurie J. Sampsel, *Music Research: A Handbook*, 3rd ed. (New York: Oxford University Press, 2019).
6. Thomas Donahue, *A Style and Usage Guide to Writing About Music* (Lanham, Maryland: Scarecrow Press, 2010). A 2nd edition of Herbert's *Music in Words* was published in 2012; a 3rd edition of Holoman's *Writing About Music* in 2014; and a 3rd edition of Crabtree and Foster's *Sourcebook* in 2015.

Introduction

1. Rudyard Kipling, *Just So Stories* (London: Macmillan, 1902), 83.
2. "Glossary of Statistical Terms: Research and Development—UNESCO," OECD, accessed December 20, 2021, https://stats.oecd.org/glossary/detail.asp?ID=2312.
3. "Annex C: Definitions of Research and Impact for the REF," REF 2021 Research Exercise Framework Guidance on Submissions, 107, accessed December 20, 2021, https://www.ref.ac.uk/media/1447/ref-2019_01-guidance-on-submissions.pdf.
4. Dylan Marney, "The Application of Musico-Rhetorical Theory to Stretto, Double, and Triple Fugue: Analyses of Contrapuncti V–XI from J. S. Bach's *The Art of the Fugue* BWV 1080" (DMA diss., University of Arizona, 2013), 8–9; and B. Vickers, "Figures of Rhetoric/ Figures of Music?" *Rhetorica: A Journal of the History of Rhetoric* 2, no. 1 (1984): 21, quoted

238 Notes

in Geoffrey Lancaster, *Through the Lens of Esoteric Thought: Joseph Haydn's The Seven Last Words of Christ on the Cross* (Crawley, Western Australia: UWA Press, 2019), 37.

5. Henk Borgdorff, *The Conflict of the Faculties: Perspectives on Artistic Research and Academia* (Leiden: Leiden University Press, 2012), 22–23.

6. Borgdorff, 25.

Chapter 1

1. Deane Root, ed., *Grove Music Online* (Oxford University Press, 2001), http://www.oxford musiconline.com.

2. Stanley Sadie and John Tyrrell, eds., *New Grove Dictionary of Music and Musicians* (London: Macmillan, 2001).

Chapter 2

1. Pauline Shaw Bayne, and Edward M. Komara, *A Guide to Library Research in Music*, 2nd ed. (Lanham, Maryland: Rowman & Littlefield, 2020); Jane Gottlieb, *Music Library and Research Skills*, 2nd ed. (New York: Oxford University Press, 2017); Laurie J. Sampsel, *Music Research: A Handbook*, 3rd ed. (New York: Oxford University Press, 2019).

2. "Cat Hope: Artist, Scholar," accessed August 4, 2021, http://www.cathope.com.

3. "The Alan Hovhaness Website," accessed August 4, 2021, http://www.hovhaness.com/ Hovhaness.html.

4. Amanda Maple, Beth Christenssen, and Kathleen A. Abromeit, "Information Literacy for Undergraduate Music Students: A Conceptual Framework," *Music Library Association Notes* 52, no. 3 (1996): 744.

5. A periodical is something that is published periodically, with a fixed time between issues. A magazine is a periodical with a popular focus, catering for a particular audience. An academic journal is a periodical directed to a specialist academic readership. Sources: *Oxford Dictionary of English*, 2nd ed. (Oxford: Oxford University Press, 2003); Paul Streby, "What's the Difference Between a Periodical, a Scholarly Journal, and a Magazine?" University of Michigan-Flint, Frances Willson Thompson Library, accessed September 24, 2021, https://libanswers.umflint.edu/faq/86816; and Cindi Nichols, "What's the Difference Between Periodicals, Journals, Magazines and Newspapers?" University of Memphis Library, accessed September 24, 2021, https://libanswers.memphis.edu/faq/34544.

6. "Is a Journal Peer-Reviewed?" University of Queensland, accessed October 25, 2021, https:// guides.library.uq.edu.au/how-to-find/peer-reviewed-articles/check.

7. The information in this table is derived from "EBSCO Music Index," EBSCO, accessed July 8, 2021, www.ebsco.com/products/research-databases/music-index; "EBSCO Music Index with Full Text," EBSCO, accessed October 26, 2021, https://www.ebsco.com/products/resea rch-databases/music-index-full-text; "Music Periodicals Database," ProQuest LibGuides, accessed July 8, 2021, https://proquest.libguides.com/musicdatabase; "RILM Abstracts of Music Literature with Full Text," RILM, accessed July 8, 2021, www.rilm.org/abstracts/; "Performing Arts Periodicals Database," ProQuest LibGuides, accessed October 25, 2021, https://proquest.libguides.com/performingarts/content; and "About JStor," JStor, accessed July 8, 2021, https://about.jstor.org/.

8. Information in this paragraph is derived from "FAQ: About JURN," accessed October 25, 2021, https://jurnsearch.wordpress.com/about/#mix.

9. Sampsel, *Music Research: A Handbook*, 3rd ed., 33–55.

10. Gottlieb, *Music Library and Research Skills*, 2nd ed., 66–98; Bayne and Komara, *A Guide to Library Research in Music*, 2nd ed., 14–18; Percy Scholes and John Wagstaff, "Dictionaries of Music," in *The Oxford Companion to Music* (Oxford University Press, 2011), accessed August 4, 2021, https://www-oxfordreference-com.ezproxy.ecu.edu.au/view/10.1093/acref/9780199579037.001.0001/acref-9780199579037-e-1939.

11. Stanley Sadie and John Tyrrell, eds., *New Grove Dictionary of Music and Musicians* (London: Macmillan, 2001); Deane Root, ed., *Grove Music Online* (Oxford University Press, 2001), http://www.oxfordmusiconline.com.

12. Ludwig Finsche, ed., *Die Musik in Geschichte und Gegenwart*, 2nd ed. (Kassel: Bärenreiter, 1994–2008); *MGG Online*, https://www.rilm.org/mgg-online/.

13. Bruno Nettl et al., eds., *The Garland Encyclopedia of World Music* (New York: Garland, 1998–2002); "Music Online: The Garland Encyclopedia of World Music," Alexander Street, accessed February 7, 2022, https://search.alexanderstreet.com/glnd.

14. Joyce Kennedy, Michael Kennedy, and Tim Rutherford-Johnson, eds., *The Oxford Dictionary of Music*, 6th ed. (Oxford: Oxford University Press, 2012); Don Michael Randel, ed., *Harvard Dictionary of Music*, 4th ed. (Cambridge, Massachusetts: Belknap Press of Harvard University Press, 2003).

15. See endnote 5 for the differences between periodicals, magazines, and journal articles.

16. "A Brief Introduction," RIPM, accessed July 8, 2021, https://ripm.org/?page=About.

17. "ProQuest Historical Newspapers," ProQuest, accessed September 26, 2021, https://about.proquest.com/en/products-services/pq-hist-news/; and "News and Newspapers," ProQuest, accessed September 26, 2021, https://about.proquest.com/en/content-solutions/news.

18. "Gale Historical Newspapers," Gale, accessed September 26, 2021, https://www.gale.com/intl/primary-sources/historical-newspapers.

19. "All Newspapers," Google News, accessed September 26, 2021, https://news.google.com/newspapers. Useful information about how to search Google News can be found at Kimberly Powell, "How to Search the Google News Archive," accessed September 26, 2021, https://www.thoughtco.com/search-tips-for-google-news-archive-1422213.

20. See also "National Digital Newspaper Program," Library of Congress, accessed September 26, 2021, https://www.loc.gov/ndnp.

21. "What are Archives?" Society of American Archivists, accessed October 4, 2021, https://www2.archivists.org/about-archives.

22. Excellent information about finding aids can be found at "What is a Finding Aid?" CSUDH University Library, accessed October 3, 2021, https://libguides.csudh.edu/finding_aid; and "Archival Research," CUNY Graduate Center, Mina Rees Library, accessed October 3, 2021, https://libguides.gc.cuny.edu/archivalresearch/archives. See also "How to Use a Finding Aid for Researching in Archives," Simmons University, Simmons College Library and Information Sciences, accessed October 3, 2021, https://simmonslis.libguides.com/using_finding_aids/home.

23. Discussions with Geoffrey Lancaster have been valuable in shaping this section.

24. Stanley Boorman, "Holograph," in *Grove Music Online* (Oxford University Press, 2001), accessed August 4, 2021, https://doi-org.ezproxy.ecu.edu.au/10.1093/gmo/9781561592630.article.13248.

240 Notes

25. Nicholas Marston, "Autograph," in *Grove Music Online* (Oxford University Press, 2001), accessed August 4, 2021, https://doi-org.ezproxy.ecu.edu.au/10.1093/gmo/9781561592 630.article.01567.

26. See, for example, "Autograph," in *The New Harvard Dictionary of Music*, ed. Don Michael Randel (Cambridge, Massachusetts: Belknap Press of Harvard University Press, 2003). For a more nuanced discussion, see Nicholas Marston, "Autograph," in *Grove Music Online*.

27. See, for example, Boorman, "Holograph," in *Grove Music Online*.

28. *Oxford Dictionary of English*, 2nd ed.

29. Marston, "Autograph," in *Grove Music Online*.

30. Stanley Boorman, "Ürtext," in *Grove Music Online* (Oxford University Press, 2001), accessed August 4, 2021, https://doi-org.ezproxy.ecu.edu.au/10.1093/gmo/9781561592 630.article.28851.

31. Sampsel, *Music Research: A Handbook*, 3rd ed., 98.

32. Nicholas Temperley, ed., *The London Pianoforte School 1766–1860*, 20 vols. (London: Garland, 1984–1986).

33. Anna Harriet Heyer, *Historical Sets, Collected Editions, and Monuments of Music: A Guide to Their Contents*, 3rd ed. (Chicago: American Library Association, 1980); George Robert Hill and Norris L. Stephens, *Collected Editions, Historical Series & Sets & Monuments of Music: A Bibliography* (Berkeley, California: Fallen Leaf Press, 1997).

34. Sydney Robinson Charles et al., "Editions, Historical," in *Grove Music Online* (Oxford University Press, 2001), accessed August 4, 2021, https://doi-org.ezproxy.ecu.edu.au/10.1093/gmo/9781561592630.article.08552.

35. The information in this section is derived from "RISM Catalog of Musical Sources," RISM, accessed July 10, 2021, https://rism.info.

36. This section draws upon information in Sampsel, *Music Research: A Handbook*, 3rd ed.; Bayne and Komara, *A Guide to Library Research in Music*, 2nd ed.; H.E.S., "Thematic Catalogue," in *The New Harvard Dictionary of Music*, ed. Don Michael Randel (Cambridge, Massachusetts: Belknap Press of Harvard University Press, 2003); Barry S. Brook, "Thematic Catalogue," in *Grove Music Online* (Oxford University Press, 2001), accessed July 3, 2021, https://doi-org.ezproxy.ecu.edu.au/10.1093/gmo/9781561592630.article.27785; and "Classical Music Cataloging Systems Explained," accessed July 3, 2021, http://electri cka.com/etaf/muses/music/classical_music/composer_catalog_systems/composer_cat alog_systems_popups/about_these_catalog_systems.htm.

37. Sampsel, *Music Research: A Handbook*, 3rd ed., 81.

38. Barry S. Brook and Richard J. Viano, *Thematic Catalogues in Music: An Annotated Bibliography*, 2nd. ed. (Stuyvesant, NY: Pendragon, 1997).

39. Tilman Seebass, "Iconography," in *Grove Music Online* (Oxford University Press, 2001), accessed July 12, 2021, https://doi-org.ezproxy.ecu.edu.au/10.1093/gmo/9781561592630.article.13698.

40. "About Association RIdIM—Mission Statement," RIdIM, accessed July 12, 2021, https://ridim.org/association-ridim/about-ridim/.

41. Bayne and Komara, *A Guide to Library Research in Music*, 2nd ed., 181–82.

42. The Smithsonian Folkways Recordings can also be accessed through "Music Online: Smithsonian Global Sound for Libraries," Alexander Street, accessed October 27, 2021, https://search.alexanderstreet.com/glmu.

43. "What are Search Engines?" Edith Cowan University, accessed October 26, 2021, https://ecu.au.libguides.com/search-engines/what.

Notes 241

Chapter 3

1. The information in this table is based on "Database Search Tips: Keywords vs. Subjects," Massachusetts Institute of Technology, MIT Libraries, accessed October 9, 2018, https://libguides.mit.edu/c.php?g=175963&p=1160804.
2. The number of search results in this and the ensuing examples relate specifically to the RILM database, and are current as at July 2021. The number will vary over time, and across different databases.
3. The design of figures 3.11, 3.13, and 3.16 is based on the model presented in "Boolean Operators: A Cheat Sheet," University of Minnesota Libraries, accessed September 7, 2018, https://libguides.umn.edu/BooleanOperators.
4. "Searching with Wildcards and Truncation Symbols," EBSCOhost, accessed October 28, 2021, https://support-ebsco-com.ezproxy.ecu.edu.au/help/index.php?help_id=137.
5. "Searching with Wildcards and Truncation Symbols," EBSCOhost.
6. "Variant Forms or Spellings," ProQuest Help, accessed October 28, 2021, https://www.proquest.com/help/academic/webframe.html?Search_Results.html#Search_Results.html.
7. "Proximity Searches," EBSCOhost, accessed October 28, 2021, https://support-ebsco-com.ezproxy.ecu.edu.au/help/index.php?help_id=55.
8. "Proximity Searches" EBSCOhost.

Chapter 4

1. Diana Ridley, *The Literature Review: A Step-by-Step Guide for Students*, 2nd ed. (London: Sage, 2012), 2.
2. Jonathan W. Marshall, email message to author, April 30, 2020.
3. Marshall, email message to author.
4. This example derives from Hannah Th'ng, "Larry Sitsky's *Century*: A Response to Selected Twentieth-Century Notation, Associated Piano Techniques, and Performance Possibility" (Master's diss., Edith Cowan University, 2023).
5. Oxford Dictionary of English, 2nd ed. (Oxford: Oxford University Press, 2003).
6. I am indebted to Amanda Myers for her input into this section.
7. Occasionally, an annotated bibliography comprises the substantive part of a thesis, preceded by a weighty introduction and followed by a weighty conclusion. There are also occasions on which an abbreviated annotated bibliography takes the place of a list of references at the end of a thesis or book. An annotated bibliography might also take the form of an independent publication. These related functions are acknowledged. In the context of this chapter, however, the annotated bibliography will only be explored as a preparatory exercise for a literature review.

Chapter 5

1. Nicholas Walliman, *Research Methods: The Basics* (London: Routledge, 2011), 147–48.
2. This abstract draws upon some of the wording in the abstract included in Victoria Rogers, "The Musical Language of Peggy Glanville-Hicks" (PhD diss., University of Western Australia, 2000).

Notes

3. These steps draw in part upon Ranjit Kumar, *Research Methodology: A Step-By-Step Guide for Beginners*, 5th ed. (Los Angeles: Sage, 2019), 327.
4. This fictitious study is based in part upon Victoria Rogers, "John Blacking, Composer," *Ethnomusicology* 57, no.2 (Spring/Summer 2013): 311–329.
5. This distinction derives in part from the definition of musicology given by Vincent Duckles and Jann Pasler in "Musicology—The Nature of Musicology, Definitions," in *Grove Music Online* (Oxford University Press, 2001), accessed May 18, 2021, https://doi-org.ezproxy.ecu.edu.au/10.1093/gmo/9781561592630.article.46710.
6. This definition is derived from Nicholas Cook, *A Guide to Musical Analysis* (Oxford: Oxford University Press, 1987), 151, and from David Symons, personal communication with the author, January 22, 2022.
7. Theodore George, "Hermeneutics," in *Stanford Encyclopedia of Philosophy*, edited by Edward N. Zalta (Winter 2021 edition), https://plato.stanford.edu/archives/win2021/entries/hermeneutics.
8. Sema A. Kalaian, "Research Design—Phenomenological Research," in *Encyclopedia of Survey Research Methods*, edited by Paul J. Lavrakas (Thousand Oaks, CA: Sage, 2008), 725–731, https://www-doi-org.ezproxy.ecu.edu.au/10.4135/9781412963947.n471.
9. James Wolf, "Self-Administered Questionnaire," in *Encyclopedia of Survey Research Methods*, edited by Paul J. Lavrakas (Thousand Oaks, CA: Sage, 2008), 804, https://www-doi-org.ezproxy.ecu.edu.au/10.4135/9781412963947.n522.
10. Henk Borgdorff, *The Conflict of the Faculties: Perspectives on Artistic Research and Academia* (Leiden: Leiden University Press, 2012), 22–23.
11. *Chicago Manual of Style: The Essential Guide for Writers, Editors, and Publishers*, 17th ed. (Chicago: University of Chicago Press, 2017). The *Chicago Manual of Style* is available in both print and online versions. There is also an abbreviated, printed version by Kate Turabian, entitled *A Manual for Writers of Research Papers, Theses and Dissertations: Chicago Style for Students and Researchers*, 9th ed. (Chicago: University of Chicago Press, 2018).
12. *Publication Manual of the American Psychological Association*, 7th ed. (Washington, DC: American Psychological Association, 2020).
13. *Publication Manual of the American Psychological Association*, 7th ed., 257, 260.
14. Laurie J. Sampsel, *Music Research: A Handbook*, 3rd ed. (New York: Oxford University Press, 2019); Turabian, *A Manual for Writers of Research Papers, Theses and* Dissertations, 9th ed.
15. Turabian, *A Manual for Writers of Research Papers, Theses and Dissertations*, 9th ed., 410.

Chapter 6

1. These two styles were discussed in chapter 5 in the context of referencing.
2. This abstract draws upon some of the wording in the abstract for Victoria Rogers, "The Musical Language of Peggy Glanville-Hicks" (PhD diss., University of Western Australia, 2000). It also replicates some of the concepts and wording in Victoria Rogers, "Avant-Garde or Postmodern? The Melody-Rhythm Concept in Peggy Glanville-Hicks's *Sinfonia da Pacifica*," in *Analytical Essays on Music by Women Composers: Concert Music, 1900–1960*, ed. Laurel Parsons and Brenda Ravenscroft (New York: Oxford University Press, 2022), 229–254.
3. The following discussion is based on James Huntingford, "Tasteful Piano Performance in Classic-Era Britain" (Master's diss., Edith Cowan University, 2021).

Notes **243**

4. This discussion draws in part upon information presented in Kate Turabian, *A Manual for Writers of Research Papers, Theses, and Dissertations: Chicago Style for Students and Researchers*, 9th ed. (Chicago: University of Chicago Press, 2018); *Chicago Manual of Style: The Essential Guide for Writers, Editors, and Publishers*, 17th ed. (Chicago: University of Chicago Press, 2017); and *Publication Manual of the American Psychological Association*, 7th ed. (Washington, DC: American Psychological Association, 2020).

5. *Chicago Manual of Style*, 17th ed.; Turabian, *A Manual for Writers of Research Papers, Theses and Dissertations*, 9th ed.; *Publication Manual of the American Psychological Association*, 7th ed.; Brian Richardson et al., *MHRA Style Guide*, 3rd ed. (London: Modern Humanities Research Association, 2015); *MLA Handbook*, 8th ed. (New York: The Modern Language Association of America, 2016); and Demar Irvine, *Irvine's Writing About Music*, rev. Mark A. Radice, 3rd ed. (Portland, Oregon: Amadeus Press, 1999).

6. This discussion draws upon three sources in particular: Irvine, *Irvine's Writing About Music*, 3rd ed.; Turabian, *A Manual for Writers of Research Papers, Theses and Dissertations*, 9th ed.; and the *Publication Manual of the American Psychological Association*, 7th ed.

Chapter 7

1. Richard Andrews, in *A Theory of Contemporary Rhetoric* (New York: Routledge, 2014), 71, offers a more expansive view of rhetoric. "Argumentation," he suggests, "is one field of rhetoric. Rhetoric also covers other meta-genres of communication, such as narrative, description, lyric poetry, everyday (non-argumentational and non-argumentative) discussion and exchange, and the distinction between fiction and non-fiction. Our definition, in opposition to that of Aristotle, is of rhetoric as 'the arts of discourse.' "

2. Merriam Webster Dictionary, s.v. "Argument," accessed October 14, 2021, https://www.merriam-webster.com/dictionary/argument.

3. These four examples are taken from Victoria Rogers, *The Music of Peggy Glanville-Hicks* (Farnham: Ashgate, 2009), 87–88, 227. Reproduced by permission of Taylor & Francis Group. Minor changes have been made to Rogers' text in techniques 1 and 4.

4. The sections on quotations and punctuation draw in part upon information presented in Kate Turabian, *A Manual for Writers of Research Papers, Theses, and Dissertations: Chicago Style for Students and Researchers*, 9th ed. (Chicago: University of Chicago Press, 2018); *Chicago Manual of Style: The Essential Guide for Writers, Editors, and Publishers*, 17th ed. (Chicago: University of Chicago Press, 2017); and *Publication Manual of the American Psychological Association*, 7th ed. (Washington, DC: American Psychological Association, 2020).

5. Ralph Vaughan Williams, *National Music* (London: Oxford University Press, 1934), 63.

6. These examples are taken from Rogers, *The Music of Peggy Glanville-Hicks*, 88, 90. Reproduced by permission of Taylor & Francis Group. Minor changes have been made to Rogers' text in examples 1 and 2.

7. These three examples are taken from Rogers, *The Musical Language of Peggy Glanville-Hicks*, 87–89. Reproduced by permission of Taylor & Francis Group. Minor changes have been made to Rogers' text in examples 1 and 2 to accommodate the in-text referencing.

8. For a more nuanced discussion, readers are referred to the *Publication Manual of the American Psychological Association*, 7th ed., 258, 276.

9. Turabian, *A Manual for Writers of Research Papers, Theses, and Dissertations*, 9th ed., 206, provides a full citation for the source within a source in both the footnote/endnote and

244   Notes

bibliographic entries. The *Chicago Manual of Style*, 17th ed., section 14.260, only provides a footnote example and does not indicate whether a "source within a source" should also be acknowledged in the bibliography.

10. The "quoted in" segment of this citation may seem to be incorrect because it is set in the style of a footnote. It is in fact correct because the second author in a bibliographic entry is cited in the order of first name then last name. It is therefore logical to format the remainder of the "quoted in" segment in the manner of a footnote.

11. Wayne C. Booth et al., *The Craft of Research*, 4th ed. (Chicago: University of Chicago Press, 2016), 206.

12. Charles Rosen, *The Classical Style: Haydn, Mozart, Beethoven* (New York: Norton, 1997), 30.

13. Rosen, *The Classical Style*, 30.

14. Rosen, *The Classical Style*, 30.

15. "Avoiding Academic Misconduct: Plagiarism," Edith Cowan University, Student Intranet—My Studies, accessed October 14, 2021, https://intranet.ecu.edu.au/student/my-studies/academic-integrity/avoiding-academic-misconduct.

16. Booth et al., *The Craft of Research*, 4th ed., 206.

17. Booth et al., *The Craft of Research*, 4th ed., 206.

18. The words "faculty or faculties of the mind," and "or which form a judgement of" derive from Edmund Burke, *A Philosophical Enquiry into the Origin of Our Ideas of the Sublime and Beautiful, with an Introductory Discourse Concerning Taste, and Several Other Additions*, 9th ed. (London: J. Dodsley, 1782), 5–6.

19. It should be noted that people who identify as non-binary in their gender designation often wish to be referred to as "they" and "their." In such cases, plural pronouns should be used as a matter of respect.

20. *Chicago Manual of Style*, 17th ed., section 5.255; and *Publication Manual of the American Psychological Association*, 7th ed., section 4.18 and chapter 5.

Chapter 8

1. The discussion in this chapter draws in part upon three sources: D. Kern Holoman, *Writing About Music: A Style Sheet*, 3rd ed. (Oakland, California: University of California Press, 2014); Thomas Donahue, *A Style and Usage Guide to Writing About Music* (Lanham, Maryland: Scarecrow Press, 2010); and James R. Cowdery et al., *How to Write About Music: The RILM Manual of Style*, 2nd ed. (New York: Répertoire Internationale de Littérature Musicale, 2006). These sources cover the subject in far greater detail than the synoptic survey in this chapter allows; they should therefore be used as references for matters that extend beyond the scope of the present discussion.

2. These definitions of proper and common nouns are derived from Mark Lester and Larry Beason, *The McGraw-Hill Handbook of English Grammar and Usage*, 3rd ed. (New York: McGraw-Hill, 2018), 281.

3. *Chicago Manual of Style: The Essential Guide for Writers, Editors, and Publishers*, 17th ed. (Chicago: University of Chicago Press, 2017).

4. Non-English terms are generally set in italics. They are discussed later in this chapter.

5. *Chicago Manual of Style*, 17th ed., section 8.195; and Donahue, *A Style and Usage Guide to Writing About Music*, 17.

6. Holoman, *Writing About Music: A Style Sheet*, 4.

7. This is consistent with the *Chicago Manual of Style*, 17th ed. (section 10.4), which advocates the omission of periods from abbreviations comprising two or more capital letters.
8. For a more detailed discussion of numbers, see Kate Turabian, *A Manual for Writers of Research Papers, Theses and Dissertations: Chicago Style for Students and Researchers*, 9th ed. (Chicago: University of Chicago Press, 2018), 330–333.
9. For a more detailed discussion of numbers in the APA style, see *Publication Manual of the American Psychological Association*, 7th ed. (Washington, DC: American Psychological Association, 2020), 178–181.

Index

For the benefit of digital users, indexed terms that span two pages (e.g., 52–53) may, on occasion, appear on only one of those pages.

Tables and figures are indicated by *t* and *f* following the page number

abbreviations, 218–19
abstract
    research proposal, 106–8
    thesis, 152–53, 159–60
academic style
    elements, 174–88
    language usage, 188–97
    see also table of contents, chapter 7
acknowledgements, 157
action research, 117
active voice, *see* voice
annotated bibliography, 90–93; *see also* table
    of contents, chapter 4
anthology, 14
APA referencing, *see* referencing
apostrophe, 197; *see also* appendix F
appendix, 132, 149
archival sources, 24–26; *see also* table of
    contents, chapter 2
Archive Finder, 25
argument, 2, 76, 77*t*, 120, 164, 174, 175, 177,
    178, 226–27, 228*t*, 234
artistic research, *see* practice-based research
artistic practice as research, *see* practice-
    based research
artists' names, 207–9; *see also* table of
    contents, chapter 8
Aruspix, 115
Ask, 36
author-date referencing, *see* referencing
auto-ethnography, 117
autograph (score), 28, 33, 210–11

back matter, 123, 148–49, 154, 165–66
bar chart, *see* illustrations; *see also* appendix E
Bartók, Béla, 73
basic shape analysis, 116

BBC Proms Archive, 36
BBC Written Archives Centre, 26, 27*t*
Beethoven-Haus Digital Archives, 25
bibliography, *see* referencing
Bing, 36
Blacking, John, 45, 47, 99–110, 111, 112
block quotations, 179
Boole, George, 49
Boolean operators, 49–54
Borgdorff, Henk, 3–4, 120
British Newspaper Archive, 23–24
Buxtehude, Dietrich, 113

capitalization, 202–7; *see also* table of
    contents, chapter 8
caption, 156, 162–63, 163*t*, 164
case study research, 117
Centre for the History and Analysis of
    Recorded Music, 115
chords, 216
Chronicling America, 23–24
chronology, 178
Classical Music Library, 35
collected edition, 13*t*, 13, 28–30
colon, 197; *see also* appendix F
comma, 197; *see also* appendix F
common knowledge, 128, 174, 187
common nouns, 202–3
connecting words and phrases, 177
content, organization and presentation,
    see thesis
contents, *see* table of contents
controlled vocabularies, 45; *see also* Library
    of Congress Subject Headings
Copland, Aaron, 82–83
copyright, 151
copy (score), 28

248 Index

CORE, 36
creative research, *see* practice-based research
critical thinking, 75–76, 78–79, 84–85, 93, 176, 178
critical/scholarly edition, 28–29

database
  defined, 41
  planning a search, 57–66; *see also* table of contents, chapter 3
  searching databases, 41–58; *see also* table of contents, chapter 3
diacritics, 47, 207, 208
direct quotations, *see* quotations
discographies, 35
Doctoral Dissertations in Musicology (DDM), 22

EBSCO Open Dissertations, 22
E-Theses Online Service (EThOS), 22
editing, 226–27, 227*t*
ellipsis, 183, 197; *see also* appendix F
em dash, 197; *see also* appendix F
Empfindsamkeit, 203
en dash, 197; *see also* appendix F
Endnote (referencing software), 130
endnotes, *see* footnotes and endnotes
ethics clearance, 125
ethnography, 117
evidence, 2, 11, 12, 37, 75–76, 77*t*, 120–21, 156, 165, 174–76, 178
Expressionism, 202–3, 219–20

facsimile edition, 28, 29
feminist research, 117
Ferrera, Diego, 79, 101, 121, 149–50, 153, 154–55
figure, *see* illustrations; *see also* appendix E
filing, 79–80, 229
finding aid, 25, 26
Finney, Ross Lee, 73
focus group, 117
footnotes and endnotes, 74, 126–27, 130–31, 148–49, 167*t*, 174, 208, 228*t*
Force of Destiny, The, 49
formal analysis, 116
formatting
  references, 130
  thesis, 166–69; *see also* table of contents, chapter 6
front matter, 123, 148–49, 154, 156, 158, 174
Futurism, 202–3

galant, 203
Gale Historical Newspapers, 23
Garland Encyclopedia of World Music, 21
Glanville-Hicks, Peggy, 180–81, 184–85
Goethe, Johann Wolfgang, 103
Google, 36
Google Books, 17
Google News Archive, 23
Google Scholar, 17, 36, 58
graphs, *see* illustrations; *see also* appendix E,
graphical formats, *see* illustrations; *see also* appendix E
grounded theory, 118
Grove Music Online, 9–21, 30, 33, 207, 208

harmonic analysis, 116
Harvard Dictionary of Music, 21
Harvard-style referencing, *see* referencing
Hathi Trust Digital Library, 17
headings
  annotated bibliography, 91
  literature review, 83
  table of contents, 104–5
  thesis, 168
headline-style capitalization, 150, 163, 168, 210, 212, 213
hermeneutic research, 118
holograph, 12, 14, 26–28, 29, 31, 73, 74
Hope, Cat, 15, 36
hyphen, 197; *see also* appendix F
hypothesis or research question, 2, 109–10, 112, 148–49, 165, 176–78

illustrations, 162–64; *see also* appendices C, D and E
Impressionism, 202–3, 219–20
International Coalition on Newspapers (ICON), 24
International Music Score Library Project (IMSLP), 29
Internet Archive, 17, 19
Internet Archive 78rpms and Cylinder Recordings, 35
interviews, 118
interview survey, 118
in-text referencing, *see* referencing
introduction
  research proposal, 108–9
  thesis, 158–60

Josquin Research Project, 115
JStor, 19, 20*t*
JURN, 19

Kipling, Rudyard, 1, 4, 235
Kurtág, György, 73

Library of Congress Subject Headings, 45
line graph, *see* illustrations; *see also*
    appendix E
literature review, 72–90, 93; *see also* table of
    contents, chapter 4

manuscript (score), 28
Mendeley, 130
methodology, 113–21; *see also* table of
    contents, chapter 5
microfiche, 24
microfilm, 24
Microsoft Academic, 36
Minimalism, 202–3
monumental edition, 29
Moonlight Sonata, 48
musical examples, *see* illustrations; *see also*
    appendix C
Musical Geography Project, 115
Music and Dance Online, 35
music iconography, 33–34
music index, 19, 20*t*
Music Periodicals Database, 19, 20*t*, 56
Musik in Geschichte and Gegenwart, Die, 21

names, *see* artists' names
Naxos Music Library, 35
Neoclassicism, 202–3
Neo-Riemannian analysis, 116
Networked Digital Library of Theses and
    Dissertations (NDLTD), 22
*New Grove Dictionary of Music and
    Musicians*, 9–10, 21, 30, 33
non-English terms, 217
notes and bibliography referencing,
    see referencing
notes and note names, 214–16
note taking, 76–81
numbers, 217–18

online survey, 118
Oxford Companion to Music, 19–21
Oxford Dictionary of Music, 21
Oxford-style referencing, *see* referencing

pagination, 154–55
paraphrasing, *see* quotations
passive voice, *see* voice
peer-reviewed, 16–18, 19, 22–23, 42
performance edition, 29
performance practice, 9, 13, 45, 46, 54,
    55, 115
performance practice and early music, 49–54,
    55
Performing Arts Periodicals Database,
    19, 20*t*
person, 190–92
    abstract, 106–7
    annotated bibliography, 92
    literature review, 85–86
    thesis, 190–92
phenomenological research, 118
pie chart, *see* illustrations; *see also* appendix E
pitch class set theory, 116
plagiarism, 78–79, 89, 128, 187–88
practice research, *see* practice-based
    research
practice as research, *see* practice-based
    research
practice-based research, 72, 113–14,
    118–20
practice-led research, *see* practice-based
    research
preface, 157
primary sources, *see* primary, secondary and
    tertiary sources
primary, secondary and tertiary
    sources, 12–16
    primary sources, 12–13, 14–16, 19, 23, 25,
        31, 73, 74, 90
    secondary sources, 12, 13, 14–16,
        25, 73, 74
    tertiary sources, 12, 13–16, 25, 73, 74
Primitivism, 202–3
proper nouns, 202–3, 204, 205
ProQuest Dissertations & Theses
    Global, 21
ProQuest Historical Newspapers, 23
punctuation, 181–82, 197; *see also* appendix F

qualitative research, 117–18
quantitative research, 117, 118
quotations, 178
    direct, 179–85
    paraphrasing, 185–87
    see also table of contents, chapter 7

250 Index

Ralph Vaughan Williams Society, 19, 36
refereed, *see* peer-reviewed
reference list, *see* referencing
referencing, 126, 127–30, 228*t*
    author–date (also referred to as APA), 127;
      see also appendix B
    notes and bibliography (also referred to as
      Chicago), 126–27; *see also* appendix A
    see also table of contents, chapter 5; *see*
      also footnotes and endnotes; *see also*
      quotations; *see also* plagiarism
reflective practice, 115, 118, 119–20, 175
RefSeek, 36
répertoire internationale d'iconographie
    musicale (RIdIM), 34
répertoire international de littérature musicale
    (RILM), 41, 42, 42*f*, 43*f*, 45, 45*f*, 49, 50*f*,
    50, 51–52, 51*f*, 52*f*, 53*f*, 54*f*, 54, 55, 55*f*,
    56, 57; *see also* RILM Abstracts of Music
    Literature
répertoire international de la presse musicale
    (RIPM), 23
répertoire international des sources musicales
    (RISM), 31
research
    defined, 1
    in music, 1–2
research-led practice, *see* practice-based
    research
research proposal, 99–132; *see also* table of
    contents, chapter 5
research question, *see* hypothesis or research
    question
resources and resource portals, 12, 16–37; *see*
    also table of contents, chapter 2
rhetoric, 174
RILM Abstracts of Music Literature, 19, 20*t*,
    21; *see also* répertoire international de
    littérature musicale (RILM)
RILM Index to Printed Music (IPM), 29–30
Rosen, Charles, 186–87
run-on/run-in quotations, *see* quotations

Sammartini, Giovanni Battista, 74
saving and backing up, 227–29
Schenker Documents Online, 115
Schenkerian analysis, 116
Schubert, Franz Peter, 103
scores, editions, and collections, 26–31; *see*
    also table of contents, chapter 2
search engines and websites, 36–37

searching databases, *see* databases
secondary sources, *see* primary, secondary
    and tertiary sources
self-administered questionnaire
    survey, 118
semicolon, 197; *see also* appendix F
semiotic analysis, 116–17
sentence-style capitalization, 150
signposts, 177
Sitsky, Larry, 73
Smithsonian Folkways Recordings, 35
social media, blogs, and podcasts, 37
sound recordings, films, and
    videos, 34–35
so what? question, 96*t*, 112, 164–65, 175–78
streaming services, 35
Stürm und Drang, 203
subconscious mind, 103, 225, 226
sub-headings, *see* headings
summative statements, 177
supervision, 226
Symbolism, 202–3

table of contents
    research proposal, 104–5
    thesis, 153–55
tables, *see* illustrations; *see also* appendix D
taste in late eighteenth-century British
    keyboard music, 161
telephone survey, 118–19
tenses
    abstract, 106
    annotated bibliography, 92
    literature review, 86–88
    thesis, 192–94
tertiary sources, *see* primary, secondary and
    tertiary sources
thematic catalogue, 31–33, 48
thematic catalogue number, 209, 210–11,
    212
thesis, 2–3
    academic style, 174–88; *see also* table of
      contents, chapter 7
    content, organization and presentation,
      148–69; *see also* table of contents,
      chapter 6
    language usage, 188–97; *see also* table of
      contents, chapter 7
    musical lexicon, 202–19; *see also* table of
      contents, chapter 8
title, 102–3, 150

title case, *see* headline-style capitalization
titles of musical works, 209–14; *see also* table
    of contents, chapter 8
time signatures, 216
Tomášek, Wenzel Johann, 103
topic, 9–11

Ulrichsweb, 17–18
uniform titles, 47–49
ürtext edition, 28, 29

Vaughan Williams, Ralph, 19, 36, 182
Vaughan Williams Society Journal, 19
voice (active and passive), 194
    abstract, 106
    annotated bibliography, 92
    literature review, 88–89
    thesis, 194

Wikipedia, 24, 36
WorldCat, 16, 25, 35